PRAISE FOR

BABY PLAYS AROUND

"Rock bands are like marriages—it's only a cliché because it's so damn true—but marriages can be like rock 'n' roll as well: turbulent, energizing, heartbreaking, and ultimately transcendent. In *Baby Plays Around,* Helene Stapinski makes those connections unlike any writer (or drummer) before her, with plainspoken insight, piercing wit, and a Joisey accent that she just can't shake, and we're all the better for it."

—Jim DeRogatis,
Chicago Sun-Times pop music critic and author of *Let It Blurt: The Life & Times of Lester Bangs, America's Greatest Rock Critic*

"An anthem—a gritty, tender, unflinching, passionate anthem—to love and music. Like a torch song, *Baby Plays Around* will break your heart while promising to heal it."

—Adam Davies, author of *The Frog King*

"A dispatch from someone who got to a place where anyone who has ever played air guitar wishes they could visit . . . an honest, amusing story that is as individual as fingerprint but that will resonate like a power chord."

—*Seattle Post-Intelligencer*

"Breezy, funny and touching . . . Ms. Stapinski captures perfectly the queasy mixture of euphoria and trepidation that all new band initiates experience."

—*The New York Observer*

"Whether writing about the slow transformation of posthoneymoon bliss to the under-the-same-roof estrangement that plagues many

marrieds or the first-datelike jitters and commitment phobia of bandmates, Stapinski keeps the pace brisk."

—*People*

"A freelance music writer and wannabe drummer watches her two greatest achievements—her marriage and her band—fall to pieces in this biting Manhattan memoir."

—*Us Weekly* (Hot Book Pick)

"If you've ever dreamed of being in a band, you'll love *Baby Plays Around.*"

—*Seventeen*

"Read this charming book, and you will marvel anew at the magic of rock and romance."

—*Pittsburgh Post-Gazette*

"A fun behind-the-scenes look at nightclub life in New York."

—*The Sunday Oregonian*

"Through warm, well-crafted prose and incisive wit, Stapinski recounts the months she spent playing in an indie-rock group in New York and how the demands of jelling, rehearsing and performing with a band affected her marriage."

—*The Hartford Courant*

"Well-lit, cracking memoir of Lower East Side nights . . . not so much a pretty picture as one of high contrast, all the energy and thrall caught in Stapinski's frame."

—*Kirkus Reviews*

"Skillfully balancing emotion and amusement, this is a compelling personal story of onstage and backstage relationships."

—*Booklist*

"[Stapinski] captures the strange exhilaration that comes from relentless rehearsals and performances in dingy clubs, and her exploration of her love for the music of Elvis Costello is touching."

—*Publishers Weekly*

"You don't need to be a music fan to appreciate the dual love story—and the linked subtext of betrayal and second chances—in *Baby Plays Around,* all delivered in vigorous but nuanced rhythms suitable to a sometime rock drummer."

—*The Hamilton* (Ontario) *Spectator*

"Bouncy . . . a good-natured look at life on the fringes of the music business."

—*The Columbus Dispatch*

"Who does she think she is, Cher?"

—*Leader-Post* (Regina, Saskatchewan)

BABY PLAYS AROUND

also by helene stapinski

Five-Finger Discount:
A Crooked Family History

a love affair,
with music

helene stapinski

baby plays around

VILLARD NEW YORK

2005 VILLARD BOOKS TRADE PAPERBACK EDITION

Published in the United States by Villard Books,
an imprint of The Random House Publishing Group,
a division of Random House, Inc., New York.

VILLARD and "V" CIRCLED Design are registered trademarks of
Random House, Inc.

This book was published in 2004 in hardcover by Villard Books,
an imprint of The Random House Publishing Group,
a division of Random House, Inc.

LIBRARY OF CONGRESS CATALOGING-IN-PUBLICATION DATA
Stapinski, Helene.
Baby plays around: a love affair, with music / Helene Stapinski.
p. cm.
ISBN 0-8129-6789-5
1. Stapinski, Helene. 2. Journalists—United States—Biography.
3. Drummers (Musicians)—United States—Biography. I. Title.
PN4874.S64A3 2004
070.92—dc21 2003053844
[B]

Villard Books website address: www.villard.com

Printed in the United States of America

987654321

Book design by Elina Nudelman

FOR MARTIN
(NOT HIS REAL NAME)

• PRELUDE •

I had this dream. It wasn't just a hope. Not just that kind of dream. After the breakup, it became an actual dream, one that I would see in my sleep. It was a recurring dream; a happy fantasy to help wipe away the sadness of the days that stretched before it.

Some mornings when I woke up I couldn't remember if it had actually happened in my life or not. Whether the dream—or even the horrible reality—was a ghost in my imagination. Whether the whole awful episode, and my escape, were real at all.

The dream went like this:

I'm in a smoky club on the Lower East Side, a cool, off-the-beaten-path type place with a long bar and no seats, but a crowd of fans.

I down a scotch at the bar to calm my nerves and loosen up my muscles before we go on. We climb up onto the stage and take our places, instruments tuning, humming, jangling.

The lead singer, a woman, steps up to the microphone with a blue electric guitar. She smiles out at the audience while I count off in the background. One, two, one, two, three, four. And off we go. The singer strums away. Our lead guitarist, a handsome, moody dark-haired guy with a roots-out bleach job, launches into a searing guitar solo. The bass player, another handsome young guy, gives me a smile and nods his head.

I'm sweating, not just from pounding away on the drums—a vintage set of Ludwigs, the same kind Ringo played—but because of the stage lights. Blue and green and red and yellow bathing me and my bandmates in a rainbow glow that says, "Look at us. And listen."

And the audience does. It's filled with people I know and love, my friends, my family, my boss, my husband, green-eyed and handsome, smiling back at me from afar. He mouths the lyrics, about love lost, sometimes found. There are strangers out there, too. Perfect strangers, loving our songs.

All heads bob and sway as we play song after song of originals, great, hard-driving, but melodic songs with smart words—all sung in the whispery voice of our lead singer, with me and Bleach Blond on backup vocals. We've played these songs dozens, maybe hundreds of times, but the energy coming from the audience and from the music itself is so overpowering that it transforms the moment, as if the songs are being played for the first time.

It's like a first kiss. After being married for a long time, it's like a first kiss.

Elvis Costello described the moment in an interview once: In rock and roll, he said, you get in a groove and let it fly. It's either magic or it's boring. When you get it right, it's the most fantastic feeling.

Music, like love, was like that.

BABY PLAYS AROUND

• ONE •

We lived in Brooklyn on the sixth floor of a building that looked like something out of a fairy tale. It had red pointed towers, with a slate spiral staircase running up the outside, and a balcony—a breezeway, the super called it—with an ornate, black, wrought-iron railing. It ran the length of the building, past everyone's front door, like the terrace on each floor of a motel. Our breezeway looked out at the corniced tops of the brownstones across the way, out at the Statue of Liberty and down at the metal garbage cans and fire hydrants on the sidewalk, which was cracked and cleaving from the deep roots of old maple trees.

I worked in that building most days, writing musician interviews, travel stories, trend pieces, stories about New York, whatever I could scrounge up. From my back bedroom office, I looked down at the soft tops of the trees in the courtyard. The only noise, besides the incredible racket of the Tuesday morning recycling truck and the occasional car alarm, was the nearby Brooklyn-Queens Expressway, whose hum was so constant it sounded like a rushing river. Or so I liked to think.

There were better ways to make a living. But there were worse ways, too. I could be covered in yellow paint, working in the dip room of a pencil factory, like my mother had when she was young, or sitting inside the little emergency booth in the Holland Tunnel, watching the cars go by (which had to be one of the worst jobs ever), or working in a fluorescent-lit office with no windows, like my husband did most nights as a reporter at a newspaper.

I imagined the newsroom was especially depressing after nine P.M. So most afternoons, to cheer him up, I packed Martin his dinner in a plastic shopping bag. Rice and beans or pasta with homemade sauce. A piece of fruit and a few cookies. Each night, he returned the Tupperware, one of the small rituals of marriage no one ever tells you about.

We were still newlyweds. Only two years before, Martin had taken me to the top of New York, to Rockefeller Center, to the Rainbow Room, on the pretense we were celebrating the fourth anniversary of our first date, and with the glow of the city lights like votive candles flickering below us, with the big band playing "Stardust" in the background, he had proposed to me. He offered me a ring that his mother—a goldsmith—had forged. It had two thick braids of gold and a round ruby that changed from stoplight red to rose-petal pink as my hand shook that night and I hesitantly answered, "Yes."

I fingered the ring now whenever I was nervous, whenever I had trouble with an interview subject, whenever I had trouble writing a sentence. These days, I was trying to get my pen in the door of the women's magazines—cash cows with stories that paid double what my rock star interviews paid. One of my former professors from graduate school encouraged me to write a pitch to one of her old friends at *Cosmopolitan* that autumn, just as the leaves in our courtyard were starting to turn from green to taxicab gold.

As a preteen I had read *Cosmo,* which I lifted from my sister Paula's coffee table and snuck into the bathroom. It was in *Cosmo*'s pages that I had learned what a clitoris was, what a rubber was, how to one day give a good blowjob, but most important, I read a description of a simultaneous orgasm. *Cosmo* said it was like riding the Tilt-a-Whirl. I was well acquainted with the Tilt-a-Whirl. There was a Bruce Springsteen song, a favorite of mine that mentioned it. "You know that Tilt-a-Whirl down on the south beach drag, I got on it last night and my shirt got caught."

After writing an introductory letter that mentioned the *Cosmo* Tilt-a-Whirl orgasm story and dropping my professor's name, I was invited to the magazine office to look at "The Book"—the legendary sacred text of women's magazine publishing.

I learned that the Book was actually two books, two thick binders filled with story ideas that *Cosmo* had kept for years. Some ideas were typewritten brainstorms from editors, but most were pages ripped out of other women's magazines, with "Let's do something like this" scribbled at the top. I read each one carefully, trying to find the story that would inspire me.

It wasn't easy.

These stories had all been written before, and then written again, and again, and again, and again, and once again, over the years. I had read them all as a kid, as a preteen, and again as a teenager, and then again in my early twenties, until I had stopped reading *Cosmo* altogether. It was like going back to a bad soap opera after a decade and finding the same characters and plotlines.

They were all relationship stories: stories about Meeting Mr. Right, Keeping Mr. Right, Blowing Mr. Right, with an occasional orgasm story thrown in for color. The women's magazines were notorious for farming out any real, hard news stories—prostitution, drugs, domestic abuse—to their male writers. Women writers were left to catfight over the same old stories in the relationship ghetto.

After two hours of flipping, the only story that I could see myself actually writing was one called "Working the Night Shift." Not just a Love piece or a Fuck piece, but about women who worked the night shift: strippers, waitresses, cops, and nurses.

I alerted the perky editorial assistant that I had found a winner. And she led me, assignment in hand, to meet Myra, her boss. I poked a head into her office. From behind a large wooden desk she waved her long, skinny, wrinkled arm. "Come in," the arm said. "And make it snappy."

Myra's office was spacious, with a view of midtown Manhattan, and a separate, smaller desk supporting her old-fashioned manual typewriter. I wasn't sure if she still used it or if it was just for show.

Myra scared me like my math teacher in fifth grade had scared me. Miss Bertha was ancient and crumbly, with bug eyes and wrinkles, the first hard woman I had ever known. Myra made Bertha look like a cherub. I nodded and tried to smile as Myra barked out commands about my chosen assignment.

This wasn't just a first-name story, with made-up, half-fictional friends divulging exaggerated tales of love and lust, she told me. This was about real people working real jobs divulging exaggerated tales of love and lust.

If the quotes weren't quite right, she said, I should make them up.

"Make them up?"

"Yes," she said. "Didn't they teach you that in journalism school?"

Finding women who worked the night shift would be easy enough. The trick was to find women who would talk about their sex lives. I cast the net wide, asking all my friends to search their address books for potential victims.

My nurse friend, Pam Marla, found me a woman named Karen who worked overnights at St. Vincent's Hospital in Greenwich Village, tending to the overdoses and the legions of lonely people who all suffered from a similar ailment—foreign objects lodged in terrible places. There were shampoo bottles, candles, Orangina bottles, Chinese metal love balls, bananas, and lightbulbs. There was the occasional vegetable. "I was gardening and fell over and this cucumber . . ." the story went.

"Gardening naked?" she'd ask.

There was the couple that came in one night: he with a lacerated penis and she with a concussion. It seems that while he was doing the dishes, she decided to show her gratitude and practice what she'd read in the pages of *Cosmo.* While on her knees, in the act, she suffered an epileptic seizure. Her mouth clamped down, jaws freezing shut. So he hit her with the first thing he could grab, a dirty frying pan.

Maybe it was the atmosphere of St. Vincent's emergency room rubbing off, but Karen was very frank about her own sex life, which gave my *Cosmo* story the bite it needed. "Sleeping together is a big part of a relationship," Karen told me. "So we make the time. He's a big morning person, and I'm a big night person, so we do it at all times of the day now." St. Vincent's Catholic public relations department would have a collective coronary over that quote.

I interviewed a go-go dancer from a club in Manhattan. A cop who worked the graveyard shift. I found a night editor at CNN through an old girlfriend of Martin's, Linda. She put me in touch with a thirty-one-year-old single editor friend, who told me that working the lobster shift spelled doom for a dating life, but that on her commute home she got to see sunrises that most people missed out on.

I called the San Diego Zoo and tracked down the overnight zookeeper; an overnight waitress in a twenty-four-hour diner in Jersey. My friend Laura, a fellow writer who'd gone to graduate school with me, had a single friend who worked computers at night down on Wall Street and agreed to talk to me over the phone.

"Her name is Julie," Laura said. "Julie Stepanek."

So I dialed Julie's number and was surprised when a young girl answered, a young girl with a stuffed-up nose. "Can I speak to Julie?" I asked.

"This is Julie," she said, all brightness and cheer.

"Oh hi. This is Helene, Laura's friend."

"Oh hi!" she said, even more brightly.

"You sounded like a little kid."

"I'm little," she said, "but unfortunately I'm not a kid. I'm an old lady. Thirty."

"Me, too," I said, cringing a little. I told her about my story, about where it would be published, and she immediately went into detail about life with her boyfriend, Jimmy.

"We both grew up in St. Louis, but we moved to New York so he could go to graduate school. I'm supporting him," she said. "Barely." Then Julie laughed. She had a great laugh, deep but light at the same time, full of personality, like the ones that stand out sometimes over all the others on a sitcom laugh track.

I sort of knew her boyfriend, Jimmy. He had been in my writing program, which was how Laura had met Julie. To get her to open up some more, I told her about my St. Vincent's nurse and how working nights had really affected her and her boyfriend's love life. "Crazy hours and all," I said.

"Oh, we hardly sleep together anymore anyway," Julie said, not the least bit embarrassed. "We sleep separately. We get a better night's sleep that way."

"Really?"

"One night we had a fight coming home from a party. It was this incredibly stupid fight about which was bigger, St. Louis or Minneapolis." She laughed again. I liked it when she laughed. I wanted to keep her on the line, just to hear her laugh. "We fought all night about it, about which was bigger, and got so mad at each other we wound up sleeping in separate beds. I went on the futon and he slept in our bed, which was always too soft for my back anyway. And since then, we haven't slept in the same bed." She paused. I wasn't sure what I should say.

"Jimmy's a really light sleeper anyway," she said, jumping right in again. "He hates anyone touching him while he's asleep. And he hates being naked." She laughed again.

They'd been together for nearly a decade, twice as long as Martin and me. Is this what all relationships came to? Separate beds and infrequent sex? Platonic friendship by your thirties? We'd only been married a year, but it seemed to me that sleeping together was the best part of the deal. Sex? Spooning? Holding one another come morning? Wasn't this why we were together? Why people mated in the first place? To have and to hold. That's what the vows said.

I didn't want to know Julie's answers to those questions, really, but I wanted her to keep talking. So I steered the conversation away from her boyfriend in very un-*Cosmo*-like fashion. "So why do you work on Wall Street at night? Isn't trading over by then?"

"I do graphs and stuff for the people who come in during the day," she said. She didn't really have a title. "I call myself a document waitress." The pay was $25 an hour, so she worked three nights a week and Saturdays, supporting Jimmy while he wrote his masterpiece.

"And I work at night so I can write songs during the day."

"You write songs?" I asked. "What kind of songs?"

"Songs for my band."

She paused a half rest.

"Well, I want to start a band," she said, "but I can't find a drummer."

My heart started beating in triplets. Julie kept talking, but I was barely listening now. I sat mute on the other end of the line, my mind drifting while Julie babbled about her reasons for starting a band.

". . . So I was at Brownies, you know, the club, and I saw this all-girl band called Pork, and I said to myself, I can do that. I can do better than that. I mean, Pork? Give me a break. They even got a good write-up in *The Village Voice.* Unbelievable. And they sucked. They really sucked."

I had never seen Pork, had never heard Pork, but I knew what she was saying. I wanted to tell Julie all about my rock and roll fantasies. My dream. How most writers were musicians deep down inside, just waiting for someone to ask them to play in a band. Waiting for someone like Julie to step into their lives. But that's not what I said. Adjusting my voice so as not to sound too eager, I muttered, as offhand as I could, my opening line. My come-on. My pickup.

"Well, I play drums."

• TWO •

Julie, of course, knew nothing about 1974: the year I fell in love for the first time. I was only nine. Young, I admit. But a very mature nine.

To keep us out of trouble, my mother paid for us all to take guitar lessons. Before I was old enough for mine, I would strum my sister's six-string hollow-body electric. It was yellow, orange, and black, and full-figured, shaped just like George Harrison's. I would stick my small nose into the body holes to sniff the new, fresh wood. I imagined living in there, the chords reverberating all around me while I ate and slept.

Lost in my reverie, I would accidentally drop a plastic pick into one of the holes while strumming. This happened at least once a day. It was a bitch to get out, shaking the heavy Harmony guitar over my head and listening to the click-click-click, searching, searching until the pick flitted out into my eye.

But I didn't mind. I loved the guitar. Or thought I did, until my big brother, Stanley, introduced me to my true love. His set of pearl-white Ludwigs swept me off my feet.

I remember the day he got them. Worn down by his begging, my mother let him spend his after-school job money at Dick Allen's School of Music, the shop where we took our guitar lessons. Like Al himself, the instrument displays were old and dusty. There were trumpets dating back to the Jazz Age, accordions with yellowing keys, and bongo drums that predated the beatniks. Then there were the guitars, the only instruments that ever sold. Except for Stanley's drum set.

I wanted him to buy the red drums, shiny with sparkles trapped beneath, like a candy apple. But he chose the white pearl set, with mirrored center circles, which served as targets, but also guarded the drums from constant abuse. From that first day, my small palms ached to get at Stanley's drumsticks.

While Stanley practiced in the back room of our apartment, I walked, talked, and ate to his beat. I lived—and loved—vicariously through him. I practiced with chopsticks on pots and pans, using Daddy's stand-up glass and metal ashtray as a hi-hat. I played to the Beatles' "All Together Now," speeding up as the song did, sending me into a rhythmic seizure.

My idol became Karen Carpenter, the only female drummer I had ever heard of. One of my favorite tunes to play along to was "Close to You." By third grade, I had her soft fills down and even pretended to open the ashtray hi-hat up and down in a mellow "psst"-"psst"-"psst."

I loved the drums, but we were like star-crossed lovers from the start. At my Catholic grammar school, where there was no school band and no sports, the principal decided to bring in just two after-school activities: drumming and baton twirling. She was a nun with high hopes of starting a marching band, a closet majorette herself.

Sister Geraldine broke the classes into two groups, boys and girls. Boys took drum lessons. Girls were taught to twirl a baton. By the time I got up the courage to complain, the program was discontinued. Our Lady of Czestochowa produced neither drum majorettes nor drummers, regardless of sex.

My mother gently tried to discourage me from loving the drums, as if she knew what I was in for. When I was old enough, she sent me to

Dick Allen's for my own guitar lessons. On a small starburst acoustic painted in red fading to orange and then to mellow yellow, I practiced chords and notes and learned to sight-read music. But my hands were too small for the longest chord stretches.

Stanley's Ludwigs beckoned. When he wasn't at home playing them, they stood straight and still, all that energy and noise pent up inside.

While he was out one day, I got up enough courage and crept into Stanley's room, past the scary *All Things Must Pass* poster, past his old monster models—Dracula and the Wolf Man—past the baseball trophies and blowup Playboy Club pillow, and played for a few glorious hours. I snuck in the next day, and the day after, and the day after that, until playing the drums became a daily ritual, a secret obsession and addiction.

I loved the drums because they were all-consuming. They surrounded me, in the way I wished the guitar would, had I only been able to climb inside it. When I played the drums, I knew what those surfers felt like, inside the tube, the wave breaking over them, but at the same time carrying them, faster and faster, toward the shore.

I discovered that the drums played you; you didn't play them. If you practiced long enough, and hard enough, you and the drums became one, the sticks an extension of your arms, the kick pedal and hi-hat extensions of your feet. Your heart slowed to the beat you played, or sped up to catch up to the faster tunes.

Before playing every day, I would have to rearrange a few pieces of the kit, since Stanley was a southpaw and I was a rightie, but I always put the drums back in their rightful place before sneaking back out into the kitchen.

My mother never said a word to Stanley, but I gave myself away one day when I left the hi-hat on the wrong side. Ma tried taking the blame, and said she was in there dusting. But Stanley gave me an angry look and told me to keep out. I understood, even at that age. He was the middle kid, the only boy, sandwiched between two annoying sisters. The drums—and his room—were his territory.

Now, when he started playing gigs out, he would return the drums to his room, but wouldn't bother putting them back together. I discovered the horror one afternoon, after sneaking in to play: They were separated, tom-tom here, snare there, hi-hat in pieces. It was like seeing a loved one hacked to bits. But there was a cure.

I spread all the pieces out in front of me and studied them: the drums themselves, the hardware, the nuts and screws, the pedals and cymbals. Each day after school, I would study one section, assembling and disassembling it before Stanley came home from work. I was like a soldier, learning to take his rifle apart and put it back together, practicing over and over, so that when the moment of truth came, I could do it under the greatest pressure. I could even do it in the dark.

There were the myriad stands, skinny but strong, like flamingo legs. There was one for the snare, one for the hi-hat, one for the throne, for the crash cymbal and ride. I learned to tell each one apart by its length and thickness. The deep-sounding floor tom had its own little legs that slipped in and out of its body, like landing legs on a spaceship pod.

When I became an expert at one drum's construction, I'd move on to the next. The snare had a rattling band of wires beneath it, which were very delicate, and which, when moved by the vibrations of a drum hit, gave the snare its crackling sound. Because of the wires, the snare was the most breakable of the drums, and the most expensive, so I was extra careful when handling it. A switch on its side pulled the wires tighter or let them hang loose, changing the sound from a rattle to a thunk. The snare was also the most personal of all the drums, the one closest to you, since it sat right between your legs.

The tom-tom was not so delicate and screwed on top of the giant kick drum, floating and bouncing at whatever height I chose. The hi-hat was difficult, with its clamshell cymbals joined by a complicated nut. The most intricate part, though, was the kick drum pedal, with its many bones and joints, like the human foot. But once I mastered it, I realized I could raise or lower the mallet on the pedal, to avoid getting a black-and-blue on my shin.

Finally, the day came to put the parts together in the same sitting. And I did. Piece by piece. Bit by bit. And when I was done, I barely stepped back to admire my work. I quickly put a stack of records on Stanley's hi-fi, matted my frizzy hair down with his giant puffy headphones, and surrendered to the wave.

Steppenwolf's "Magic Carpet Ride" taught me how to play a skippy, syncopated beat on the snare, which I could lower and place at just the right angle between my legs, now that I understood the workings of its stand. With my new perfect fit, I sat snugly inside the zone, floating high above the tar rooftops of Jersey City. "Why don't you come with me, little girl, on a magic carpet ride?" John Kay sang.

I learned the end of the *Abbey Road* medley, with its famous drum solo. I played along to the funk of old Kool and the Gang records, to the tightly controlled Kinks, and to whatever else I could find. No matter what was happening outside that room, fifth grade, sixth grade, seventh and then eighth, prepubescence into high school, boys and best friends, twelve-inch disco singles, punk rock and new wave, Glee Club, high heels, Earth shoes, purple sparkly eyeshadow, bubble gum lip gloss, leg warmers, leather chokers, my folk phase, my Dylan phase, my twelve-string guitar phase, school dances, the Battle of the Bands, Budweiser nibs and 40-ouncers, joints and dime bags, crushes and menstruation, masturbation, tongue kissing, Tilt-a-Whirl and all, the drums were there for me each and every afternoon. My secret love. Always there and always true, no matter what I chose to play on them.

My mother walked into Stanley's room one day when I was thirteen, while I was playing the Free hit "All Right Now." It was right before my disco phase, when I was still on a heavy diet of white funk from Stanley's standard 45 collection. When I looked up and saw my mother standing there in the doorway, her mouth was hanging open.

"Oh my God," she said, as I whipped off the headphones, my hair springing back to life. I was ready to apologize for invading Stanley's space yet again. But before I could get the words out, she smiled and said:

"I thought you were Stanley."

• THREE •

Sound unheard, stories untold, Julie and I made a date.

She and her bass-playing friend had been practicing, without a drummer, for months, and were eager to play with me. After a two-week game of phone tag, we agreed to get together at a studio called Tasty Fish on a warm day in early October.

I could blame it on the seasonably warm fall weather, the kids with new book bags and shoes, the smell of school supplies still fresh and crisp in the air, notebooks barely doodled upon, but suddenly I found myself transported back to high school. I was worried about what to wear. As a freelancer, I went to work in my pajamas every day.

This wasn't the usual anxiety about what to wear out to dinner or what to wear to meet Scary Myra. This was right up there with worrying about what to wear to the St. Peter's Prep dance or the VFW Hall Hudson Catholic keg party of 1980. I hadn't missed that pit in the stomach at the thought of wearing the wrong shoes, the wrong pants, a laughable blouse. Now that feeling returned full force.

After staring into my closet for more than an hour, I decided to set it on fire. But I reconsidered and settled on olive-green Levi's with a wide, groovy, early-seventies brown belt with holes all around. It had belonged to my brother-in-law and was the real thing. I had appropriated it and cut it down to fit me sometime in the early nineties, when the seventies revival was just starting.

I chose clashing, red high-top sneakers, a dangerous move, since they were very punk early eighties. Mixing decades could end in a fashion disaster. I knew that from reading *Cosmo.* But the high-tops were the closest thing to cool shoes that I owned. To neutralize the combination, I wore a black tank under a plain beige cardigan sweater. I got hot when I played drums so the layers were for convenience.

"What do you think?" I asked Martin, my arms out, showing him my ensemble. "Honestly."

"I think it works," he said, nodding, his hands in the pockets of his bathrobe. "She'll love you." He leaned over and planted a coffee-scented kiss on my forehead.

I had never played in a studio before and wasn't sure if I needed to bring any hardware. I didn't want to ask Julie, worried she would know I was a rank amateur. I asked Martin, who had played bass in a band as a teenager.

"What would a drummer need in a studio?"

He thought for a minute and then placed a hand on his bacon-wrinkled forehead.

"I can't remember if they usually have the cymbals there or not. My God, that was so long ago. That was like fifteen years ago. Can you believe it? I was in the Zones fifteen years ago."

He faded away into a teenage reverie, but right now I was having a drum emergency. I had no time for a walk down memory lane with Martin and his old band, the Zones. I left him in the haze of nostalgia and called my brother.

"What's up?" Stanley said. Unlike my sister and me, my brother and I rarely called each other to chat. We loved each other, but spoke on the phone only out of necessity.

"I'm going to a studio to play drums with this girl I met. Do I need to bring anything besides sticks?"

"Some places want you to use your own cymbals."

"Oh," I said, waiting for him to offer. He wouldn't offer.

"Well, can I borrow yours?" I asked.

He had to make me wait a few seconds, even though we both knew what the answer would be. Stanley's cymbals were locked, unused and dusty, in the basement of his house in New Jersey. For several years now, there had been no crash finales for Stanley. Pyramid, his last band, had broken up a decade ago.

"Yeah," he said finally. "You can take them." I was still his pain-in-the-ass little sister, but he loved me anyway.

I made the emergency trip to Jersey, and Stanley and I went on an archaeological dig to find his drum kit. Beneath the layers of Little League trophies, furniture and clothes, boxes of pictures and eight-track tapes, the cymbals sat smooth and cold, just like I remembered them, with rings working their way out from the center to the edge, like the rings in a pond after you've thrown a pebble. It was so good to see them again. Stanley watched as I walked out onto the porch with them.

I should have felt victorious, finally, after years of begging and pleading and assembling under pressure. I should have waved them over my head, or smashed them together in a triumphant clang. But Stanley looked so sad standing there, watching me and his cymbals leave the porch and make our way down the street. His little sister taking his crash cymbals away.

I promised to return them as soon as possible. Looking over my shoulder as I walked away, I thanked him about seventeen times until he was no longer in shouting distance. With the booty in a large black duffel bag and my drumsticks in my backpack, I took the train to Manhattan, then the F train to the Delancey Street stop on the Lower East Side.

Tasty Fish was on Ridge Street, in the shadow of the Williamsburg Bridge, across from an empty schoolyard. There was no sign on the studio, just a red door with TASTY FISH written in black marker in very small letters, like a secret password. I checked my watch: 2:35. I'd purposely arrived a few minutes late, so as not to seem overly excited. When I pushed the red door open, I was happy to find I was not the first to arrive. The bass player was there, searching through a stack of wrinkled and ripped music magazines: *Musician, Rolling Stone, Modern Drummer.*

There was a foam-hemorrhaging couch and a "clock" consisting only of hands that pointed to numbers drawn onto the wall. Tasty Fish was low-rent chic, in a neighborhood that was slowly replacing its Dominican, Puerto Rican, and Eastern European families with rock clubs, upscale thrift shops, and practice studios. When you walked down the streets of the Lower East Side these days, you were more likely to hear a drummer drumming than a fishmonger mongering.

When I went to NYU, Alphabet City—Avenues A, B, C, and D—was dangerous, filled with burned-out crack houses and bums. No taxis, no carefree pedestrian hipsters. Back then, it was just plain people unfortunate enough to live there, scurrying from one rickety doorway to another. The Bowery was still a rest stop for passed-out drunks, a lost cause, the butt of a cruel joke.

But now the Bowery was where models hung out, so it had become a different kind of joke.

The bass player barely looked up from her magazine when I walked in. Dark stringy hair hid her eyes.

"Hi," I said, a little too brightly.

"Hi," she mumbled, from behind the fringe. I could see she was checking out my clothes, my seventies belt, my uncombed hair, my high-tops. She had the same look on her face as my high school best friend Sharon, the day she informed me I would have to wear brown suede wallabies, not penny loafers, for the cool boys to like me.

"I'm Helene." I offered the bass player my hand to shake.

"Elizabeth." No smile.

She had on checkered sneakers (low-tops), a striped shirt, a silver nose ring, and, I would later learn, a navel ring. She was Williamsburg bohemian all the way, the kind of girl who could wear a slip as a skirt and feel confident, who could pull off wearing a housedress ironically. I was Cobble Hill, with a husband and a growing collection of Pottery Barn furniture, including a dresser with a drawer filled with slips that would never be outerwear.

"I'm not a very good bass player," she announced.

"Well, I'm not a very good drummer." Maybe we could bond after all and make very bad music together.

But then Elizabeth asked, "What kind of music do you like?"

It was a cruel question, one I hadn't been asked since freshman year, September 1979. I listened to a lot of things, but probably not the right ones. What was I doing here? Maybe I should just turn around and leave with Stanley's cymbals, just take the train to Jersey City and hand them back, silent, defeated. I was too old for this.

My record collection had stopped growing in the late eighties, and since then had been augmented with singers like Lucinda Williams and k.d. lang. The only cool music I owned was from rock star interviews I had done and had had to prepare for, like PJ Harvey, Babes in Toyland, and Lisa Germano. I had never been in a mosh pit and probably never would be. To me, rave was, and would always be, a verb.

I felt very old, and gave Elizabeth the answer that old people often give.

"Neil Young."

I had listened to him and played his songs as a teenager because they were easy to figure out on acoustic guitar. And by some miracle, he had become cool again, thanks to a recent collaboration with the band Pearl Jam. Elizabeth nodded. I sensed approval.

"What else?"

Was she kidding? Did she want me to just lay down and die right here on the Tasty Fish floor?

I was at a loss. I didn't listen to the cool bands I should be listening to, like Stereolab or Built to Spill or Pavement. When the name Dean was mentioned, I pictured Dean Martin, not Dean Wareham, the front man from the band Luna. I hadn't even gotten around to listening to his first band, Galaxie 500. I had given up trying to keep up years ago.

Bless me, Elizabeth, for I have sinned. I just purchased the new Sting album.

I began to sweat, and stalled by taking off my sweater. There was an extremely long pause, littered with mumbles of, "Oh, I like so many bands. It's so hard to choose."

But then I thought of Yo La Tengo.

They were a cool indie band based in Hoboken, the city bordering Jersey City. I had stumbled upon Yo La Tengo at a few outdoor fairs and once or twice at the Hoboken club Maxwell's. They even had a girl drummer, Georgia Hubley. I knew her father had created the cartoon character Mr. Magoo. I even knew that the band's name was Spanish for what ballplayers say when they're about to catch a fly: I've got it. And there I was, going in for the catch.

"Yo La Tengo."

Elizabeth nodded slowly, unconvinced. Before she could quiz me on my favorite Yo La Tengo songs and albums, though, Julie walked in the door and rescued me. She looked exactly like she had sounded on the phone, a pixie with short, strawberry blond hair, a turned-up nose, and perfect teeth complementing a perfect smile, which she was not too cool to use. She was dressed in a black T-shirt, jeans, and Doc Marten boots. She had a line of silver earrings in her ear and a silver chain and pendant around her neck, gifts from Jimmy, I would later learn. The picture was made complete by the black guitar carrying case slung on one tiny shoulder and the small amp she pulled on a handcart.

Julie had an energy that changed the chemistry of the small, shabby room, something that Elizabeth, Steve, the Studio Guy, and I lacked. She made everything at Tasty Fish all right. Tasty, really.

She was cute, tomboy cute, with delicate bones, like a child's. The thing that got you, though, was her glow. The It. Whatever It was, Julie had It. It wasn't beauty or complexion, more a charisma, but not the kind aerobics instructors or motivational speakers possess. You couldn't fake It. It was the charisma of starlets and rock stars. I assumed lots of people had It, but I'd only witnessed It a few times in my life.

I had seen Lucinda Williams open for Rosanne Cash in Central Park once. I hadn't noticed It was missing until Cash got onstage beside Lucinda. That was the thing about It. You didn't know you were missing It until It actually showed up in your life and stood next to you. Like right now with Julie.

Rosanne Cash had been born with It. It had been passed down from her father. She had no choice but to become a performer. As soon as she took the stage and opened her mouth, she took command and left Lucinda in the shadow of her glow.

I had seen Nils Lofgrin, Bruce Springsteen's guitarist, at the Bottom Line once, and he, too, had It. He was a tiny guy, but the energy coming from his body and his guitar was enormous. It was hard to describe really. But as soon as he came onstage, you recognized It. It was the reason Springsteen had chosen him from the many thousands of guitarists in the world.

Springsteen, of course, had It. When he played with the E Street Band, It was hard to discern sometimes from all that commotion and the many instruments and voices layered one atop the other. There was so much going on onstage that It sometimes got lost in the shuffle. But Springsteen proved It to me one night when he played solo at the Beacon Theater. Alone, with an acoustic guitar, Springsteen conjured the soul of Tom Joad, with a whisper in your ear, but as loud as can be. He could take you into his hand and carry you off to a remarkable place, then bring you back again, the here and now new and improved, all at his will, with the sound of his voice and the flick of his wrist.

Like Cashes and kings, rock stars and queens, Julie had It. And luckily, she carried It with her into Tasty Fish.

All I had to carry were my cymbals, which were completely useless. There were cymbals in the studio already and a decent set of black drums with a pillow in the bass drum to muffle the sound. While I got comfortable, Elizabeth searched around for the right amp to plug into.

"Last time we were here, things were set up different," she said. "I'm not sure which amp is the bass amp."

"Just use any amp," Julie said, plugging her black Japanese Fender with the whammy bar into her little Mesa/Boogie amp.

The moment Elizabeth plugged into the big brownish box against the wall, she regretted Julie's advice. Feedback flooded the room. She pulled the cord out quickly, as if the amp might explode. There was a soft knock on the studio door. Steve, the Studio Guy, popped his head in.

"Did you see my keys?" he asked. For a second, he watched a shaken Elizabeth in her desperate search for the right amp. The keys were an excuse.

"Did you plug into this amp?" he asked Elizabeth, placing his entire forearm on the top of the big box. "This isn't a bass amp. Don't ever plug a bass into this amp. This is my baby. I love this amp."

"It's my fault," Julie said. "I told her to plug in there."

Steve snatched Elizabeth's cord and plugged it into a two-tiered bass amp. If she had been a guy, he never would have grabbed her cord like that.

Elizabeth slouched. Julie rolled her eyes while Steve made his way to the door. He paused to touch his precious amp, probably debating whether to take it with him or not, then slammed the door behind him.

"If it's his fucking baby, he should have said something before we got in here," I said.

"No," said Elizabeth. "It's my fault. I'm supposed to know which is a bass amp."

I hit the tom-tom a few times, tried the snare, and pumped the hi-hat to knock the tension out of the air. Julie walked up to the microphone and started strumming. Elizabeth recognized the song and fingered a simple bass line.

With Julie and Elizabeth leading the way, I leaped right in. Playing the drums isn't as complicated as playing the guitar or piano. It's easy simply to play along on drums even if you've never heard the song before. All you need is a tempo and a few gestures from the lead singer, and you're on your way.

We tiptoed through a dozen songs, most of which had no official title. There was the Shower Song ("You think you love her so you take another shower"), which used the bass line from a Violent Femmes song. So we called it "The Violent Femmes Song." There was a dark brooder that sounded like a Nirvana song; we called that "The Nirvana Song."

They had pretty, bright melodies disguising harsh lyrics. It was something Julie had picked up from bands like the Smiths, who had successfully matched a pretty melody with the words "Heaven Knows I'm Miserable Now."

My favorite Julie song was "The Next Big Thing."

I've been looking in magazines
And I've been looking on the movie screen
Everybody is so beautiful but
They don't say anything to me.

I'm waiting for the next big thing
To come along and tell me
What it is I've been doing wrong

I filled the spaces with crash cymbals and a big, sloppy sound. I could picture us playing it in arenas and football stadiums, a tongue-in-cheek anthem to superstardom and fame. It started out slow and quiet, but built louder and stronger and faster. Faster was a problem. The speeding up was my fault. I needed to stay calm and keep the tempo even.

This was the first time I had ever played original songs. Playing covers was one thing. Coming up with original fills and rhythms was something I hadn't thought about when coming to play. I had no one telling me, or showing me, what to do. No record, with fills all laid out for me to copy. It was all up to me. It was exciting, but crippling, if I worried about it too much. Should I use the drumsticks or a tambourine, my jingle stick or my mallets? I had to listen to the music to try and hear what it was calling out for. So I played quietly, gently, trying hard to listen.

"I like the way you play," Julie told me. "You play like Mo Tucker. You're a gentle drummer."

I shrugged and smiled, embarrassed.

Tucker, the drummer from the Velvet Underground, was the queen of all female rock drummers. She had, not a moment too soon, replaced Karen Carpenter as my number one.

There were the Go-Go's and the Bangles. But I didn't count them, since hardly anyone could name their drummers. Well, maybe a few rock critics could. There was Sheila E., Prince's former girlfriend. But she was more of a percussionist. There were lots of female percussionists, tapping the shit out of triangles and rapping away at conga drums, like Joe Jackson's percussionist, Sue Hadjopoulos, whose name, even if I could remember it, I could never pronounce. Female percussionists were overqualified drummers that nobody knew what to do with.

I just concentrated on staying steady and keeping it simple, like good ol' Mo. Elizabeth struggled to keep up and not lose her place. She shot Julie a nasty look every now and then until finally Julie explained why. "I convinced her to buy a bass and learn to play," Julie said, nodding at Elizabeth.

"I was there at Brownies the night she saw Pork," Elizabeth complained. "I've only been playing a few months."

Because this was all her idea, Julie couldn't really give Elizabeth a hard time when she lagged behind. Whenever the bass line turned muddy, Julie would stop singing and lay her head alongside the neck of her own guitar as if posing for a photograph. Definitely the album cover, I thought.

"Just thump along," Julie said to her. "Don't worry about it."

"That's easy for you to say," Elizabeth said. "You know how to play."

Julie had a natural sense of rhythm and liked to take a more relaxed, "let's skip a chorus, or is that a verse? I always get the terminology mixed up" approach. She wanted to jam. But Elizabeth couldn't.

Julie turned to me and asked, "So what do you like to play?" The question had none of the contempt or cruelty of Elizabeth's questions. I didn't answer, though. Not verbally. I immediately fell into a more skippy "Magic Carpet Ride" rhythm, using all my limbs and really digging in. Julie jumped in on guitar, and encouraged a silent Elizabeth to join us.

"You know I can't," Elizabeth moaned, looking both embarrassed and homicidal at the same time. I was afraid she would beat us both to death with her bass, then run out and smack Studio Steve in the forehead for good measure. So I stopped, less out of pain for her than fear for myself. I hadn't even worked up a sweat.

It was past 4:30, though. Our time was up at Tasty Fish. Two hours had slipped by unnoticed, like the first date with the new love of your life.

• FOUR •

When I was an undergraduate at New York University, all journalism students were required to intern at a newspaper, magazine, or broadcasting station. I chose *Down Beat,* the jazz magazine, but by the time my internship rolled around, their New York bureau had closed. Faced with the prospect of working a whole semester at *American Airlines* magazine (my advisor's solution to the problem), I called *Musician* magazine and asked if they had an intern program.

Peter, the guy who answered the phone, was just that—the guy who answered the phone. And Peter was sick of answering the phone. He was sick of being sent for coffee and sick of being generally abused by the staff of editors. When he heard the word *intern,* he pounced.

"Well, we've never had an intern, but we'd love to have one," he said, overenthusiastically. I should have hung up right then, but I was too young to know that you should never trust anyone who wants you that much.

Working at *Musician* for four months convinced me that I was an amateur when it came to loving music, that I thought I loved music but was, in fact, an impostor. Loving music took an orthodox approach in a world devoid of other distractions, including women. Though it was one of my favorite magazines, *Musician* was for guys—mostly single guys who fancied themselves musicians but had day jobs, which left lots of disposable income for the equipment advertised in *Musician*'s pages. Unlike the other gearhead magazines, though, *Musician* landed the biggest rock star interviews and always went into detail about songwriting.

The magazine's main office was in Gloucester, Massachusetts, which is where its founders, the Baird brothers, Gordon and Jock (*Jock!*), lived. *Musician* was published out of a remote fishing village. It made sense in a way. You hardly ever found a woman on a fishing boat, either.

The magazine had a much smaller office on Times Square, where I worked. It was a tiny suite in the 1515 Broadway building, the skyscraper with the square crown on its head, which housed *Billboard* magazine, record labels, and countless other musical enterprises. Someone claimed to have actually seen Madonna on the elevator once.

The *Musician* crowd was, for the most part, your typical collection of grown-up music geeks. There was a nasty little man, about four foot eleven, with thick glasses and a smug look that said, "Even though you're taller than me, I'm smarter than you." His claim to fame was that his once-Afroed head was in the background of a much-reproduced poster of the crowd at Woodstock.

Another editor was a former electronics salesman, the guy who would humiliate you at Radio Shack into buying better woofers and tweeters than you would ever really need, the guy who played the electric guitars himself, scaring away potential customers with his renditions of Eric Clapton songs.

The guys at *Musician* spent their days listening to rare bootlegs and, every now and then, writing stories for and selling ad space to others like themselves. Other guys who knew what *MIDI* stood for. I still wasn't sure what it meant. I lived in fear that someone would ask me. So I finally looked it up:

Musical Instrument Digital Interface, wherein electronic devices interact with other electronic devices. For instance, a MIDI connection allows a keyboardist to play ten different keyboards from just one keyboard (!) and to sample sounds from computers and other digital devices.

I did my homework and tried hard to fit in, but I was still not allowed into the *Musician* club. I got the feeling I was the only person with two X chromosomes who'd ever set foot in the office besides the cleaning lady. The editors were all in their late thirties and early forties and hadn't yet married, aging monastic brothers joined by their very excellent sound system. The nasty little Woodstock editor once said that he didn't believe in marriage. Yeah, right, I wanted to say.

The only editor in the office who hadn't been spurned his whole life by pretty girls, the only one who hadn't hidden behind his rare vinyl and concert tapes, the only one who was actually married was a guy named Bill Flanagan. He was so cool and comfortable and confident around women and rock musicians that he had a model for a wife. Just like Mick Jagger and Keith Richards did, Rod Stewart and Billy Joel and, ugliest of all, Rick Ocasek. If they had model wives, why shouldn't Bill?

Susan, Bill's wife, was the beautiful blond woman who had been in the Cars video "You Might Think I'm Crazy." Though Bill was a good-looking guy, he wasn't good-looking enough for Susan. It was that rock star confidence that made him attractive.

Bill was the only person, besides Peter, who ever dared to have a full conversation with me. It was Bill who had arranged for me to sit in on an editorial meeting once, and Bill who arranged for me to come to the office Christmas party in Gloucester.

Bill was so cool that he actually was friends with Elvis Costello. The best part of my job—by a long shot—was answering the calls made by Elvis to Bill every few days.

"Is Bill there?" the London accent would ask.

Even though I knew who it was each time he called, I'd make him say so, just to hear him say his name. It was the only fringe benefit I had. No medical, no dental, no pay. Just Elvis Costello on the line. Not even calling for me.

"Who's calling?"

"It's Elvis," he'd say. "Elvis Costello." (I thought maybe once, just once, he'd slip and use his real name, Declan McManus. But he never did.)

I wanted to tell him how much his music meant to me, how great the Attractions were, how cool it was that he had recently married Cait O'Riordan, the bass player from the Pogues. But I was too shy. All I could muster was,

"Hold on. I'll transfer you."

"Thank you," he always said. So polite.

The only thing I learned that semester—aside from being able to recognize Elvis's voice instantly—was a bit of wisdom from Bill.

Bill told me that you could judge whether a song was good or bad by stripping it down to its basics. Take away the fancy production, the echoes and string section, extra percussion and synthesizer, Eric Clapton guitar solos. Have the singer sing it, and strum along on guitar, and if what you're left with is any good, then the song is good and the singer has talent.

It was sound advice.

At the end of that first practice, I gave Julie my address, hoping she would send me a demo tape of her songs. But I wasn't sure I'd ever hear from her again. My drumming was amateurish, my outfit a greatest hits compilation of the seventies and eighties. I was sure she and Elizabeth found me unworthy.

But three days after our practice, there it was, the tape in my mailbox. Like the tiny word John Lennon had spied after climbing to the top of Yoko Ono's white avant-garde ladder: Yes.

Julie's songs were all recorded on a small four-track that she had at home, with her on guitar and vocals, just like Bill had said. Sometimes she played keyboards. But the songs were always stripped down to their basics. And they sounded great.

The next time Julie and Elizabeth and I got together at Tasty Fish, Studio Steve graced us with the bigger studio room, better lit, with air-conditioning. The only problem was that it smelled like feet.

"Probably rug mildew or something," Julie said. "One of my friends had a place that smelled like this. It was the bong water he spilled on the rug."

The Bong Water Room, as it came to be known, was much better than the old room; the drums were decorated in red-and-white swirls, very Brady.

This time, Elizabeth knew better than to plug into the wrong amp. Studio Steve kept his distance. I recognized all the songs from the demo and some from that first practice together. Elizabeth was much more engaged, and even had some drum advice for me on the Nirvana Song. "You should maybe use the kick drum during that break," she said. "You know, this one." She played the bass line leading up to the void. And I filled it with four kicks.

It felt so good to be behind a set of drums again. It felt right. Snug and right, like spooning with your boyfriend. Or husband.

We met again that fall. Then, in winter, there was no heat at Tasty Fish, so we had to wear gloves and coats while we played. With my wool gloves on, my sticks kept slipping out of my hands. So for our next practice, I cut the fingers off to get a better grip.

"How'd it go today, girls?" Studio Steve asked as we were leaving.

"It's getting better," I said.

"You're such an optimist," Julie said, rolling her eyes.

We played again and again, until we learned all the songs on that demo tape, songs that I wouldn't mind listening to, even if I weren't playing to them. There was the pop ditty, the Haircut Song ("I cut my hair for you. I painted my toenails, too. I painted them black to get you back").

There was the Fuck You song, about Julie's job on Wall Street. And another song, called "Document," which was a pretty lullaby about growing up, about childhood lost, all the little things you'd forgotten, about penmanship and drinking Shirley Temples and Roy Rogers. The lines I loved went like this: "Don't forget to say your prayers, is what she said to me. Jesus lost and found, over and over again."

It sounded like nonsense, but the lines resounded for me. "Jesus lost and found" was a mantra my fifth grade teacher had taught us. When you lost something, all you had to do was repeat those four words, while you looked for whatever it was you'd lost, and sooner or later, Jesus would help you find it. According to Mrs. Wojtowicz, the prayer dated back to the time Jesus was lost in the temple as a boy. Julie, having grown up thousands of miles away from me, knew this very same story, and this very same prayer.

All winter, as the snow accumulated on the breezeway, I practiced at home to Julie's tapes, using a rubber practice pad to bang on. It was black and looked like a wide-brimmed flat hat, with a raised section in the middle for smacking. One January afternoon I got too carried away, banging with my foot on an imaginary bass drum. Our downstairs neighbor came up and complained.

Martin listened to the demo tapes with me before going to work and sometimes even played along on his old Fender bass turned down low while I banged on the practice pad. No feet.

I loved to watch Martin play bass. He was happy, blissed out, the same way I felt when I played drums. Martin had a great sense of rhythm and very nimble fingers, which moved up and down the neck, just like Paul McCartney's. He moved his hips when he played, ever so slightly, and made a concentrated face, moving his lower jaw but keeping his eyes fixed.

It was the same face he made when we had sex. Playing bass, or any instrument, was as close as you got to doing it. It was a labor of love, which, if practiced right, could climax in a way that made your knees all noodly.

One afternoon, excited by Julie's new songs, Martin dragged out his old tapes from his Zones days. He rarely talked about the band, but I could tell it was part of his glory days, his lost golden era. He seemed not to like his job very much. Martin had always been a pretty happy person; these days, he looked a little down.

Sometimes he wouldn't even bother to shave before going to the office, or, horror of horrors, he would wear wrinkled pants to work. Martin wasn't the type of guy to wear wrinkled pants to work. In the middle of dinners out, weekend trips away, and home-cooked meals, Martin would start staring off into space and mumbling to himself, having private fights with people at work.

"What did you say?" I would ask, to try and draw him out.

"Oh, nothing," he'd say, then continue to mumble and curse.

When Martin listened to those Zones tapes, he forgot all about the paper. I was surprised at how professional the recordings were and how good the band sounded for a bunch of teenagers. Especially now, having played in a band a whopping four months, knowing how hard it was to find that chemistry.

Many of the Zones songs had been written by Martin and his friend Dave, who had been our best man. Every now and then, at a party or on a night out in Brooklyn, I would run into some woman who had gone to the same high school as Martin and Dave—Edward R. Murrow High.

"Oh, my husband went there," I would say. And within seconds, the Zones would be the main topic of conversation. The girl, no matter who she was or where I met her, was likely to have had a crush on either Martin or Dave. Those girls knew the Zones' lyrics better than I did, knew how Martin had combed his hair, what kind of sunglasses he had worn. And every time I bumped into one of Martin's old groupies, I would get jealous. Not for the normal reasons a wife should get jealous. I would get jealous because I wanted to be in a band.

The Zones' music had an eighties edge, with heavy keyboards, syncopated beats, and a touch of reggae here and there. Like those girls lost in their high school memories, I could just picture the Zones with their skinny ties, Ray-Bans, and greasy hair jumping around on a high school stage, melding into one cohesive entity, becoming much more than the sum of their parts.

I had played drums with Stanley's band, Pyramid, once, at my sister's anniversary party. I sat in for two songs while Stanley sulked in the corner. And just in those two numbers, "Satisfaction" and "I Saw Her Standing There," I had entered that zone, the zone that the Zones had inhabited. I had melded with the other band members, connected, in a rhythm, moving steadily, surely, to the song's finish.

I craved that band dynamic, that groove that I had only briefly tasted at Paula's basement party. But it didn't come again until Julie.

One February afternoon at Tasty Fish, Julie was singing, strumming away to the Nirvana Song, and Elizabeth was hitting all the right notes, filling the spaces left by my hi-hat and then, when things built louder and louder, my ride cymbal. And suddenly, we were coasting on that wave, lost inside that zone, that Tilt-a-Whirl spin, three of us, all together. We all nodded and smiled, even frowning Elizabeth. There she stood, with a big, toothy smile on her sour puss. We were grooving. Or, like Afro-Cuban musicians liked to call it, in *clave:* a state of perfect equilibrium.

"That wasn't half-bad," Julie said, all giddy, when the song was through.

Elizabeth smiled again. It was a record: two smiles in one day. I smashed my crash cymbal in celebration.

We had no name, no gimmick, but in moments like that, it felt like maybe we should. "Maybe we could call ourselves Girls, Girls, Girls," I said.

Julie bent her head to the side and gave it some thought. "That's not bad."

"I don't like it," Elizabeth said, frown back in place.

The next week, still on that high, the three of us made a tape of ourselves playing together in the rehearsal studio. The production values were pretty low—a boom box with one red button: RECORD. But when I got the tape home and played it, loud, just like Martin liked his music, we were both shocked.

"You sound pretty good," he said, his arms folded.

"We do," I said, more surprised than he was.

We actually sounded like a band. Between our conversations about the men in our lives and about what plans we had for the weekend, you could hear those moments when we had bonded.

In *clave.*

• FIVE •

A band was a lot like a marriage, Martin had told me. Like being married to two or three people at the same time. There was commitment and hard work, but there was an emotional side as well, something that didn't come with just any job. The music, like love, kept you together, made some days miraculous, and other days unbearable.

Of course, Elizabeth, Julie, and I were still just going steady, trying to get to know one another. Still in the freefall of love.

Elizabeth was holding out on me. But between songs, I learned the lyrics to Julie's life. Not just the choruses, but the verses. She was the youngest of seven and had been raised Catholic, like me, but she didn't believe in marriage, actual marriage, and didn't want kids. Being the youngest of seven could do that to a person. She had spent her formative years in Nebraska, in a town called Broken Bow, but had moved with her family to St. Louis when she was ten.

Julie and I started socializing outside the studio. We went to shows together, to see Aimee Mann, Ben Folds Five, and the HORDE show, an ill-conceived Woodstockish affair that unwisely placed Beck and Neil Young on the same bill. I liked both of them, but you had to be a moron to think Neil Young fans were going to sit through Beck's latest stage show, a tribute to/send-up of seventies disco. Beck actually led the crowd in chanting "Sergio Valente" at one point. Joking, of course. But the Neil Young fans, hairy, sloping-foreheaded Neanderthals, didn't get the joke.

We grimaced as the Neil Young fans screamed obscenities at Beck. By the time their main man came on, their Lee jeans coated in beer, they were standing on their seats, screaming out the names of their personal theme songs, like "The Needle and the Damage Done." You could see Neil Young cringe.

"I hope we don't have fans like that," I said.

"Hey." Julie laughed. "I'll take anything I can get. Let's get their addresses so we can put them on our mailing list someday."

It was at HORDE that Julie confided in me about her problem with Jimmy.

Jimmy had just done work on a movie called *Tromeo and Juliet.* It was a dark rewriting of the Shakespearean classic, with lots of violence, fourth-grade humor, and gratuitous sex. Julie's only contribution to Jimmy's movie was a voice-over for a TV bit in the film, which you never see but simply overhear. On the TV playing in the background, you can hear Julie's sweet little voice. "Eat shit," she says.

The female lead in the movie was a woman named Jane Jensen, who was not only an actress but led her own pop band, Jane Jensen and the Dolls. *Spin* had just run a full-page photo of Jane, a pretty blonde with a long braid. Julie was afraid Jimmy was going to sleep with Jane. He had already directed her in several nude scenes. I told Julie she was right to be suspicious.

"I think all Janes are evil," I said. I regaled her with tales of an old roommate of mine named Jane. "She left our back door open one morning and this giant pile of dirty dishes in the sink. So when I got home from work there were like twelve thousand flies, half of them dead and floating in the sink, the other half on one of the window screens. You know, like out of that movie *The Amityville Horror*?"

"Yikes." (Julie was one of the few people who could say "yikes" and get away with it.) "What did you do?"

"I ran away. I went to Martin's apartment and didn't come back for like three days."

I told Julie how most Janes I had known I had hated, or at least actively disliked. "I actually had a second roommate named Jane who was even worse than the first. She was so clueless, she had no idea which of the Beatles were still alive."

"How old was she?"

"Our age!"

"No!" Julie said.

"She made cookies once and used salt instead of sugar. Complete idiot."

"So you think there's something inherently bad about being named Jane?"

"I do," I said. "Maybe it has something to do with those books we were forced to read when we were little. See Jane run. See Jane talk. After a while, you don't want to see Jane anymore. You know what I mean? Like, give me a break, Jane."

"Exactly," Julie said. "Fuck Jane."

"We don't want him to fuck Jane."

To make Julie feel better, I told her that things weren't always so great with me and Martin. "Believe me, we've had our problems."

"Like what?" she asked.

I told Julie about how, after a year of dating, Martin had wanted to get married, how he had hinted at it, and how I had run away in a panic and taken a job at a radio station in Alaska.

"You *what*?" she asked.

"There was no reason *not* to get married," I said. "Things were so good I got scared. I guess I was afraid of the idea of getting married. I mean, come on, how many happily married couples do you know?"

She shook her head, at a loss. "So I just took off to Alaska and promised to come back after a year."

"And did you?" she asked.

"I'm here, right?"

"Wow," she said.

"Even after I got back, though, I still wasn't sure I wanted to get married. When he finally proposed, I was pretty freaked out."

"But you seem pretty happy now," she said.

"That's the crazy part," I said. "I am happy. I'm really happy I married him." I shrugged. "Happily ever after."

After practice one day, over coffee at a Polish restaurant, we shared our first-concert stories. Mine had been at age five, at Madison Square Garden to see Elvis Presley with my mother and my Aunt Millie, a career waitress who was a very big fan of the King.

"All I remember is his white cape swirling around," I said, my finger twirling in the air. "We didn't have very good seats. We were all the way up in the blue section." My mother had called it Blue Heaven.

"But still," Julie said. "Elvis Presley!"

I had impressed her.

Julie's first show had been at Six Flags Great Adventure to see Scott Baio. "You know, Chachi from *Happy Days*?"

"Oh, I know. I had his picture on my wall, from *Tiger Beat* magazine."

"But my first real stadium concert was the Police," Julie said, "during the *Ghost in the Machine* tour." She raised her eyebrows and nodded her head in mock pride.

"Oh, yeah," I said. "I had that album. Remember that song "Spirits in the Material World"? I always thought they were saying, 'We are nurses in the maternity ward.' "

"Really?" Julie laughed.

"Really."

"I was one of those new wave girls in high school," she said, "a fan of the B-52's."

"Oh God. Me too. Remember the night they were on *Saturday Night*

Live?" I said excitedly. "I remember I was up late because I had a sunburn. It was the summer and I couldn't sleep. I was covered in Noxzema. And they came on. It was like, what is this? But it was so great."

"I remember," she said, smiling, distant suddenly, lost in that summer memory, too, of Fred Schneider singing "Rock Lobster," of the women in their beehives providing backup.

Julie and I wound through friendships and months and years, comparing notes and synchronizing the events in our lives. We talked about when we were teenagers, when music still mattered, when it was an integral part of your life, like water, air, or food. The music you played wasn't background music, but was the soundtrack to your life. It made all the difference in the world which songs you chose, because the plot—your plot—would be affected by the tempo, the mood, and the lyrics.

When you closed your eyes, you could glide on the rhythm and, if you listened hard enough, feel the melody etch its way onto your heart. And then there were the words, which touched you like no Freshman Lit poetry ever could.

Rock and roll explained what it was like to be a teenager, to hold on to those last, panicked moments of childhood lost, the magical time when escape was imminent, your parents were stupid, and the world was yours for the taking. Adolescence was the first twilight in your life, the first intermission between acts, the one that seemed the most painful, only because it was the first. You had no idea there would be more painful times ahead. How could there be? And those lyrics explained that pain, that suffering, and the release that came with the melody.

I told Julie that whenever I heard Elton John's "Don't Let the Sun Go Down on Me," I was reminded of sitting in my room and crying because I had no date to the St. Aloysius junior prom. My boyfriend, a stoner named Sean, had just broken up with me, and though I didn't miss him all that much, with his droopy eyelids, yellowed fingertips, and hacking cough, I was devastated about not having a prom date. It was a week away. I had already bought the dress, had ordered the flower for his lapel, had even paid for the pictures in advance. I sat on the edge of my bed and played that sad, sad Elton John song over and over again on my turntable, its piano bouncing off my lavender walls and tormenting me. And whenever I heard the song now, I couldn't help but feel a little desperate, a little bit like that sixteen-year-old girl without a date.

By the time the senior prom rolled around, I made damn sure I had secured a steady, reliable boyfriend. And whenever I heard a Culture Club song, any Culture Club song, I thought of John. It was the early eighties, and so Boy George's voice was the soundtrack to the summer we went out, the soundtrack playing on John's car radio, particularly the song "Karma Chameleon." I laughed every time I heard that song because John had misheard the chorus as "Become a comedian." As in "Become Become Become Become Become a comedian."

I told Julie about my first really serious boyfriend, Tony, who required a more serious song. When I first set eyes on him, Tony was quietly singing a verse from one of my favorite Beatles songs, one of John Lennon's grimmest. "The eagle picks my eye, the worm he licks my bone . . ."

" 'Yer Blues'?" I asked him. When he nodded, I should have run the other way.

Tony and I went out for over three years. We were like twins in a lot of ways. We had grown up within a couple of miles of each other, had escaped our working-class towns, and both had the same moody temperament. Most important, we listened to all the same music, and were both big Beatles fans.

I was the first girl Tony had met who knew as much about the Beatles as he did. And in those first, tingly weeks of dating, we would try and impress each other with our vast knowledge of the band.

"Did you know that the wood that coffins are made of is often imported from Norway?" Tony asked me one day.

"Huh?"

"As in 'Norwegian Wood.' That's where Lennon got the song title."

"Ohhh. Okay," I said. He waited a beat.

"Not really," he said. "Lies About the Beatles."

This was a little game we played, something that Tony dreamed up, and I was the first woman who had ever played along. Every once in a while, instead of stumping each other with real Beatles trivia, we'd throw in some made-up factoid.

While he was driving one day, I turned to Tony and said, "So did you know George Harrison was secretly married for like four weeks in 1962?"

"Really?" he asked, his ears pricking up.

"No. Lies About the Beatles."

The biggest difference between Tony and me was our ages. He was three and a half years older than I was, so he knew what was going to happen in life before I did. It sometimes came in handy, but what I learned with Tony was that you just didn't want to know what was heading your way. You didn't need another person just like yourself. It was like having two melody lines. With Tony, it was like we were singing the same tune out of sync, always correcting each other when we got it wrong.

Whenever I heard the album *Murmur,* by R.E.M., I was reminded of the time I cheated on Tony. *Murmur,* in its entirety, reminded me of Rob, my first lesson that being in love was no defense against falling in love with another person. I had gone to Italy for my summer abroad thinking, knowing, that Tony and my relationship was secure. But then I met Rob. And, with the help of the sweet Tuscan air, fields of sunflowers, and R.E.M. playing on Rob's boom box at the head of his bed, I learned that you could, in fact, love two people at the same time. It was a terrible thing, really, probably the worst of all human traits: the ability to give your heart away when it was already spoken for.

But while it was all happening, with your soundtrack of love playing in the background, cheating didn't seem so terrible. The pangs of guilt were easily overwhelmed by the euphoria of falling in love. I remember seeing a sticker of Charlie Chaplin in Rob's closet one afternoon after having sex. Tony and I had recently been to a Chaplin festival in New York. I was suddenly plunged into a pit of betrayal and guilt, but as soon as Rob walked back into the room and pushed PLAY, those feelings evaporated and love lifted us up where we belonged, where the eagles fly, blah blah blah. Try singing that one to Tony.

He knew right away, of course, that I had cheated on him. On a long-distance, transatlantic phone call, Tony noticed my voice sounded different. "Have you met someone else?" he asked. My silence was my confession.

Julie told me about her first loves, Bobby Younger in high school, and Tom Unger, her grade-school sweetheart. Younger/Unger. It sounded like a song coming on. There was Chris, in graduate school, who wanted to marry her. And Jim, who was in a rock band with his best friend, Jimmy. Jimmy had had a crush on Julie from when he was a kid. So after she and Jim broke up, Julie wound up going out with Jimmy. Which brought us up to her romantic present, more or less.

While I was still dating Tony, and answering phone calls from Elvis Costello, Julie's mother was diagnosed with cancer, she told me. Julie stayed at home with her, riding the train every day to school, where she was studying philosophy. "On my commute, like a half hour each way, I'd listen to my headphones," Julie told me. "That was the extent of my music education: the Smiths, Style Council, Billy Bragg, Elvis Costello. It was all boy music," said Julie. "I didn't listen to any girl music."

Julie's rock dream was born after she had moved to New York, a few months after her mother died. Her mother had been dying for years, and finally gave in while home alone in St. Louis, drinking dry martinis.

"I didn't know what I wanted to do with my life," Julie said. "But then I realized that you die and everything you do is meaningless. I thought, 'I'm twenty-eight years old. Fear or courage or shame is irrelevant. You only get eighty-five good years at the most and then it's over. You can make boring-ass movies or interesting movies. Good music or no music at all.' "

So that summer, Julie bought her first guitar—a red Epiphone with a small amp.

"I ordered it by mail," she said, "because I couldn't bear being humiliated by the guy in the music store."

I nodded. I knew that guy from *Musician.*

• SIX •

I told Martin everything about Julie, everything about the band, like a girl with a new crush. And sometimes he would tell me a little bit about the Zones. They had played out a lot, including a bunch of gigs at 2001: Space Odyssey, the Bay Ridge club where John Travolta had danced in *Saturday Night Fever.* By the time Martin, Dave, and the other guys played there, it was an all-male strip club six nights a week. They played on the seventh night, though the sign in the dressing room still warned, NO PUBES ON CUSTOMERS!

When Martin and I first met, still getting to know each other, I was happy to learn that he had been in a band. He hardly had to tell me. I could see that Martin banged on tabletops and his knees, playing to the beat playing inside his head. I was the first girl he'd ever known who was not driven insane by the habit. I loved him more for it. As a kid, he ruined his mother's fancy living room chairs by banging on them. After that, he used the phone book as his tom-tom.

"It gives it a nice, deep sound," he explained. And I knew right away what he was talking about.

It was one of the many reasons we got together. But not the only one. Elvis Costello helped, too.

Martin and I had met while both working at a newspaper in New Jersey. Newspapers were filled with frustrated musicians. There was Jim, the columnist who was also a drummer in a Hoboken band. And Ken, the photojournalist by day/alto saxophonist by night. And Allen, the struggling guitarist.

I was the crime reporter/closet drummer and Martin was the obituary writer/recovering bass player. We were assigned to the same desk, different shifts. I banged on it during the day; he took over at night.

Just as I was finishing up my police horror story for the day, my phone would start to ring with calls for Martin. Calls from the funeral parlors.

I would e-mail him that he'd gotten a call. But one night, after overhearing a conversation he was having about Elvis Costello's latest album, *Spike,* I sent him this message, quoted from a song from the record:

> *"Now I'm dead, now I'm dead, now I'm dead, now I'm dead.*
> *And I'm going on to meet my reward."*
>
> *Call Failla Funeral Home*
> *They've got a stiff for you.*

Martin loved that message. And he loved that I loved Elvis Costello. I loved that he loved that I loved Elvis Costello. I was the only woman he knew who knew Elvis was married to Cait O'Riordan. I even knew that they had written a song together on *Spike* called "Baby Plays Around." I was the only woman Martin knew who knew that Elvis's band, Bruce, Steve, and Pete, was called the Attractions, and that they had recently broken up. I knew they weren't on *Spike.* And I knew Elvis was mad at Bruce, the bass player, for writing a new tell-all book about the band.

Martin hoped that Elvis would change his mind about Bruce and about the band. But our hopes were not high. Those guys had been together way too long. Ten years. As long as the Beatles. Longer than most married couples I knew.

That summer, I went to see Elvis on his *Spike* tour at the Garden State Arts Center with Tony, who was still my boyfriend. In an act of betrayal worse than adultery, I relayed Elvis's set list to Martin at work on Monday. There was one song, a slow, pretty number that Tony and I had never heard before, so I asked Martin the name of it. I sang him a line.

"Thank you for the days. Those endless days, those sacred days la LA la."

I couldn't remember any more lyrics. I hummed the rest of it. I had the melody down.

"I never heard that before," Martin said, shaking his head. "I don't think it's an Elvis song."

"Are you sure?" I said, singing it again and again, frustrated, hearing the tune clearly in my head.

"I don't know it," he said, wincing, slightly embarrassed, not wanting to disappoint me.

A few months later, after Tony and I had broken up, Martin and I became a couple. And for the first time in my life, I really understood that *Cosmo* orgasm story I had read as a little girl, about the ride on the Tilt-a-Whirl.

But it wasn't just great sex. Martin was patient and kind and loved me unconditionally, even when I ran away to Alaska. He came to visit me, in the middle of a blizzard. And when I came back home, he made that proposal from the top of Manhattan. He calmed me down when I grew anxious and made everything all right.

One time, when we were lost on the New Jersey Turnpike, with my mother in the backseat, I started to unravel. Martin opened a map, turned to me, and gently said, "Don't worry. We'll find our way." And we did. My mother liked to use that story as an example of how wonderful Martin was. Tony and I would have wound up screaming at each other and the whole thing would have ended with me kicking him out of the car at the Vince Lombardi Rest Area.

Then one night, not long after, Martin and I went to see a Wim Wenders film, *Until the End of the World.* In the middle of the movie, Elvis came on the soundtrack and sang, "Thank you for the days, those endless days, those sacred days you gave me."

Hearing it was like being an amnesia victim and getting hit in the head with a baseball at Yankee Stadium, and suddenly remembering who you were.

"Oh my God," I said to Martin. But when I turned to him, in my excitement and disbelief, he nodded. He already knew what I was about to say.

"That's it," he whispered. "Isn't it? That's the song."

I nodded and hugged his arm.

That night, we walked hand in hand down Thompson Street to my SoHo apartment, the song, "Days," playing in stereo inside our heads. We watched the lights of the Empire State Building snap off at midnight. Like something out of a song.

Now my marriage—the band marriage—was on the rocks. Julie, Elizabeth, and I had barely exchanged vows, and there we were, in need of group therapy. Julie and I were growing closer. That wasn't the problem. Or maybe it was. Maybe Elizabeth was jealous.

One week, Julie took a new step in our relationship when she asked me if I would baby-sit her dog, a small, white, fluffy Havanese. Aubrey was Julie's baby, and having her trust me with her baby was monumental.

Aubrey stayed with Martin and me for a week while Julie went to visit her friends Dave and Mary in Philadelphia. It was great having a dog around the house, to keep me company the long nights Martin spent at work. Then Aubrey and I would both be overjoyed when Martin came in the door around midnight. Aubrey would do a little dog dance, jumping from the coffee table to the couch to the armchair and back to the coffee table, to the couch to the armchair, over and over, in a crazy circle. Martin laughed and laughed.

So one night, when Aubrey had gone back home to Julie, I did the same thing when Martin came in from work, looking sad. I did the Aubrey dance. Joking, of course. But meaning it really. I hopped from the coffee table to the couch to the armchair, around and around. And we laughed. And we hugged. And did it on the couch.

The week Julie came back, Elizabeth called and told her something had come up and she couldn't make it to practice. She confided in Julie later that she was unhappy with the new songs Julie had written, especially one keyboard number called "Epigone."

Julie and I tried playing without Elizabeth, but we discovered that we had become dependent on her cues. A band needed a bass player, even a bass player as unenthusiastic as Elizabeth.

It was important that the bass player and drummer get along. That they groove. Not now and then, but always. And as hard as we tried, there was no real groove between Elizabeth and me. She would not practice on her own, either out of laziness or shyness; I never got close enough to find out.

Then one afternoon in the late winter, with the days growing longer, Julie added another band member, a keyboard player, to fill in the holes that Elizabeth and I were leaving in our groove thing. It was as if Julie had invited a stranger into our bed to spice things up, as far as Elizabeth was concerned. His name was Steve. Not Steve the Studio Guy. But Sleepy Steve. That's what I called him.

Steve wasn't a total stranger, but worked with Julie and Elizabeth at Goldman Sachs, earning money by day so he could survive as a jazz pianist by night. Steve had an easy smile and relaxed posture that made you feel comfortable right away. My favorite thing about Steve, though, was his voice, not his singing voice, but his speaking voice, which you hardly ever heard, since he was not much of a talker. It was smooth and baritone, with a brightness that didn't seem to fit his appearance. He had the voice of a deejay.

Steve was cute, with sandy brown hair and an open face, but he had a bad habit of letting his mouth hang open while he played, which made him look stoned or asleep. When he kept his mouth closed, Sleepy Steve could pass for a genius. He played keyboards the right way. The tasteful way. Like Joe Jackson, not like the guy from ELO. He preferred piano to synthesizers, which was an important distinction when deciding whether a keyboardist was cool. But a week after Steve joined the band, Elizabeth refused to come to practice.

"I have to do my laundry," she told Julie.

"You'll always have to do laundry," Julie said. "Your dirty underpants will always be there. But the band is here now."

Elizabeth refused to play with Steve because she had a strange hatred of keyboards. Julie defended Elizabeth at first, and said she was simply a "purist." I wasn't sure what that meant exactly, how hating keyboards was somehow "pure." It seemed like an unfair prejudice to me. What had the piano ever done to Elizabeth? Had the black keys frightened her as a child? Was she scared away by an especially loud arpeggio? Whatever it was, Elizabeth gave Julie an ultimatum: "The keyboards or me."

Julie chose the keyboards.

Elizabeth wasn't the one to make the choice. Julie told her to leave. When it came down to it, Julie broke up with Elizabeth. I was not the other woman. But I felt like the other woman. I could have saved Elizabeth. But what for? A band of miserable women getting nowhere, singing to one another a few times a month? But I knew that I felt guilty about Elizabeth for a reason. I was the one who had planted the seeds of a great new idea in Julie's head.

In a moment of inspiration, I realized it was my turn to propose to Martin, to get down on my knee and change his life, to convince him that life could surprise you and make you happy after all. So one night, over dinner, I popped the question.

• SEVEN •

"No, absolutely not," Martin said, when I asked him to join the band. It was the obvious next step in our lives, I said. I had no bass player. He was a bass player.

"It's just simple addition and subtraction," I said.

But he put his big bass-player hands over his ears, then waved them in the air for emphasis. "I don't play in bands anymore. It always ends badly."

"That's not true," I said, trying hard to think of a band that hadn't ended badly. But there really were none.

"See? You can't think of one, can you?"

"Yes. Yes, I can. There are just so many."

I considered teaching Lauren, my sixteen-year-old niece, how to play bass, but she was too young to play out in clubs. And that was Julie's dream, playing out. Her goal was to one day play Brownies, where she had seen Pork the night she decided to start a band. But Lauren couldn't even get into Brownies. So I kept at Martin. And that spring, just as the snow started to melt on our Brooklyn street, Martin gave in.

"Okay. Okay," he said, finally, after my most recent attack in our living room. "I'll play with you until you find someone else."

Martin doled out $100 to get his old black-and-white Fender Precision bass fixed, to rid it of a nagging hum that had plagued it for the past fifteen years, ever since he'd played in the Zones. He got new tuning pegs and shiny new pickups and had the neck straightened.

If I had been a man, bringing my significant other into the fold would have been impossible, a mortal sin frowned upon by the fraternal order of banddom. It was the sin committed by John Lennon with Yoko, and Paul McCartney with Linda.

Martin threatened from the start that he would only stay long enough so we could record a few songs in a studio and get a demo to help us find a permanent bass player. Since he worked nights, Martin could rarely play gigs, so it would be dumb to keep him on. He could pick up and leave anytime he liked.

Like a session player, Martin fell right in. It helped that he knew all the songs already, since I'd been playing them incessantly for months. He already had a few bass lines mapped out, and put them right to work. It also helped when he and Sleepy Steve hit it off. With the guys in the band, we could never call ourselves Girls, Girls, Girls. "Unless Martin and Steve wear dresses," Julie said. "That could be our gimmick."

"You don't want to see Martin's legs in a dress, believe me. That's no gimmick. That would just be scary."

"Maybe we could all dress as boys then," she said.

"We already do," I said, looking down at my jeans, T-shirt, and red high-top sneakers. Julie was the only girl I knew who was more of a tomboy than I was. I had yet to see her in a dress or skirt. Maybe her legs were as bad as Martin's.

"Maybe," Julie said, "we could be Boys, Boys, Boys."

Still anonymous, we started practicing in midtown so that Martin could play and then run over to his job at the *Daily News.* Ultra Sound studio was on West 30th Street, a block with tall stone buildings whose sidewalks held the homeless spillover from Penn Station. The sun never shone on 30th Street, so there always seemed to be smelly puddles on the block, urine runoff and stagnant water from days-old rain that refused to evaporate.

Ultra Sound was in a building that housed a dozen or so other studios that were used by grown-up, frustrated musicians who worked real day jobs. It was worlds away from Tasty Fish and lacked something Julie called "indie credibility."

Though it wasn't as hip as the Lower East Side studios, the building had a certain professionalism to it. The wrong kind of professionalism maybe. It was filled with dreamers and quasi-talented musicians who talked big, but would probably never get anywhere. The place reeked of desperation, especially at night, when accountants and other "professionals" came to play. They had state-of-the-art equipment, the latest keyboards, the most expensive guitars and mics, as if great equipment would make them sound better. They used MIDI. And read *Musician* magazine.

The type of person who practiced there was best illustrated by this flyer posted on a building bulletin board:

> Working band looking for guitarist, bass player and drummer.

There was a bar downstairs called Down Time where these musicians "jammed." The bands that played there had given the studio black-and-white professional photos of themselves, which they, sadly, had autographed.

The new studio made us feel like grown-ups, not just kids screwing around, mostly because it was more expensive, almost twice as expensive as Tasty Fish—$12 an hour, so you really cherished each moment you spent there. Most important, Ultra Sound had heat. And did not smell like feet or bong water.

It felt as though Julie and I had graduated to the next level of banddom. Elizabeth's blood stained our hands, of course. But we kept our hands busy, with the help of Martin and Steve.

One afternoon at practice, Martin told Steve and Julie just how much he hated his job.

"My boss got fired this week," Martin said.

"Is that good or bad?" Julie asked.

Martin shrugged. "Everybody thought he went to the bathroom. He told one of the reporters to call him back in twenty minutes with some information and when she called back, they said he didn't work there anymore."

"Is that what life is like at the *Post*?" Julie asked.

"The *Daily News,*" Martin corrected her.

"Oh," Julie said. "Sorry."

"Yeah," said Martin, answering Julie's question. "That is what life is like at the *News,* actually."

Steve piped in, uncharacteristically. "You used to work at *New York Newsday,* right?" Martin nodded. "That was a great paper," Steve said. "That was like my favorite paper."

"The guy who got fired was the editor of *New York Newsday,*" I said. "He moved over to the *News* when the paper folded."

"This is the terrible story," Martin said. "They hired him as the metropolitan editor of the *News.* The owner hired him. All the guys in between, in middle management, didn't want him. So they made his life miserable for three months. He had a three-year contract."

"That sucks," Steve said.

Martin nodded again. "I wanted to go to work a little early today and make sure I have my job," he said, looking uninspired. "I don't want to be late or unenthusiastic."

Most of Martin's spare time was now spent with the band and me. Julie and Martin collaborated well on songs, throwing out ideas and trying them on for size on Steve and me. When Julie wrote a new song, she'd give a demo of it to all of us, with a written copy of the chords to Martin and Steve. We'd listen at home. Depending on the tempo, I'd think up drums parts: skippy beat, straightforward beat, or waltz beat. My repertoire was pretty limited. Martin worked out his bass lines.

Once we were at practice, we threw it all together. We tried modulating once on a song, jumping from one octave to the next between choruses. We slowed songs down, and sped them up. I sprinkled my playing with auxiliary percussion instruments that Martin had given me for my birthday. There was my new jingle ring, which screwed onto the hi-hat; my cabasa, a spool wrapped in ball bearings that made a shaky, grinding sound; and my claves—two thick wooden sticks that made a sharp clacking noise when smacked together. They were popular with Afro-Cuban jazz guys. As in "in *clave.*"

We played well enough to make changes, and then revert back to the old way if we hated it. And still remain in *clave.* We could criticize one another, and live to see the morning. Julie was forever telling me and Steve to play more quietly, afraid we were playing over her voice. I was constantly telling her to stick to the melody line. She had a habit of writing new melody lines on the spot, like Billie Holiday or Frank Sinatra. Except we needed her lyrical cues to keep it together.

"Once you get as big as Billie or Frank, you can change the words and melodies," I told her. "But for now, let's just learn the song." Julie taped each and every practice, then made us copies of the tapes each week so we could hear our parts and the progress we'd made from the week before. And we were making progress. With Martin in the band, the songs soared to new heights.

There was something mature about the bass player and drummer being married, something solid upon which to build the rest of our songs. It had worked for Talking Heads, for Tina Weymouth and Chris Frantz. Maybe it could work for us. There was something sexy about it, too, about two people with intimate knowledge of each other finding a rhythm.

Those were the romantic and poetic reasons for having a husband-and-wife rhythm section. The real reason was that Martin and I weren't afraid to argue, like the time I told Martin to stop looking at me during a song. I felt like he was sizing me up, inspecting my drumming, and he was making me nervous. The next time we played the song, Martin, as instructed, did not look at me. Which made me miss the bridge, since Martin's nod had always been my cue.

"Why didn't you look at me?" I yelled, as the band came to a crashing halt.

"You told me not to!" He turned to Julie and Steve and laughed. "You know, playing in a band with your old lady can really be a pain in the ass."

"Shut up," I said. "Just shut up."

"You know, Steve Nathanson never gave me a hard time like you do," Martin said.

"Why don't you just marry Steve Nathanson then?" I shot back.

"Thank God I wasn't married to Steve Nathanson," Martin said. "It felt like I was sometimes."

"Who the hell is Steve Nathanson?" Julie asked, laughing.

"The drummer in the Zones," Martin and I said in unison.

Then there was the time Martin accused me of giving him a dirty look while playing "The Next Big Thing." "Look at that look she's giving me," Martin said to Sleepy Steve. Martin turned back to me. "You're looking forward to the day I'm out of the band, aren't you? You're thinking, 'God, why did I ever bring him into this?' "

That wasn't true. My problem was that I was too busy concentrating to smile. I actually dreaded the day Martin would leave. Whenever there was a dispute about how to play a part, he and I voted as a block, and usually won. At worst, the vote ended in a tie. While playing a song called "The Bomb," Julie wanted an oom-pa-pa drumming approach. But Martin wanted a lighter, more straightforward waltz beat.

"Can't we just try it my way once?" he asked. "It's not like we're recording the White Album here. We can just try it."

"It's not what I want," Julie said.

"You two should just wrestle on the studio floor and the winner can decide," I said.

Still, I fell more on Martin's side of the argument and made it a jazz waltz.

"You get preferential treatment because you're the husband," Julie said.

"That's the problem when the rhythm section is married," Martin said. "You're not there late at night or in the morning when I'm whispering in her ear to do it my way."

The best part about having a married bass player and drummer was that the rhythm section could talk in shorthand. Like this:

MARTIN: You need to do it more like bom BOM.
ME: Bom BOM?
MARTIN: Yeah. You're doing it too quick.
ME: You mean delay it a little?
MARTIN: Yeah. Like bom BOM.
ME: Is that what you want? (*bom BOM can be heard in the background*)
MARTIN: That's it.

That was a problem that an unwed rhythm section could take several practices trying to solve. But with us, it took twelve seconds. By the end of the practice, that song, "The Other Side," was perfect. It was like a child riding a two-wheeler for the first time: clumsiness and stumbling effort transformed into freedom of flight.

Martin was bouncing along, swinging his hips to the rhythm we were creating. Steve was no longer sleepy, his rocketlike keyboards rising subtly in the background. Julie was strumming, smiling her way through the actual melody and lyrics, lyrics that seemed to be Elizabeth's elegy:

She was my best friend, but no longer
Girls can be cruel, but now I am stronger . . .

That same afternoon, we nailed "The Bomb," about an old woman who sits on her porch drinking martinis and thinking about the glory days of the Eisenhower years. I pictured an elderly Julie rocking in a rocking chair, slowly wasting away, bombed out of her mind. To make up for the harsh lyrics, as always, there was a pretty, simple melody.

It started gradually, with Martin playing a slow but bouncy line, with me falling in on soft hi-hat and snare, then Steve on the piano playing a pretty wraparound melody. Then Julie's guitar, and finally her wispy voice, until the song was grinding along, its piano tinkling, bass bouncing, me building, until Julie reached her crescendo, that sad lady sitting on her porch sipping a tumbler of gin and vermouth, thinking about what the world was like before we were born.

Until that practice, we had finished the song all together, neatly. But Martin had an idea. "We should fade out with the bass and then the piano, like in the beginning, only in reverse."

We all knew what he was saying. Our shorthand was spreading. And it worked. The song really worked. Steve's playing was pretty, but it stopped just short of the cheese. Julie's singing was fragile and powerful all at once. And Martin and I helped keep it all together. "The Bomb" gave me chills when we played it. And if I was in a melancholy mood to begin with, listening to it on our practice tape could make me want to cry.

"We really do sound good," Martin said, listening to that song with me on one of the practice tapes. We were home, in our living room, sitting next to each other on our ratty brown velour couch, tethered by our set of headphones, listening to songs we had helped create. I couldn't hear what Martin had said. But I could read his lips. Those big, full lips. *"We really do sound good."*

"We do," I mouthed back, wanting to kiss him all of a sudden. Martin smiled at me. And I smiled back. He turned away, but I kept looking at him for a long while as he listened and nodded his head to the beat, to our songs. I couldn't stop staring at him because what I saw was so wonderful. It was something I hadn't seen in months, close to a year, really.

Martin looked happy. Really happy.

• EIGHT •

Just as Martin stopped talking to himself, and just as the band was really grooving, I left and went to Alaska. Not permanently, but for freelance reasons. How was I to know it was the beginning of our troubles? When things fell apart, when everything truly went to hell, I would look back at this very moment and wish I'd never gone to the airport. I wished I could rewind the practice tape of my life to that very instant, and cab it back home to Brooklyn. But this was no practice. No dress rehearsal. No song, even. This was for real. And sometimes, in real life, you just hit the wrong note.

I was trying to sell a travel piece on Alaska and thought a trip there might nail a contract. The plan was to stay for three and a half weeks. I'd stay with friends I'd met in Nome the year that I had lived there.

"Do you really have to go for that long?" Julie asked. "Three and a half weeks?"

"It's so far away," I said. "It takes more than a day to get all the way up there, and then a few days just to get used to it. It's like landing on the moon." Julie rolled her eyes. "It'll fly by," I said. "Don't worry." But Julie continued to sulk.

"It's my job, remember? This is what I do for a living. I'm a freelance writer. It would be nice to be a drummer full-time, but—"

"I know," she said, cutting me off and forcing a smile. "You're right. I'm sorry. You need to make a living. I wish I could pay you to stay."

Unlike Julie, Martin never complained about my trip. He encouraged me to go because he knew I could get a great story out of it, even though the very thought of me going up to Alaska again gave him hives.

I safely tucked our practice tapes away in my suitcase so I wouldn't forget my drum parts. On my Walkman, I listened to our songs on the long flight. My drumming was really coming along. It was still pretty amateurish, with straightforward, sometimes hesitant beats. But each song was starting to distinguish itself.

Almost as soon as I landed on Nome's barren dustscape, a story idea materialized. A photographer named Rob, who was living with one of my old roommates, Nikki, had a proposition for me. He asked me if I wanted to come with him on a trip to St. Lawrence Island, a rock in the middle of the Bering Sea, just a short plane ride from Nome and just thirty-six nautical miles from Siberia. Rob was heading to the island for a whaling festival and thought we could team up on a travel story.

But there was a catch. There was always a catch.

Rob had another reason for asking me to come along. He had dated a Yu'pik Eskimo woman on St. Lawrence Island over a decade ago and had mistakenly given her grandmother—the family elder—a present: a new tea set, which, as it turned out, was a symbol of his intentions to marry her young granddaughter, Edna. Rob hadn't returned to the island since.

When he asked me to come along, it wasn't so much as a reporter, but as a woman. According to village custom, if Rob returned alone, or with one of his buddies, Edna and her family would be the joke of Gambell, the tiny Eskimo town. Rob needed to return with a woman.

"As long as I don't have to hold your hand," I said. "Or kiss you."

Rob, six foot three, with a beret, a photographer's vest, and a big scar on his face from another failed romance, was not my type.

"No problem," he said, laughing. Rob had no designs on me, save for the cash he could make from the travel piece. "That wedding ring will come in handy," he said, pointing to my finger. "They'll think we're married."

We'd be staying with a friend of his, a guy named Charles, whom Rob had met in Anchorage a few months earlier. "Separate beds." Rob smiled. "Just pretend you actually like me. And keep those rings on."

I had no worries about Rob, really. But I was slightly worried about telling Martin about being Rob's beard. I thought about not mentioning it at all, but the night before we left for St. Lawrence, once I got on the phone with Martin, everything spilled out.

"You should definitely go," Martin said, without a moment's hesitation.

"You won't be jealous or anything?"

"Should I be?"

"No, no, not at all. You should see this guy. He's a real piece of work."

Though I was relieved, I was also a little disappointed Martin wasn't the least bit jealous. I thought about how other husbands would have reacted to news like this: your wife flying off to an island with a tall stranger and pretending to be his wife.

"Thank you," I said. "For trusting me, I mean."

"You're welcome," he said. "It's gonna be a great story. You'll see."

That Friday morning Rob and I flew out on Bering Air and in forty-five minutes landed on the hundred-mile-long island, with its sweeping cliffs and rocky beaches, scattered every few yards with giant whale skeletons. This is what I loved about freelancing. One minute you could be interviewing Lou Reed for *New York* magazine in all his cranky glory and the next you were counting whale ribs on a beach four thousand miles away.

I had heard about the village of Gambell while living in Alaska, and knew that it had one of the worst reputations of all the Eskimo villages. Its people were known for their violent nature, their habit of shooting at anything that moved. It came with the territory. Living on a frozen rock in the middle of the Bering Sea for millennia meant you had to kill whatever you could to survive.

Changes had come in the last twenty years or so: Stouffer's frozen food, welfare, booze, and drugs. But the villagers were still hunters at heart. Which explained the whaling festival.

Our plane wobbled a bit in the strong Bering Sea wind before touching down. When the door opened, I noticed how cool it was compared to New York, even compared to Nome. Before we set foot on the island, there was the sound of four-wheel all-terrain vehicles (ATVs) buzzing over to offer us a ride into town. We'd have to pay a few dollars, but it was better than slogging through the gravel and rocks. We jumped on one guy's roomy backseat.

"Where you headed?" he asked, in his choppy native accent.

"We're staying with Charles," Rob said.

The guy turned around, eyes and smile wide, and asked, "You got dope?"

Charles, it turned out, was the village drug dealer. He was the son of a wandering Scottish father and Mary, a Yu'pik Eskimo who still lived a few gravelly blocks away. When we pulled up into his front yard, the guy on the ATV waved off Rob's attempts to pay him. "No charge," he said, nodding demurely—practically bowing—toward our host.

Charles was almost as tall as Rob—an anomaly for an Eskimo—but he was twice as wide. Not fat, but wide, with broad shoulders, a bit of a belly, dark, curly hair, a large nose, and a ball of a chin, inherited from the Scottish side. He didn't even notice our ATV driver; he was too busy barking orders at a friend and at his own eldest son, Charles III, whom he called Big Boy. He was teaching the eleven-year-old how to hook a halibut line for a big fishing expedition they'd be taking over the weekend. Large metal hooks with long lines hung from barrels outside his house. It was a shack, really, but the nicest shack on the street.

"Use your brain," he was yelling at Big Boy. "You've got a brain. Use it."

He turned around and finally noticed us standing there, sleeping bags, photo equipment, backpacks hanging all around us.

"Welcome to the Rock," Charles shouted, opening his arms, rushing over to embrace Rob.

"This is Helene," Rob said. "She's a writer. Do you think you can find some room for her?"

"Sure," Charles said, giving me a wink, convinced I'd be sleeping with Rob anyway. "We got lots of room." He threw open his wooden front door, so hard and fast I thought it might fly off its hinges. Inside, there was a long, plush couch, a big-screen TV, a state-of-the-art stereo system with giant speakers, tools, rifles, the latest videos from the Lower 48, and toys scattered everywhere from Charles's one-year-old son, Baby.

"What's his real name?" I asked Charles.

"Lance."

"Lance?" It was a strange name for a little Eskimo boy. Very white, I thought.

"I wanted to call him Harpoon, but Pickle wouldn't let me."

Pickle? She stretched out a small hand, as small as mine, and slipped back into the dark corners of the house. Pickle was Charles's wife, or longtime girlfriend, or something. His woman.

Their house was much more spacious than any other Eskimo home I'd ever been in. But there was no plumbing, just a honey bucket, and no hot water, except for a big pot boiling on the stove.

"You guys hungry?" Charles asked. Before we even answered, the steaks were out, the chicken was defrosting, and Pickle was busy mixing some potato salad. I parboiled the chicken and made some barbecue sauce while Rob grilled the steaks. Charles watched as I made the sauce.

"A little bourbon would be nice in there," he said.

"Sure. Got some?"

He laughed.

Gambell, I hadn't realized, was dry. There was no liquor—officially—on the island.

While I waited for the water to boil, I noticed a bucket full of knobby, tumorlike objects holding the back door open. "What are those?" I asked Pickle.

"Sea peaches," she said. "I have to clean them." She bent down and lifted the bucket, letting the back door slam closed. She placed them on a wooden table and filled the bucket with water from the stove.

Maybe we could call the band the Sea Peaches. That was pretty catchy, I thought. Ladies and gentlemen, the Sea Peaches!

With a knife, Pickle peeled the reddish-brown skin from the sea peaches—*uupa,* she called it—revealing a sea-urchin-orange goo.

"We scrape these off the bottom of the ocean floor with a big rake," she said, "then let them sit for a few days to die. They're a delicacy." She slit the middle of the orange blob with a knife and squeezed out some greenish white fluid, which, she said, was poison, dunked them in the now grimy water in the pail, and then set them aside. It was the single most disgusting thing I'd ever seen. Maybe the Sea Peaches wasn't such a great band name after all.

When our meal was ready, we gathered out on the sunny wooden deck. While we ate the rare steaks and chicken dripping in the sweet, hot sauce, flies migrated from the cleaned whalebones on the beach to our full plates. I swatted; Charles told stories.

"The feds finally got me about two years ago, coming home with two fresh-cut walrus heads. Me and Big Boy on the ATV. It was part of that Operation Whiteout."

I knew from my time in Alaska that the federal government had arrested those who had violated subsistence laws, head-hunting for ivory's sake and leaving walrus meat on the beach to rot. And Charles was one of their main offenders, trading ivory for drugs, they claimed, and then selling them to the locals.

"They wanted me to talk. But I kept my trap shut. So they sent me outa state. Oregon. A year and a half I spent there. I told the other inmates, 'Don't fuck with me. I'm an Eskimo. The Eskimo impaler, and I'll have all your heads on sticks.' I taught one guy to write with his eyeball." Charles laughed and took a bite of his steak.

"Write with his eyeball?" I asked, my mouth full of chicken.

"Stuck a pencil right in his eye." Charles jabbed his fork for emphasis. I swallowed my meat and looked over at Rob, sending him psychic messages. What the hell did you get me into? What kind of husband are you?

"No one fucked with me much after that," Charles was saying.

I cleared our dishes and headed to the kitchen. I considered doing the dishes, but there was no sink and no running water, only the slimy sea peach water. So I left the dishes piled on the kitchen table.

"We should probably head over to the festival," I said to Rob.

"I'll give you a ride over," said Charles, from outside.

"No," I said, headed into the still-bright evening sunshine. "That's okay. The walk will be good."

"Walk? It's nearly a mile. You can't walk through this shit," Charles said, kicking at the gravel under his feet. "Come on. It'll take two seconds."

Rob and I climbed on the back of Charles's ATV and zipped across town to the high school gym, where the festivities were being held. The high school was like any other in suburban America, a sprawling, modern, featureless mass that looked more like a prison. As we pulled up, all heads turned our way.

Now the whole town knew we were Charles's guests. "I'll see you guys tonight," he said, before rumbling away. I nodded and forced a smile.

When Charles was out of shouting range, I turned to Rob and punched him in the arm. "What the hell is that all about? Didn't you know who this guy was?"

"He seemed like a nice guy in Anchorage. How was I supposed to know he was the Eskimo Impaler?"

Inside, the Eskimo dances were already under way. This, I remembered, was why I'd come here.

A line of eight elders from Point Hope, a village on the mainland, led the song. Men with wrinkled faces were seated on folding chairs and held long willow sticks in one hand and drum paddles in the other. The paddles were shaped like oversized tennis rackets—a handle leading up to a big, beige, slightly transparent, stretched walrus-gut surface. In unison, they beat their paddles and sang.

I had heard Eskimo songs before, but not since being in a band. To the untrained eye, it looked like these guys were just banging away. But if you watched, really watched, you could see that each smack was different. Some drum hits were lighter than the others. Some hit the edge of the paddle, while others only skimmed the rim. Some were on one side of the paddle, some on the other. From song to song, the beats varied. And these guys never missed a beat. And never said a word.

One of them, the guy in the middle, slightly more wrinkled than the others, seemed to be in charge, and was the reason they all kept it together. He was leading them, looking back and forth and making sure they were all keeping time. Playing in unison wasn't as easy as it seemed. I knew that from the band.

Some songs required fewer drummers, so now and then, a couple of the players would get up and wander away, then suddenly reappear just in time for the next number. There was no set list. What would it say, anyway? Walrus Song Number One? Walrus Song Number Two? Whale Song? Second Whale Song? Another Walrus Song? It was all unspoken, as if they could read one another's minds. They had been playing together for so long that the set list was nearly part of their metabolism.

Newcomers on the island were those who had arrived 400 years ago. These families had lived here for thousands of years. And these songs, these rhythms, had been passed down for that long, never written down. These were oldies, real oldies. These songs had weight and meaning, had been sung in houses and reindeer-hide tents and emergency igloos through blizzards and births and deaths and seasons of hardly any walrus, when stink flipper from last year was all that you had to go on.

The songs sounded like Native American songs, but were a bit more melodic. The lyrics were more guttural, more mumbled, as if the singers had a mouthful of the beach gravel we'd just driven over. The beat was primal but catchy, working its way into our bones and forcing most of the crowd onto its feet.

The old men's voices carried over the children running wild in the gym, over the tattooed faces of the old women. Some kids sat on modern wooden bleachers. Others joined the dance, not self-conscious in the least.

The official dancers were dressed in simple matching costumes. The men were in solid black anoraks, pullovers. Eskimo fashion did not include zippers. The wind cut right through them. The women wore traditional dirndled *kuspuks*—knee-length pullover dresses with a bottom ruffle—made at home from flowered material.

Men and women moved to the music in sync, without touching. The guys were allowed to move their feet, making sudden, jerking motions and stomping loudly on the gym floor, their legs far apart. But the women were bound by tradition not to move their feet, to keep them close together.

In the past, I'd always resented that the women weren't allowed to move their feet. How could you dance without moving your feet? But I'd never really watched them very closely. Until now. Whatever they needed to express had to come from the knees up. They bent down gracefully, tipped their hips, but mostly waved their arms and hands, telling the story through sign language. It was beautiful, really, much subtler than the jarring movements of the men.

The unofficial dancers joined casually, getting up off the bleachers, wandering into the growing crowd. One bent old woman with a blue-ink goatee on her face threw her cane down and led one dance, practically starting up a *Soul Train* line, all the young people enthusiastically jumping up and joining her.

"That's her father's song," Mary, Charles's mother, explained to me, pointing to the old, tattooed lady. When the song ended, abruptly, the crowd exploded in applause. It was Point Hope's last tune.

"Savoonga is next," Mary said, nodding toward the dancers waiting to come onto the gym floor.

Savoonga was the only other village on St. Lawrence Island. Their group was much larger than Point Hope's, because they didn't have to pay for plane fare to get here. They had canoed over, hugging the shoreline. Their line of drummers was almost the length of the gym. The island's oldest residents, ninety-four-year-old Mr. Toolie and eighty-nine-year-old Mr. Aningayou, banged away, never missing a beat.

I tried to figure out the stories behind each dance. The lyrics were a mystery, until you simply watched the dancers' movements. A young boy with a very round head and a sure step got up with the Savoonga dancers. He was wearing an anorak, fur mitts, and sneakers. He had a definite style of his own—very strong, exact, and powerful, jabbing horizontally like a hunter, then using his hands gracefully to imitate walrus tusks. One dance had him down on the floor, legs to the side, leaping sideways like a walrus.

I sat there and watched, until Mary dragged me onto the dance floor. "Up, up," she said, taking my hands. "Last chance. This is the last song."

I took a deep breath and followed her out, as if wading into the cold, deep water of the Bering Sea. I kept my feet together and moved my arms and hips to the music, trying to feel the rhythm in my bones. At first I watched the professional dancers for clues to the lyrics, so I could act them out as well. But then I closed my eyes and surrendered to the rhythm.

When the song was through, I opened my eyes, and there was Mary and her elder friends applauding, not just the singers and dancers, but applauding me, too. "You looked like one of us for a minute," Mary said, jabbing me with her elbow.

When the drummers and dancers cleared the gym floor, the village held its annual blanket toss, in which a person stands in the middle of a reindeer hide and gets flung into the air by the people pulling all around. Even I got flung, at Mary's urging.

Blanket Toss, I thought, in midair. Now there's a good name for a band.

• NINE •

When I got back to the August heat of New York, it seemed I'd been on another planet, gone for a millennium. While I was in Alaska, I did and saw almost as much in three weeks as I had in the whole year I had lived there. After the blanket toss, Charles and Pickle took Rob and me seal hunting. Stoned, of course. And though we didn't kill any seals, we saw tens of thousands of migratory birds make their way, all together, in a tornado funnel of flapping and darkness, over to Siberia. We spied a huge whale off the side of our small metal boat, a dry patch in the freezing waters of the Bering Sea. It lingered there for what seemed like a month, threatening to tip our boat over and drown us. After I silently recited a full decade of the Rosary, the whale took mercy and moved on.

The next night we visited the burial ground of Charles and Pickle's ancestors. The coffins, the newest ones anyway, were exposed, due to permafrost, since it was impossible to dig into the frozen ground. The burial ground hit me in a visceral way, the way that our own proper, manicured, green cemeteries never could. Like everything else in Alaska, it was just out there, exposed and raw and in your face.

Before I left the island, Charles showed me some of the ivory pieces he had carved, beautiful seals and birds, walruses and whales. "Some of his work is on display at the Smithsonian in Washington, D.C.," Pickle said proudly. Looking at the smooth, graceful artwork, I wondered if I had been too quick to judge Charles. He had been a gracious host. He wasn't such a bad guy. Maybe that man in prison deserved that pencil in his eye.

After I returned to Nome, Nikki and I visited my favorite place on earth, a hot spring called Pilgrim, which had been an orphanage for Eskimo children left alone by the great diphtheria epidemic of the 1920s. The place was in a ring of a weather system, with mountains all around it. The clouds would bounce over, and the hot springs kept the ground warm, creating a circle we called the Pilgrim Ring. Pilgrim was always green and always under blue sky. It was a magical, heavenly spot.

On the Fourth of July, I tended bar at my favorite roadhouse outside Nome and saw the whole town get drunk, the mayor included, then drove back to town sober at dusk—at midnight—and watched the sun barely set over the Sawtooth Mountains. It was a blink more than a setting, since the sun came right back up only minutes later.

Finally, with some friends of Nikki's, I climbed the highest peak on the Seward Peninsula. Or, I should say, I tried to climb the highest peak on the Seward Peninsula. I barely made it into the valley below the peak. It was a ten-mile trek through treacherous, mosquito-infested bog. We ran up against a herd of wild musk oxen, disgruntled and defensive of their young. And we narrowly escaped a bear attack. It sounds like hell on earth, but when it was through, I felt more alive—and grateful to be alive—than I ever had before.

The whole trip left my nerves jangled, but my head clear and awake. Alaska did that. It woke you up somehow to the power of the world around you and made you feel small, but at the same time, a part of that mystical whole. Whenever I got back to New York after being in Alaska, my life felt like a sweater that was too small for me, like something that had shrunk in the wash and no longer fit. It took me days, sometimes weeks, to readjust.

Coming home after a long trip away from the other was always exciting for Martin and me and always a bit awkward at first. It was hard to tell Martin—to explain, really—all that I had seen and done.

Whenever I got back from Alaska or any freelance trip, it was like we were dating again, just getting to know each other. We always went out to dinner first, and talked and flirted before actually sleeping together again. Being apart for a little while kept things fresh.

But this time was a little different. That first night back, after having dinner and welcome-home sex, I fell asleep and dreamed vivid dreams of Charles and Pickle and riding on a boat in the Bering Sea. I woke up and looked over at Martin. But I didn't recognize his full lips, or his nose, or his perfect eyebrows. Who was this man sleeping next to me? I sat up in a panic and then thought, relieved, that I was just dreaming, that in a second, I would wake up and know my own husband. But a minute passed. And then two. Then ten minutes. And more. And still, I couldn't recognize Martin. I was wide-awake and he looked like a complete stranger to me. What was wrong with me? I'd probably just been gone too long.

"This is your husband," I told myself. "Martin. Your husband." I lay back down finally, and tried to sleep.

After two hours, I finally fell back asleep. And the next morning, when I hesitantly looked his way, I was relieved to find I recognized Martin once again. I hugged him and told him about my freak-out. "I didn't know who you were," I said. "For the longest time. It was really creepy." I shook my head.

Martin looked concerned, but comforted me. "You were just gone too long," he said, hugging me tight to his chest.

That first week back, we learned Julie's song "Epigone," the one Elizabeth hadn't liked. Martin tried hard to figure out a bass line to wrap around the piano part that Julie had written, the part that Steve was now playing.

"It took me a long time to figure out my part on guitar," Julie said to Martin. "I wrote it as a piano song and had to transfer it. I think it's a diminished chord."

"Is there any coffee?" Martin asked. Sometimes Julie brought more than one cup with her.

"You getting tired?" I asked.

"I'm slowing down," he said. He had gone out with some friends from work and had gotten home around three A.M.

"You look like you had a rough night," Julie said, strumming her diminished chord.

"Did you know diminished chords were illegal in the Middle Ages?" Martin asked. He was just a font of musical knowledge, even on a few hours of sleep.

"Why?" Julie asked.

"I think it was considered a demonic sound," he said, tooling with the melody.

"Is that the same thing as a blue note?" I asked.

"I'm not sure," Martin said, finally hitting the right note, the devil note.

Later, as we were packing to go, Martin said, "You know, we should record a demo soon. I don't know how much longer I can stay in the band."

While I was away, he had decided that we were getting too good not to play out, and because of his job, he couldn't really commit to any gigs. The pressure of working a full-time job and playing out and practicing was too much for him. "You guys really need to find a permanent bass player," he said. "I can't do this forever." He saw the look of disappointment on my face. On Julie's face. On Steve's face, too.

"I'm sorry," he said. "Don't do this. Don't make me feel bad. I told you guys . . ."

"It's all right," I said. "We knew you couldn't stay."

His rationale was sort of like the rationale behind breaking off a love relationship because it was getting too serious. Like running off to Alaska because you loved someone so much, afraid you'd have to finally get married. I understood. As much as Martin wanted to be in the band, he couldn't really. He had his job, which seemed to be getting a bit easier. He looked a little less stressed these days. A little lighter, somehow. Maybe the band had helped him get through the rough patch.

That autumn, we booked time at a studio called Night Owl on the same street where we practiced. Our goal was to record seven songs. Martin gave me a pep talk before our all-day Saturday session. "You're going to have these songs on tape for the rest of your life, so make sure you like the way you sound. If you want to redo something on the drums, tell us. Because it'll be there forever."

I knew he was thinking about his Zones demos, adolescence preserved, etched in tape forever. I nodded and bit my nails. "Remember," Martin said, "you only have to get it right once."

There was no need to bring any drums to the studio. The large room was fully stocked with instruments and mics and amplifiers, too. Steve was treated to a full grand piano. And Julie, the most nervous, got to sing by herself, secluded in a soundproof glass booth. She was like a princess in there, like Snow White in that glass coffin, set aside from the rest of the dwarves.

For each song, Martin, Steve, and I played together in one big room, with Julie on guitar, from that glass booth. Later, Julie re-recorded her vocals from the same glass booth. While she sang, we all sat on a couch in the waiting room. Steve and Martin flipped through issues of *Guitar World* and *Bass Player* magazines, while I read through a new issue of *Musician.* I hardly ever read it anymore, but whenever I did, I always went to the masthead first to see who was still there from the old gang. One by one, over the years, they had all disappeared into the vast void of the rest of the wide world, until finally, now, even Bill Flanagan's name was missing. I flipped through the magazine, a little disappointed, while Julie sang her songs, over and over again, until she got them right.

We recorded for a full day, and by the end, my brain was buzzing, I was so tired. But the songs sounded terrific. There we were, preserved forever, on digital tape. To have and to hold. For better or for worse. Until death do us part.

Seven songs were enough for a full set for a gig, so we convinced Martin that Julie should send the demo around as an audition tape to clubs. Not just to find a new bass player. "You could at least play one or two gigs with us," I said.

Martin agreed. "But we're gonna need a name if we play out," he said.

Girls, Girls, Girls was out. And Boys, Boys, Boys was just plain stupid.

"How about Ugly Step Sister?" I offered. "Stapinski. Stepanek. Get it?"

Julie made a stink face. Martin and Steve shook their heads.

"How about Swing Set?" Julie said.

"Not bad," I said.

"But that's not it," Martin said. "It doesn't fit the music."

"How bout Blanket Toss?" I said. "Or Stink Flipper?"

"Uber Kitty?" Julie offered. "Snaggle Tooth?"

"Charo's Guitar," somebody said.

"The Guillo-teens."

"I Hate Jane," Julie said.

"I know you do," I said.

"For the name of the band, dummy," she said. "I Hate Jane."

A week after Christmas, I Hate Jane premiered at the Pyramid Club. I thought it was sad, and strangely ironic, that the club had the same name as Stanley's last band.

The Pyramid was on Avenue A, in the upper reaches—near 7th Street—next door to the tenement where Julius and Ethel Rosenberg had once lived. Not good karma. Over the front door of the club was painted a pyramid like the one on the back of a dollar bill, with the eyeball in the center. That eyeball, with a cocked eyebrow, had watched the neighborhood slowly morph from a drug market to anarchy central to hipster heaven to its current state—a real estate developer's wet dream.

The Pyramid was catercorner from Tompkins Square Park, where squatters living in the abandoned buildings in the area had staged riots in the summer of 1988, after the city—and developers—had come to reclaim the housing stock. The developers won the fight; their victory flag was the sign outside the neighborhood's first sushi bar.

The Pyramid itself was a historic site. Not only had Nirvana actually played there before hitting it big, but the place was the East Village's first drag queen bar, where the likes of RuPaul and Lady Bunny had gotten their start. Back in the day, in 1984, it was on the Pyramid site that Lady Bunny got the inspiration for Wigstock, the annual drag queen festival, the concert and free-for-all that, until just a couple years ago, had been held across the street in the park's bandshell. Wigstock had gotten too big for the park, though, and had been staged at the Palladium dance club the previous year.

Drag queen legend went that in olden days, before Julius and Ethel Rosenberg had even arrived, beneath the Pyramid Club was buried a Freak Magnet, a mystical object that drew crowds of powerful, unusual people to it. And each year, Lady Bunny would harness the power of the Freak Magnet to attract her thousands-strong throng to Wigstock. We hoped the Freak Magnet would draw in a crowd for our show. Nine or ten people would make me happy. I'd even settle for the ghosts of Julius and Ethel Rosenberg.

Our show was listed in *The Village Voice.* A start, at least. But it was a tiny ad with letters so small you needed a magnifying glass to read it. If you squinted and held the paper close enough to your nose, there we were:

I Hate Jane.

The night of our gig, Martin and I got going early. The sun hadn't yet set, but it was already freezing, hovering somewhere around zero. What I liked to call Alaska cold.

First, I had to pick up my in-laws' red Toyota station wagon, the only car big enough to fit all our equipment. Then I had to drive to Jersey to pick up Stanley's drums.

"How long will you be taking them for?" he asked, standing in his hallway and scratching his elbow. It was a nervous habit. I lugged the giant bass drum down his front porch. Cold drafts of air flooded the hallway, but Stanley didn't seem to notice.

"We have this show, and one more scheduled." I wedged the drum into the hatchback, already sweating from the manual labor. "That could be it. Or maybe we'll get more gigs. I'm not sure. It depends if Martin stays in the band."

I carefully carried the snare out, the tom-tom, floor tom, cymbals and then the cymbal stands, one by one, as if dragging each one of Stanley's kids away. "I'll bring them back as soon as I'm done with them." I slammed the hatchback. "Do you think you can come tonight?"

"I'll try," Stanley said.

"Okay then," I said, climbing behind the wheel. "So maybe I'll see you later." I waved from the driver's seat and gave a quick honk as I drove toward the Holland Tunnel. I felt like a kidnapper. I tried to get one last guilty look at Stanley through the rearview mirror, but his biggest baby, the bass drum, was in the way.

I headed home to change, and Martin took the Toyota to borrow a bass amp from our friend Tony, who was in a band called Smash Mouth. We called him Smash Mouth Tony, to distinguish him from Tony my ex-boyfriend, who I was still good friends with and who was now living in Nashville. Smash Mouth Tony kept his amp at his bandmate's Brooklyn apartment, in an old tenement in an industrial neighborhood near the Manhattan Bridge exit ramp. Smash Mouth's drummer, John, rented the apartment downstairs from Andres Serrano, the artist who had found fame and fortune by submerging a crucifix in a jar of urine.

Because of Serrano, other artists were always mailing strange illustrations and photos to the building. One of those flyers—of a bucktoothed, knife-wielding, encephalitic baby—wound up in John's mail slot by accident. Smash Mouth co-opted the image and gave T-shirts to us and all their friends featuring the band name on the back and that bald, bucktoothed, knife-wielding encephalitic baby on the front. Or maybe it was an alien. I never asked. Whatever it was, it was disturbing, much like Smash Mouth's music.

Their song list included a power-punk ditty entitled "Arthur Kill Road," about the joys of driving on Staten Island. My favorite was "The Joe Pesci Song," which included the lyrics, "Don't fuck with me, you fucking fuck." Hearing that song—full on, week after week—might upset some neighbors. But not the *Piss Christ* guy.

Since the area was so deserted, the band was able to rehearse their power chords in the front room of that floor-through apartment, which was a mess with equipment, amps, and instruments. We needed an apartment like that for I Hate Jane. Tony liked to call it their "fortress of solitude," the one place in the city where three guys could get away from the chaos of New York and their girlfriends and create their own noise.

With John the drummer's help, Martin carried Tony's bass amp down a flight of slanting wooden steps and loaded it into the station wagon.

We showed up at the Pyramid at eight P.M., the time the booker had told us to arrive. I had wanted to get there early, since I hadn't set the drums up in years and needed plenty of time to screw up. I dreaded the hi-hat nut and the construction of that foot pedal.

But when we got there, the club's black metal grate was pulled down. No drag queens. No throng. So much for Lady Bunny's Freak Magnet. It was just Martin and me, sitting outside, illegally parked. We waited for someone to show up. And we waited. And waited.

"This is why I'm not in bands anymore," Martin groaned.

"Sorry," I said, sliding down in my seat.

Finally, Steve arrived, carrying his portable keyboard on a handcart. He would have liked to have brought his piano, but it was much too heavy. Steve climbed into the car, since it was so cold outside. Julie showed up soon after, with her small amp on a handcart and her black guitar case slung over her down coat. We waved at her from the windows. She climbed into the warmth and immediately began to unzip her guitar case. "I have a surprise for you guys," she said. She slowly pulled open the top of the case, smiling wide all the while. We all craned our necks to get a look.

Inside was a brand-new baby blue Stratocaster, an American Standard, with a whammy bar, a white pick guard, and silver-colored tuning pegs.

"I went into Sam Ash to buy a new strap, but I was so excited about our show that I bought this." She lifted it like a newborn.

"Niiice," I said.

"Congratulations," Martin said. Steve, his mouth hanging open again, even more than usual, strummed the new strings, which glinted in the street lamplight.

For over an hour, I Hate Jane, in its entirety, instruments and all—bass guitar, bass amp, guitar amp, tom-toms, snare, hi-hat, cymbals, throne, bass drum, keyboard, new baby blue guitar—sat in the station wagon, its windows fogged. We kept the motor running so the heater would blow wafts of warm air on our fingers. To keep the blood in my hands flowing, and to save myself some precious, panicked moments, I assembled my foot pedal in the front seat.

I hadn't planned on eating dinner until after the show, since I thought I might throw it up onstage. But we got so bored that Martin bought some sushi at one of the new restaurants on the block and brought it back to the Toyota. We couldn't leave the equipment, for fear the car would get stolen, or towed. And the equipment was all too heavy to drag into the restaurant. So we huddled together in the car and ate our raw fish, like cozy Eskimos inside an igloo.

When the bouncer arrived, he didn't even apologize for being late. He rolled up the gate and gave us a dirty look.

A few friends showed up as soon as the doors opened, taking spots in the subterranean, dank club. Maybe the Freak Magnet was working after all. We had only invited a few close friends: my friend Sara; Martin's friend Ben, a photographer who planned to shoot some pictures; Smash Mouth Tony and his wife, nurse Pam Marla from St. Vincent's; former Zone Dave; our friend Laura, who had introduced me to Julie. And my brother, Stanley.

I set my drums up, the way I had taught myself nearly twenty years earlier. I was slightly taller now, but the setup was pretty much identical. Bass drum first, with its kick pedal, all ready to go. Tom-tom screwed on at just the right height, around chest level. Snare between my legs, snug and tilted at a slight, 85-degree angle.

The booker arrived and told us to hurry up, that they were behind schedule. I screwed on my hi-hat nut. It was so much harder than I remembered, maybe because I was under such pressure to do it in a hurry. Maybe I could just leave it assembled when we were done so I wouldn't have to go through this again. If you couldn't screw on a hi-hat nut, maybe you shouldn't be playing out, I thought. What was I doing here?

When I finished, I sat up on my cushioned throne and noticed that there were two black poles at the front and center of the stage, practically blocking the tiny audience's view of Julie. Who puts poles in the middle of a stage? We were better off playing in Stanley's basement in Jersey. Then I wouldn't have to lug the drums at least. And I wouldn't have to worry so much about the hi-hat nut.

My only comfort was having Martin onstage with me. He was dressed in one of my favorite shirts, blue and purple paisley, with his jeans and black Converse high-tops. His bass was slung low, down past his hips, the way he liked to wear it. He smiled at me while running through a scale, but I knew he was nervous, by how bright red his ears were. No one else could tell.

Julie was another story. She was so nervous, she seemed happy about the poles onstage. She was trying to hide behind them, tuning and retuning her new guitar. The booker gave us yet another dirty look for taking so long, so I nodded at Martin and he nodded back. I counted down to the tempo of our first song. One, two, one, two, three, four.

We started with "Epigone," a wink at the audience, for those who even knew what the word meant. I had to look it up the first time I heard it. (*Epigone:* a lame imitator of a creative thinker or artist.)

But the song was about as original as you could get, with its diminished chords that Martin and Julie had worked out, a xylophone sound on Steve's keyboards, and the rhythm of my cabasa. My hands were trembling so much, I was afraid I would drop it. The raw tuna from my tekka roll was now lodged in my throat. But the song we had created together shot back out at us from the monitors along the small, foot-high stage.

I see you there, your thrift store clothes and your practice pose
I must admit I used to be so terribly impressed.

During the first break between songs, I was surprised by how bright and hot the stage lights were. It felt like I was being interrogated. I wished I were back out on the cold sidewalk. Sweat was pouring down my back, soaking my brown velvet striped shirt. (Note to self: Never wear velvet onstage again.) The lights made it nearly impossible to see the crowd, which, considering how nervous I was, was a good thing. Not seeing the audience helped stave off complete and utter panic. The audience was a shadowy lump in the distance.

I searched the dark lump for Stanley.

Julie was still lurking behind those poles, and her nervousness showed in her vocals. Mine were worse, so off-key, that after that first song, I decided I shouldn't sing anymore. I kept my mouth shut for the rest of the show.

Between songs, Julie spent what seemed like an eternity tuning her Fender. She was a relative newcomer to guitar and hadn't really gotten the process down. Having a new guitar, with new strings, didn't help. At practice, taking forever to tune up didn't seem to matter, but now that we were onstage, with a waiting audience, it was a real problem. There was the top E string, which she hit about fifty-seven times, followed by the A, which she hit maybe fifty-eight times, and then the D, and so on and so on. I was worried the club manager would bring another band onstage to fill the gaps between songs.

By the third song, "The Other Side," we had all warmed up a bit. Julie's voice was more in control, not jumping octaves or veering off somewhere. When the song was through, she introduced the band, tuning all the while.

"Thanks for coming out tonight. We're I Hate Jane."

It wasn't until that moment—hearing the name announced over the sound system, bouncing off the club walls—that I Hate Jane seemed like a bad idea. Right off, we were alienating anyone named Jane, anyone who loved a Jane, whether a girlfriend, child, or mother. I started scanning the audience, trying to identify who was out there, running down a list in my head of their loved ones.

"I hope there are no Janes in the audience," Julie said over the mic, verbalizing what I was thinking. "If you are a Jane, don't take it personally."

By the time we hit "The Bomb," the name problem was forgotten. We were lost in the beauty of Steve's tinkly piano and the bounciness of Martin's bass. I chugged along with my waltzing beat, stumbling here and there, trying to appear confident. Most people would think I was doing fine, but I knew that my fills were hesitant. I was afraid of hitting the drums too hard, that I might make a mistake, as if it were easier to go back and correct a softer stray beat. But the beats were where you put them, and would stay there forever, hanging in the stale air of memory.

Between Julie's marathon guitar tunings, we sang the Rip My Tongue Out Song, which repeated the line, "I will rip my tongue out first" ten times. Ten. Ten times. It wasn't until you were amplified and playing out in a club that you realized little problems like these.

We played "Document," with my favorite "Jesus lost and found" line. And finally, Julie tuned up for "The Next Big Thing," our show-stopper. One last time, I shaded my eyes from the harsh blue and white interrogation lights hanging above me and looked for Stanley's face. But he wasn't there. I sighed, a bit of air easing its way out of my tense body.

I counted down for our finale and we began. The sound system was awful, the lighting worse. But I was in a definite groove.

And then it was over, almost as soon as it had begun.

There was not a moment to savor it, either. Before Martin's last bass note finished reverberating, as the few pairs of clapping hands did their best, the booker was upon us, shooing us away. As we packed our gear, the next band charged the stage and practically mounted us.

These guys were straight out of Down Time. Their drummer had set up his kit during our set and was ready to get going, lifting the already assembled drums onto the stage as I stepped off. He had about a dozen pieces, with a huge, arcing set of rototoms, so many that they completely hid his upper torso and head from the audience. He gave the drums a rococo roll, like Neil Peart from Rush would have fifteen years earlier. It seemed pointless to set up so many drums for so few listeners. A good rule of thumb: Never have more drums than audience members.

The bass player gave Martin the thumbs-up as he ascended the tiny stage. Martin returned the gesture, then nudged me. "Look at that bass."

It had the neck and head of a cobra, carved in dark wood. He had it strapped high up near his neck, and he slapped away at it with his thumbs like a madman, the cobra's head dancing and jerking away, looking like it might bite him in the neck. I had to sit down for a minute and watch these guys, they were so ridiculous.

We made $15 that night, all from our dedicated friends who had dragged themselves out on the coldest night in memory. We considered evenly dividing it among them, giving it back, but decided that was more complicated than it was worth. We kept it for studio time, to practice for our next big thing.

In early February, I Hate Jane played CB's Gallery, an acoustic-oriented add-on to CBGB, the graffiti-filled hole in the wall where Talking Heads, Television, Blondie, and Patti Smith had gotten their start. The name CBGB stood for Country, Blue Grass, Blues, the original intent of its owner, Hilly Kristal, who had been a fan of that music.

But back in 1973, when Kristal opened, there was no place for an unsigned band to play original music in New York City. So Kristal obliged, and the punk scene was born. There were great stories about CB's, about how Clive Davis had come down himself and signed Patti Smith during her seven-week run there. About how the fire department had to be called one night when one of the Bowery bums out front set his mattress on fire with a lit cigarette, and nearly burned the club down.

The bums were now gone. And so was most of the good music.

CBGB was holy ground, but like most musical holy ground, it got invaded by teenagers from New Jersey sometime in the eighties and was now a parody of itself. The Jersey kids tried desperately to look hard-core, with safety pins in their noses and ripped black T-shirts, cursing anyone over thirty who came near the entrance. CB's 313 Gallery, next door, was for the over-thirty set. For us.

It was where I Hate Jane played our rooftop *Let It Be* goodbye. We practiced every day for a week, growing tighter and more confident. And louder. I pounded the drums harder. And Julie got a little worried.

"I think maybe we're too loud," she said. "CB's Gallery is an acoustic venue, you know."

"I've seen electric bands there," Steve said.

"And what are they gonna do anyway? Kick us out?" I said.

"Imagine that!" Martin said. He saw everything in headlines. "Band Kicked Out of CB's for Being Too Loud."

"That would be good PR, actually," said Steve.

"Okay, okay," Julie said. "I'm outvoted."

For the show, Julie bought a cool, sixties-era polyester blue and white check minidress with a zipper in front, like something our mothers would have worn while cleaning the house. When she tried it on in the Macy's dressing room, it was the first time I'd ever seen her legs. They were very muscular; she had some very serious calves.

"I was a gymnast when I was teenager," she said, reading my mind. "A guy told me in high school that I had legs like a linebacker." Her legs were sexy. She had no reason to feel self-conscious.

"Don't you know guys love former gymnasts?" I said. "They think you're gonna do back handsprings on them or something."

No matter how many guys you piled onstage, they were no match for a single woman. Especially a single former gymnast. Though we could only see her from the back, Julie looked great onstage in her new dress.

The she-vibe was why so many bands had female singers. Never mind their voices, which were generally much better than the average male singing voice. The sex appeal and power of the mere presence of a woman made most teenage rock fans crazy. Maybe it was their smell, their estrogen edging itself over the top of all that testosterone. Or their curves, fitting more closely to the lines of the guitars onstage.

To avoid showing her panties, Julie had to do a deep-knee bend every time she bent over to grab her bottle of iced tea. Before we started, Smash Mouth Tony winked at Martin from the audience, then came up to the stage and whispered, "Nice view you got there."

We ran through the same set as the Pyramid show, a little less sloppy, a little less nervous. There were no poles in the middle of the stage for Julie to hide behind, so she really hammed it up out there, shaking her hips back and forth behind her baby blue guitar. Martin was swinging his hips, too, ever so slightly, doing a little sideways dance across the stage. He looked so happy he was glowing.

The only difference in our set was that "The Next Big Thing" had a new ending, an even grander finale. "Don't forget to turn around and look at me," I said to Martin. His nod to me was my cue to end the song.

All went well. My backing vocals were on key, and balanced Julie's, which were much more confident. My fills fell in the right places, stronger and harder than before, filling the spaces they were meant to fill in time. Just when we were coming in for that home stretch, when it looked like we were going to finish on the right note, finish big, Julie missed the ending. Drove right over it.

She kept playing, an extra four bars worth, as the three of us struggled to start again and catch up. Martin ran over to Julie and shouted something and we ended with me crashing the cymbals as loud as I could muster in John Bonham fashion, trying to distract from our fuck-up, our fitting swan song.

"Sorry," Julie said, but no one in the audience seemed to notice anything was wrong. They were roaring: my sister, her husband, all my friends, Smash Mouth Tony, Pam Marla, even the few strangers who had drifted into the club for a drink.

"What's the name of the band?" one of them yelled.

Julie shouted it one last cathartic time. Shouted it right at Jimmy. Right out into the world where her Jane and my Janes and the rest of the planet's population were passing the night, unaware of our very existence.

• TEN •

In the late summer of 1962, when the Beatles recorded the first few takes of "Love Me Do" at London's Abbey Road studios, producer George Martin wasn't happy with Ringo's drumming. He hired a studio drummer named Andy White to replace him.

I could just see Ringo, sulking, sitting on the other side of the recording booth, on the silent side, glaring out at his mates and his replacement. Of course, Ringo was just getting a taste of instant karma. A few years earlier, he had replaced the Beatles' drummer, Pete Best. And now, he was being Pete Bested himself.

For years, only a few overly devout Beatle freaks knew that Andy White had played on the final version of "Love Me Do," not Ringo. But then *The Beatles Anthology* was released and there was Ringo, being interviewed, obviously still pissed about it, nearly forty years later.

Not long after our CB's show, I interviewed Andy White for a story I was writing for *Request,* a Minneapolis-based music magazine. White now lived in suburban New Jersey. We met for coffee at a diner in

Kearny, which, I was to learn that very afternoon, was the Scottish capital of the United States. Who knew?

White, a Scotsman, had a mustache and a receding hairline covered by a wool cap. He was a decade older than Ringo, and already in semiretirement. He no longer sat in with bands, but taught Scottish drumming to kids in kilts. He also worked in the audiovisual department of the Montclair library. When I met him, White had just moved into a new house in Caldwell, big enough for him to set up his drum kit for the first time in a long time. He looked like a happy kid, though he was sixty-five.

"We have a basement now," he said enthusiastically, in a Sean Connery accent. "I guess I'll have to do some soundproofing down there."

Over coffee and Danish, White told me about the historic afternoon he spent with the Beatles. "At the time, I didn't even know it was the Beatles," he said. "That happened all the time at sessions. They just called you in to Abbey Road and asked you to play."

He remembered the session vividly, though. How funny the Beatles were, quick-witted and charming. How they played off one another's humor. Except for Ringo, of course, who was in a very bad mood. He remembered how mad Ringo was, but how he had swallowed his pride finally and wound up playing tambourine in the background.

Ringo was an easygoing sort, the one who got along well with all his band members. I thought of him as the glue that had held the Beatles together, the regular Joe who kept them all grounded.

When the Beatles became overnight sensations in Britain and then the United States, White couldn't get over it. "I was surprised at how big it all got," he said. "There was always the question, why didn't you join the Beatles? Well, I was from another decade. I was ten years older than John. Besides," he smiled, "Ringo was already there."

White was a jazz-trained drummer who played with the likes of Anthony Newley, Chuck Berry, Bill Haley and His Comets, Herman's Hermits, Marlene Dietrich, and Tom Jones. He had played on the song "What's New, Pussycat?" Not as cool as Ringo, but more technically proficient.

"My drums are a much better sound," he said. "At the end of the bridge with the harmonica on 'Love Me Do,' there's that cymbal crash. In my version, you can hear the cymbal crash. Ringo's is a bit muffled." I nodded as if I knew what he was talking about.

"I was a professional," he said. "A professional," he said again, and laughed. "Guess it sounds like a dirty word."

White was from the old school, and said that you could spot a good drummer by the quality of his drumroll.

When the interview was through, he climbed into his Toyota to head over to the nearby Argyle Restaurant, where he planned to pick up some kidney pies for his mates back at work. He offered to drop me at the train station on the way. As I climbed in beside him, I told White that I was in a rock band, and that my drumroll was not very sophisticated.

"I never had lessons," I said, dropping a hint. When he didn't take it, I asked him if he would be open to giving me a few pointers sometime.

"Sure," he said, in that 007 accent. "Give me a call and we'll see what we can arrange." I got out at the station and he pulled away, his Toyota coughing down the street.

We kept in touch for a while, White and I. He sent me a tape of his version of "Love Me Do" versus Ringo's version; sure enough, his was better. The way you could tell them apart was by the tambourine in the background, Ringo's tambourine, a touch of jealousy beneath the jingle.

Julie didn't seem very excited when I told her I might take drum lessons. Maybe she didn't want me to bang any louder over her quiet, girly vocals. So I put off the White lessons, until too much time passed and I forgot all about them.

With Martin gone, I thought Sleepy Steve would become even sleepier. But the CB's show really revved him up. He couldn't wait to find a new bassist and play out again. He was even intent on playing a bit of guitar.

Julie tried to recruit a bass-playing woman for the band. In March, she put an ad in *The Village Voice:* "Looking for female bass player for melodic pop band. Influences include Luna, Pavement, and Built to Spill."

Only men responded. If a guy didn't sound completely insane over the phone, Julie would send him a tape of I Hate Jane songs and tell him to call her back. If he called back and didn't say something incredibly stupid about her songs, she would invite him to play with the two of us. Steve got to sit it out for the auditions. Lucky stiff.

A guy with seven different effects for his bass showed up. He was all equipment, no soul, a MIDI-Musician. Julie and I grimaced at each other as he plucked and popped away at his five-string fretless bass. It had no tuning pegs up top, but was cut off at the end, like an amputee, the stub of the fretboard sticking out all lonely and awkward. Ten minutes into the audition, I was hoping someone would come in and lop his fingers off.

"Thanks," Julie said, as he packed up his instrument. "We'll be in touch."

There was another guy, who hadn't even listened to the tape. "Why are you wasting our time?" Julie asked him. He just shrugged, grinning like the teenager he actually was. You could tell what was passing through his meager brain, as he nodded and looked us over: "Chick band. Cool. Two chicks. One guy. Guy is me. Hey. Maybe I'll score. Threesome! Cool!" I think he actually drooled on his bass guitar. Unfortunately, he was not electrocuted.

Then there was the guy with the long ponytail who played New Age bass. He was sent packing, back to the mother ship. A few punk kids with mohawks arrived, one after another, as if we had made a casting call for the Broadway version of *Sid and Nancy.*

"Did you listen to the tape I sent you?" Julie asked them. They would shrug and play on, harsh chords and feedback drowning out the sounds around them.

There were lots of guys who'd never been in a band before. And those who didn't even know how to play bass.

Dan was one of those guys.

He called Julie one afternoon, while I was on a trip to Oregon, interviewing the founder of the Tazo Tea empire for a business magazine named *Success,* an unsuccessful periodical that eventually wound up going bankrupt. Julie called me in Oregon, long distance, all worked up.

"This guy Dan showed up with a guitar," she said. "Not a bass. But lead guitar."

"The nerve," I said.

"Well, at first I was like, what's with *this* guy? But then he started playing."

"And?"

She paused.

"I told him he could join the band."

"You what?"

"It's okay," Julie said. "You'll meet him. You'll see."

When I got back to New York, Dan, Julie, and I got together at Ultra Sound. As soon as I saw Dan, I became uncomfortable. He was very good-looking, almost too good-looking, like that guy you had a crush on in high school who never even knew you existed, or at best was your friend and talked to you about the blond, big-chested girls in your class, oblivious that you, too, had breasts.

He had high cheekbones and intense, black eyebrows and short, dark hair that was dyed blond. He was young enough to carry it off, young enough that his favorite show was *Space Ghost* on the Cartoon Network. He was also young enough to wear crazy shoes, a red plastic pair that only he could get away with. Young enough that he rode his bicycle to his audition. But Dan was old enough to have a day job, working in some office somewhere that he hated.

Only weeks earlier, Dan had moved to New York from San Francisco, the swing capital of the country. "My girlfriend and I used to go swing dancing all the time. Do you guys know of any places to go in New York?"

He took his girlfriend swing dancing. This guy was too good to be true. And I hadn't even heard him play yet.

Then, right there in the studio, to warm up, Dan started doing guitar impersonations, disguising his voice like Axl Rose's and singing like an old toothless man, "No one knows what it's like to be the bad man. To be the sad man." Julie and I cracked up laughing. He immediately morphed into Eddie Van Halen for three seconds, making his red Fender Stratocaster bark and squeal in a frenzy of incredible cheese. Then he stopped, the silence shocking us, and said, "You guys ready?"

I counted down, a smile still on my face, and Julie and I started playing "Letters," a new ballad she had written. Dan picked out a beautiful countermelody to Julie's strumming. And then, on the chorus, he stepped up to the microphone and opened his mouth, to sing harmony to Julie's lead vocal.

This is how the news arrives . . .
My tongue was tied and I saw stars,
But I didn't cry.

What came out of Dan's mouth almost made me stop playing the drums. I was suddenly just a visitor. Dan belonged here.

All I wanted to do was shut up just so I could sit back and listen more closely as their voices wrapped around each other, guitar lines dancing, joining and breaking free again, then back, over chorus, verse, and chorus. Dan's voice echoing Julie's. Her lines repeating his lines. Dan and Julie melding like lovers, like brother and sister, like twins, like they had played together for years and years and had found each other again, across the miles, across that big bulge of the United States, after all this time.

I wondered if maybe Julie and Dan would become an item, which, I figured, would add a whole new dynamic to the band. Their chemistry was great, but it tipped the delicate balance that was the band marriage. Somehow, having Dan in the band meant Sleepy Steve was out. We were headed to rock and roll divorce court one more time.

According to Julie's purist theory, you couldn't have lead guitar and keyboards in a band. It was one or the other. Steve also kept insisting on playing guitar himself. With Dan, a real guitarist, in the band, he would have to go. "You can't have three guitars in a band," Julie rationalized. She was right about that. Three guitars bordered on rockestra territory—those all-star jams at music awards shows where everybody plays guitar and the result is a nasty din. Rockestras were always a disaster.

"But if he played keyboards, you wouldn't have three guitars," I said, in Steve's defense.

"But you can't have keyboards *and* lead guitar in a band."

It was a catch-22 for poor old Steve. He just couldn't win. Julie had made the decision to break up with him; there was nothing anyone could do. No severance package, no explanation, no résumé-writing workshop, no goodbye party.

So long, Steve.

Partly in solidarity, partly out of fear of being too old for all this, feeling a little intimidated by Dan's talent, I offered to quit.

"Maybe it's time you got a real drummer," I said to Julie after our next practice, after Dan had packed up and gone home. "I mean, now that you have a good guitarist. I'm not a real drummer, you know."

"You can't leave," she said, quietly, simply. "I need you."

It was true. It wasn't my drumming Julie needed exactly. I wasn't dumb enough, or brazen enough, to believe that. Julie needed my amateurism. She needed another girl on her side to bring her solidarity, to bring her confidence, to stand up against the boys who would show up for auditions. I knew that. And I stayed anyway.

I never even got to say goodbye to Steve. I considered calling him, but had no idea what I would say. Like with Andy White, I put it off, until so much time went by that it was too awkward to call.

• ELEVEN •

I thought Julie had a crush on Dan. But so did I. He was so cute, you couldn't help but have a small crush on him. He was too young, though, to seriously consider dating. Not that I was in the market.

I had to remind myself that I was married sometimes, since these days I didn't see much of Martin. He was promoted to an editor's position that spring, and so he left for work earlier and worked even later than usual. Sometimes it was great to have the apartment all to myself. I could play whatever CDs I wanted, and not have to worry if it was something Martin would like, too.

Those nights, I would play my G. Love and Special Sauce CD, which Martin couldn't stand. G. Love was a white hip-hop blues boy who sounded drunk all the time, or retarded. I liked him for some reason, maybe because I had several retarded people in my extended family. But Martin hated G. Love. I could only play him when Martin wasn't at home. I also could watch whatever I wanted on television late at night. Whenever Martin was home, he'd flip around and invariably end up on the History Channel, watching some World War II documentary. I called it the Hitler Channel, since it always featured a Nazi rally or tanks moving on Poland.

But I missed having him at home. And I missed having him in the band. Some nights, I barely noticed he was with me in bed. We hardly ever had sex anymore, since I was always in deep REM by the time he got home. And he slept later than I did in the morning. By the time he got up, I was already on the phone doing interviews or out practicing.

I was spending so much time alone these days, without Martin, that I wondered if this was what marriage was supposed to be like. I had nothing to compare it to, and was too embarrassed to mention it to anyone else. I remembered that first conversation I had had with Julie for *Cosmopolitan,* about how she and Jimmy hardly ever slept together. Maybe this was normal.

I didn't want anyone to think I was unhappy or anything. Because I wasn't exactly. I was a little lonesome sometimes and disappointed. But I wasn't going to complain to Martin. He had enough problems from his new job and was so nervous, he started smoking again, a new brand, Parliaments. One afternoon, as we passed each other briefly in the living room, I nodded to the blue and white hard pack on the coffee table.

"What's with the Parliaments?" I asked.

"I like the recessed filter," he said.

"Maybe you should do a commercial."

I didn't want to be one of those wives who nags her husband to stop smoking, or bugs him to come home from work earlier, who stops her husband from seeing his friends for a beer or two. But with Martin's new hours, I actually felt like I was single again.

Home alone at night, flipping through our music collection for something I wanted to hear, I'd come across a CD case with a yellow Post-it note flagging a favorite song. The notes were left over from our wedding, from three years ago, and they made me a little sad sometimes when I saw them now.

The Post-it notes had been for Dave, former Zone and best man, who offered to make mix tapes for the wedding from our CDs. We had decided there would be no deejay, no band. No playing of Kool and the Gang's "Celebration." There were no gushy love songs, no "In My Life" or "Here, There and Everywhere." Martin and I trolled through our joint CD collection together, looking for smart songs about getting married, like "Big Day" by XTC: "Could be heaven, could be hell in a cell for two-oo-oo-oo-ooh."

We reserved a casual Cajun/Italian joint in Brooklyn for the reception. While Martin had his suit custom made, a schnazzy double-breasted charcoal number, I spent only $105 on my dress, though it looked pretty fabulous, I have to say. I had always felt like Maryann from *Gilligan's Island,* but in this dress, I was Ginger, the Movie Star. It hugged my body and came to a quick flip about three quarters of the way to the floor; off-white, stretchy lace, for maximum maneuverability, and very low heels, in case I decided to make a break for it.

When I ordered the cake, I told the baker it was for a party; and when I ordered the bouquet, I said it was for a school play.

My wedding ring would be a tiny gold band we had found in Martin's grandmother's safe a few months after she had died, just a few months before the wedding. Inside it were written the words, "God Bless You." I was the only one with fingers small enough for the ring. Martin's mother, the goldsmith, would forge his ring, a simple gold band.

In buying the cake, the dress, the bouquet and rings the way we did, and getting Dave to make the mix tapes, we could save money. That's what I told people anyway. And it was partially true. But the truth was, the real truth was, that I was scared to death.

Shit scared, as my family liked to say.

I pretended this wasn't a wedding at all. It was a big party with good music and good food to celebrate our union. We were already living together. So getting married was really no big deal. Right? Because what if he wasn't the one? Though I could never tell anyone my doubts, I wasn't sure he was the one I was supposed to spend my life—my whole life—with. The one I should have kids with. The one who my kids would look like. I could leave Martin if I had to, but what about those kids? They'd have his features, miniature eyes and noses and those big full lips of his, a reminder of Martin, an advertisement for Martin, for the rest of my life. You had to be sure about these things. Didn't you?

I needed a sign. A new sign that we were meant to be together. For always. It would have to be a pretty big sign, billboard size. Earthquake-like, at least a 7.0 on the Richter scale.

In keeping with the casual nature of things, our ceremony would be in Martin's mother's backyard, in Park Slope, Brooklyn, where he had grown up. Presiding over the ceremony would be an Episcopal priest friend of mine whose church had been destroyed back in 1990. It had been hit by lightning and burned to the ground.

George, the priest, was one of my heroes. He was, among other things, a great banjo player. It was hard not to love a banjo player (you even had to love that retarded guy in *Deliverance*). To add to his coolness, George was married to a priestess named Katrina. They would perform our ceremony together. We even went through pre-Cana with them, a three-session, mini premarriage counseling in which we talked about our desire to have children, our desire to be together, and the stories about our past girlfriends and boyfriends. We told them all about Linda and Tony. And everyone else who came in between.

The day of the wedding, I pretended to be pretty nonchalant about the whole thing, though I was still worried, searching the backyard for that sign. Any sign. My whole family got stuck in traffic from the San Gennaro street festival in Little Italy, which was smack in between New Jersey and Brooklyn. Not a good sign.

Though it was late September, it was a hot, hazy day. I was dripping. I wasn't sure if it was the heat, or my rising anxiety, that was causing me to sweat.

Everyone arrived, including most of the Zones: There was Jamal, the old singer, who was now working as an undercover detective at Macy's. And Dave, the best man, who made the mix tapes and was still playing keyboards for a living, mostly as a session musician. Matt, the former guitarist, was on tour somewhere in Europe with his ska band, the Toasters. With a small crowd gathered in the lush backyard, I pushed PLAY on the portable CD player. Stanley walked me out to the strains of Vivaldi's Concerto No. 15 for Guitar in D Major.

My niece, Lauren, her hair a frizzy halo, her teeth still in braces, read a minimalist poem about love, smiling that metal smile all the while. In the same way I had watched Lauren grow from an infant to a toddler to a kid and into a teenager, Lauren had watched Martin and me grow closer and closer over the years. We were the first couple Lauren had ever watched meet, fall in love, and now get married. She had heard firsthand about our first dates, experienced our short breakups, watched me cry through them, had rooted for us, and was now, here, taking part in our wedding.

My sister, Paula, my matron of honor, read a Bible passage, to make George and Katrina happy. There they were, in their elaborate Episcopal robes, performing their double-barrel ceremony. Then came the tiny God Bless You ring and the vows.

Suddenly, the crowd was gone. And it was just Martin and me up there, looking at each other. If it had been a movie, the lens would have zoomed in on us, one of those quick, tunnel-vision zooms where everything else on the periphery falls away. No George and Katrina. No parents. No Lauren or Paula. No best man, roses, or gardenias.

There we were, getting married. I almost started crying. Not because I was scared anymore. And not because of Vivaldi's Concerto No. 15, though it always made me cry, it was so pretty.

I was crying because I realized, in that zoom lens, all-alone-up-there moment, that I really did love Martin. I loved his new wedding suit and his big, gentle hands and the way they banged on tabletops and played bass and the way he moved his hips and the fact that he had brought me to the top of New York to ask me to marry him and the fact that he loved me while I was away for a year in Alaska and I loved his shoes and the toes inside them and his face and his voice and everything I knew and didn't even know about him. I imagined him in the delivery room with me, calming me down while I screamed my head off. I wanted my kids to have his head melded onto the tops of their bodies, tiny little bodies that would have his features, his eyebrows and toes and hopefully his hair, not mine. I wanted to know what he would look like in fifty years. I wanted to grow up with him and grow old with him and be with him and take off and land with him and even jump from planes with him. Over and over again. For the rest of my life, even. I wanted to suddenly shout it from the tops of the Brooklyn brownstones. But I was too choked up to get past a whisper.

And in that moment, that quiet moment where I vowed to forsake all others, to love him for richer, for poorer, for better, for worse, in sickness and in health, to have and to hold, until death do us part (Death, mind you. Not another cute guy. Or a bad sex life. Or a bad year. Or anything but death), I was converted.

In that split-second transformation, I became the happiest bride in the world. No longer embarrassed by the flowers and the dresses and the ceremony, I wished, suddenly, that I had ordered several tiers for my cake, hundreds of bouquets to throw to my single friends. I wished that the sappiest love songs, like "Colour My World" and "Evergreen," had been on my wedding mix tapes. Well, maybe not "Evergreen."

The worst cynic might say I was just caught up in the moment, in the happiness of the wedding moment. We danced and laughed and drank champagne and ate from platters of Cajun shrimp and pasta and were told by dozens of people—dozens of particularly grumpy New York people—that it was by far the most fun they'd ever had at a wedding. The happiest wedding they'd ever been to. People refused to leave.

Dave gave the toast: "Coney Island. The Cyclone. A run-down, rickety, downright, played-out institution that has somehow managed to remain standing after all these years. This roller coaster offers an impending sense of doom for some, an exhilarating thrill of a lifetime for others. With a little courage and a couple of bucks in your pocket, you can ride as long as you like.

"Five years ago," Dave said, "I met Helene in front of this roller coaster. A perfectly appropriate place, it turns out. Who knew the ride we were all in for?" Big laugh.

"I met Martin thirteen years ago at a little ice cream parlor a few blocks from here. After being in the same high school, the same neighborhood, and the same band together, he earned the distinction of being, among other things, the greatest songwriter I've ever met or will ever meet, for that matter." Martin's ears turned red.

"Despite my limited experience as a married guy, I can tell that they are a perfect combination. Martin and Helene," he said, raising his glass high. "Here's wishing you a pocketful of quarters and the ride of a lifetime."

Everyone cheered. Martin blushed some more. "We're gonna have a lot of fun from now on," he said, raising his glass to mine.

We spent half our honeymoon in Amsterdam, eating space cakes. (My idea.) Nothing happened after we ate them, and we thought maybe we'd been ripped off. Then, about a half hour later, we were sitting next to a canal watching a tour boat go under a bridge and Martin said, "Look: The bridge is moving and the boat is standing still." I had noticed the very same thing.

We tried to walk it off, but were suddenly so stoned that Martin sat down in the middle of the sidewalk in the Red Light District. Martin wasn't the type of guy to just sit down in the middle of a sidewalk. He had on nicely creased dress pants, which he had to hike up a little before sitting down.

When we finally came to, we took an overnight train to Paris (Martin's idea), where we snuggled in a tiny hotel on the Île St. Louis. Paris was so beautiful, and for the first time, I looked over at Martin and called him my husband. Husband. He was my husband. And I was still happy.

When we got back to our fairy-tale building in Brooklyn, I cooked and worked and made our bed after we made love in it. I didn't even mind when he played his music too loud. I didn't mind the Hitler Channel, really. I kissed him when he left for work in the afternoon. And kissed him when he returned late at night.

Soon after we were married, Elvis Costello recorded "Days" on an album of covers. "Days," the song I had heard in concert and had sung to Martin in the newsroom, the song we had heard the night we watched the Empire State Building snap off at midnight, had been a Kinks song, which explained why Martin had never heard it.

More important, Elvis reunited with the Attractions the year we were married. But that wasn't the only sign all was right in the world.

On their album *All This Useless Beauty,* Elvis and the band were pictured on the inside sleeve standing on a Paris street, the same Paris street where Martin and I had stayed on our honeymoon. The good, sober part of our honeymoon. Out of all the thousands of streets in Paris, out of all the alleyways and boulevards, avenues and squares, Elvis Costello and the Attractions had chosen our tiny street, on the Île St. Louis.

Not only were they on our street, but they were standing right in front of the hotel where we had stayed. It was the sign I had been searching for all that time, the sign we were meant to be together.

• TWELVE •

In the spring of 1997, Doug became my other half.

He, like Dan, was a lead guitarist. He had seen *The Village Voice* ad, too, and called Julie about being our new bass player.

Julie and Doug hit it off before they even met. They liked all the same bands and decided to meet each other at a Yo La Tengo show, for which they both already had tickets. Midway through the Yo La Tengo set, Julie took Doug's hand and dragged him up to the front of the stage. He went right along, laughing all the way. From then on, Julie and Doug were buddies.

There was just one small problem. I didn't like Doug. His playing was fine. Nothing spectacular. Nothing in bad taste.

It wasn't the music. I just didn't like *him.*

For starters, he wore a baseball cap to his audition, just like Hootie. Adult males who wore baseball caps were either members of a college fraternity, in an arrested state of development, or simply going bald. I had nothing against bald guys. But just be bald already. Shave it all off. Or just leave it alone.

The baseball cap was annoying, but not the only reason I didn't like Doug. He was very chilly to me. Snotty, almost. He wouldn't even acknowledge my presence throughout his audition. He refused to make eye contact with me. And he didn't seem the shy type. I was the drummer, for Chrissake. I was already in the band. Shouldn't I get a little respect? Maybe girl drummers weren't good enough for him.

"So what do you think?" Julie asked after his audition, after he and Dan had already left.

"What about that other guy?" I asked. "The guy I liked?" There was a bass player who had come to try out a week ago, a quiet guy whom I had really hit it off with.

"He's too old."

"Too old? He's the same age as we are."

"He's just too eighties," she said, shaking her head.

Doug was a kid, a brat from Seattle, and like Dan, had just recently arrived in the city. Julie figured that the only way to get good players in the cutthroat music world of New York was to get them hot off the plane from another city.

"Well, I really like Doug," Julie said, as she wound up her guitar cord. "I'd like him to play with us for a while." She paused. "Do you not like him?"

"No," I lied. "It's not that." I didn't want to be a pain in the ass. I didn't want to complain. But Julie could tell I was lying to her.

"Maybe once you get to know him," she said. "He has real indie sensibility."

Over the next few weeks, I did not learn to love Doug and his indie sensibility. He skateboarded everywhere and always wore that stupid baseball cap. Something about his swiftness and his tall lanky frame reminded me of a professional hockey player. And hockey was my least favorite sport.

He was in his mid-twenties, though he looked like he was sixteen, and had such a baby face, I wondered if he even shaved regularly. But his real age was given away whenever he took off that baseball cap, which was not often. Doug was starting to lose his hair, just as I had suspected. Maybe if he had taken his hat off at his audition, Julie would have rejected him for being too old.

Doug often brought a six-pack with him to drink while we played. And he smoked in the studio, which was not allowed. He smoked Parliaments, just like Martin. I wondered if it was a trend. I started smoking, the first time since smoking menthols back in high school. He did not bring out the best in me, that Doug.

But he loved Julie, you could tell, and he loved her songs, but he was often nasty to her, like the boy in seventh grade who expresses his emotions by punching you or making fun of you in front of his friends. Julie found it somehow endearing.

Once, during rehearsal, Julie spent about ten minutes futzing with the switches and dials on her guitar.

"What's the problem?" Doug finally asked.

"I don't want the distortion for the verse," Julie said.

"That's why there's a foot pedal," Doug said, pointing to Julie's new distortion pedal, which clicked the distortion on and off. "You just push it." And he did. It was a simple suggestion, but Doug's tone and body language were mocking. He might as well have put "idiot" at the end of the sentence.

Dan, seeing Julie's red face, tried to calm her down. He chastised Doug with a simple, exaggerated "Now, now."

I just kept quiet. I wanted Julie to get so mad she'd kick Doug out of the band and hire that other guy, Older Eighties-Looking Guy.

"If I want your advice, I will ask for it," Julie said to Doug, in as snotty a tone as she could muster.

"It's not advice, it's a suggestion," Doug said.

We played the song again, but this time Julie used the distortion pedal—as Doug suggested—and the problem was solved.

"I'm sorry," yelled Doug. "But that sounded a lot better."

"I'm sorry," Julie said, giggling. "I love your suggestions." They practically kissed and made up. Dan scowled. I wanted to stick my finger down my throat.

I considered quitting yet again, since it didn't look like Julie would ever get rid of Doug. But something whispered in my ear and made me stay. Not Martin this time. But Julie.

One night, Doug took us to see his favorite musician perform at a small club, a subterranean place called Fez. I don't think he even invited me really. I think Julie asked me to come. The musician's name was Elliott Smith; he was a singer from Portland, Oregon, whom Doug had discovered and had been listening to for the past year. I had my doubts, but Julie had heard a tape of Smith that Doug had given her, and convinced me to come along.

When Smith came out, he sat on a plastic chair, all alone on the tiny stage, just a few feet from us. He was introverted and dark with bad skin and posture, and for those first few minutes, I felt like we had suddenly intruded on his private space. If it hadn't been for a sparkly curtain and the bar, it would have felt like Smith's living room or, worse, his bedroom. Like we were about to see something we shouldn't be seeing. Overhearing something we shouldn't be overhearing.

Smith hadn't even opened his mouth yet, and I was already embarrassed for him, already annoyed at Doug for bringing us here. He looked so uncomfortable up there. It was beyond stage fright. It looked like any minute he was going to slink away, crawl under one of our cocktail tables and die. But then he touched his hand to his strings and opened his mouth, and everything around him, and us, disappeared. We stopped existing for him. All the tension and uneasiness were washed clean by a simple A minor chord.

The songs he played, played for us that night, were delicate, sensitive, and amazingly powerful. How could Doug like this guy? There was one song about sitting in a bar and knowing that it's raining outside just from the sound of the tires on the pavement. And there you were, suddenly, leaning on that bar with him, that sad, empty bar, having just been dumped by your girlfriend.

When the song was through, we all climbed back to the surface of reality, to the here and now. Doug and I made eye contact. He nodded ever so slightly, as if to say, "See. I told you so."

All of Smith's songs were sad, but in the way that made you want to wallow in the sadness. To dive headfirst into depression with him. Sit with him and have a drink. George Harrison, my favorite Beatle, was his favorite Beatle, too, Smith told us during a very uncomfortable moment of mumbled onstage banter. He didn't need to tell us, though. You could tell.

And that night, with the help of Elliott Smith, I softened ever so slightly and decided that maybe Doug wasn't so awful after all.

Maybe it was an unwritten rule in banddom, but every time we got a new band member, we had to find a new studio to practice in. It was like moving out of the apartment you had shared with your lover. The lover you were leaving.

Paul, the studio guy who had recorded I Hate Jane earlier that year, had bought the Night Owl studio and had moved it. He called Julie to let her know, so we started practicing at the new Night Owl. The place was small, about half the size of the old Night Owl, with a main, glassed-in studio for recording and two claustrophobic practice spaces, plus a tiny waiting room up front—so tiny that you were forced to wait in the hallway for your space to open up. Over Paul's desk were a calendar and a dozen of those black-and-white autographed photos of Down Time bands no one had ever heard of. The space was cheaper than the other studios in the building, but there was good reason for the bargain.

"You know, it stinks in here," Doug said one afternoon. "I go home and I can smell it on my clothes."

"I can smell it, too," I said, burying my nose in the shoulder of my shirt. It smelled like musty indelible marker.

"I think it's these old amps getting heated up or something," Doug said, lightly kicking one of them for emphasis.

"It gets in your stuff," I said. "My bag smells like it when I get home. And my hair." The smell was so strong some days that you had to take a shower when you got home from practice, as if returning from a tryst with the smell of sex on your body.

"My theory being that smoking in here can only help it," Doug offered, pulling out his pack of Parliaments.

"I think you're right." I reached for one. "And spilling beer helps, too."

"There you go," Doug said, laughing. "That's the spirit." I counted down, two, three, four, and we started playing again, lit cigarettes dangling from our lips.

We played a song called "So Far," about a friend or a boyfriend who had changed so much they were unrecognizable. "You smoke too much," Julie sang. "Those cigarettes, they cloud your thinking. So you pour yourself another drink. What are you drinking now?"

Practice after practice, I grew to appreciate Doug, like a song you don't like on first listen, but learn to love over repeated playings. I came to like him more and more, cigarette by cigarette, mix tape by mix tape, which he made us, from his vast indie label collection.

I came to have a secret crush on him, too, actually. Kind of like the crush you'd have on your little brother's best friend. Sick, in a way, but innocent in its impossibility.

At various stages, I had crushes on everyone in the band, never simultaneously, but in a round-robin fashion. Whenever Dan sang with Julie, I just wanted to marry him, he was so sexy. His harmony was so pretty and his guitar playing brightened every song it touched. Julie was like my old flame, who could make me smile no matter what was happening around me.

My crush on Doug was different, since it was the only one that manifested itself in an erotic dream. The next time we practiced, I suddenly remembered the dream—Doug going down on me—and I'm sure that I blushed when I entered the studio. I tried to avoid eye contact with him that afternoon, but it was hard, since we were the rhythm section.

It was the music, really, that brought me around to liking Doug. It was hard not to develop a close relationship with the other half of your rhythm section. Like Martin and me, Doug and I finally clicked, filling in the spaces that the other was leaving, echoing beats and rhythm lines.

I found that as long as you were on Doug's side of the jokes he cracked, you could get along with him. But if his adolescent, insulting humor turned your way, it was excruciating.

While walking down 30th Street once, after practice, on our way to the F train, Doug kicked me in the ass. I got so mad I wanted to hit him. So I did. A nice jab to the chest. I was buff from a year and a half of banging on tom-toms.

"Ow," he said, rubbing his chest. "What'd you do that for?"

But he knew. And he never kicked me in the ass again.

As Doug and I grew closer, our rhythm section improved. One of our strongest bits was the song "Nightlight's Glow." It had a bassy, low-to-the-ground sound that Doug and I helped create. I played the floor tom through each of the verses to get the sound right. Doug's bass matched it with an underwater, *Creature from the Black Lagoon* quality. The introduction sounded as if it were being played from the ocean's murky bottom, so deep down you could barely see the sea monsters around you.

Dan added counterpoint to all that by playing a guitar part that sounded like sparklers, the kind you ran around with on the Fourth of July when you were a kid. His guitar work twinkled and glowed, just like the song title said. And over it all was Julie's simple strumming and her whispery, spooky, little-girl voice, pulling it all together.

The song was my niece Lauren's favorite. At one of our Night Owl practices, I propped up my new cell phone on a music stand and the band and I played the song for her in New Jersey, her own private satellite hookup.

Lyrically, it was the most adolescent of our songs, the one that Julie's boyfriend, Jimmy, had written. But it was the song most likely to be played on the radio and become a hit. We actually considered making a low-budget video of it, through a friend of Dan's.

"We should all wear pajamas," Dan said, at the bar around the corner from Night Owl—the Molly Wee Pub. We went there for a drink after practice just to talk about the video script.

"Yeah," Doug said, "we could all be tucked in for sleep in, like, one big, giant bed."

"Then the mom would come in and turn out the light," Julie said.

"Then you could all jump up and grab your instruments and play them standing on the bed," I said. "I could get one of those little kid sets of drums."

"Yeah, yeah," Doug said. "We'll all still be in our pajamas."

"And then when the next verse comes around," Dan said, "we'll be tucked back in again. We could just come out on the chorus."

The last line of the chorus—"And we can pretend that Mom and Dad are dead"—was repeated over and over again, to the pleasure of our imaginary, youthful, parent-hating MTV audience. It was completely infantile. But it was our best song, a dark, brooding number with the flickering light of Dan's guitar work.

One afternoon Lauren came with me to Night Owl for our practice. The new band thrilled her even more than the old band, since there were now two cute young guys playing guitar, neither one of them her Uncle Martin.

She sat quietly in a corner, and smiled and listened, mouthing the words now and then. When we came to "Nightlight's Glow," her eyes brightened even more than usual. A favorite song could do that.

As Doug and I swam in the depths of the rhythm, and Dan layered on his bright night-light flickers, Julie—and Lauren, quietly, to herself almost—came in on vocals.

Red fingertips
Turning off the light switch
She says, Lay your heads down.
She says, Shut your mouth.

So we pretend
That we're asleep
Until we hear footsteps down the hall,
And out the door and down the street

And then we awake
Gonna start an earthquake
We are alone in the Nightlight's Glow.

We don't care
What you think about us
We know that the world is for the misfit girls

Lauren clapped. And then rose in a single standing ovation.

"How old is she again?" Doug asked, leaning in close to me.

"Seventeen," I said, suspiciously. "Why?"

"She's kinda cute," he said, shrugging.

"Don't even think about it."

"Ow," he said, as I punched him in the arm.

"Sorry," I said.

"No you're not."

"You're right," I said. "I'm not."

• THIRTEEN •

Lauren wasn't the only one who came to visit the new band. Martin stopped in now and then, on his way to work in the afternoon. It was one of the few times I saw him. Once he came to the studio because I had left my house keys at home. He came to drop them off, then wound up sticking around a few minutes to watch us practice, standing sadly in the corner with his raincoat on and his hands in his pockets. I could tell the way he watched us that he wished he were playing along, too. The glow he had the night of our CB's show was long gone. Then his beeper went off and he left Night Owl in a panic.

For my birthday, when Martin asked me what I wanted, I told him I wanted to spend the night in a fancy New York hotel. No beepers, no phone calls. Just Martin and me. He loved hotels, so I knew he'd go for the idea. My ulterior motive, of course, was to have sex. In a new setting, we could close that hotel door and finally relax. It would be like a second honeymoon. Just like Paris. Just like that magical street on the Île St. Louis.

Martin made a reservation at the Parker Meridien. All the rock stars loved the place, and it was considered a music industry hub. I had interviewed Isaac Hayes there once for a story. When Martin had been a teenager, he had waited in the hotel lobby for Elvis Costello and the Attractions to go by. He chatted with Elvis that night. I had heard that story about 500 times, but never got tired of hearing Martin tell it.

So on my birthday, we ordered room service, a bottle of champagne, and a movie that neither of us had ever seen, Alfred Hitchcock's *Spellbound,* with its Freudian overtones and Dalí dreamscapes. When we got into the big king-size bed, Martin held me close, but made no moves to undress me. When I made a move toward him, he gently took my hand away and held it, then kissed me on the forehead and got into snuggle mode, pulling me warmly to his chest.

I couldn't decide if I should cry or yell, if I should feel sorry for him or for myself. I lay there paralyzed, afraid to even touch him.

He drifted off to sleep and I rolled over to my side of the bed. Maybe he had some physical problem. Maybe he needed a penile implant or one of those pumps or something. Maybe he wasn't attracted to me anymore. Or maybe this was just a downbeat in the rhythm of marriage. Maybe it was one of those patches they talked about. A dry patch. Like that patch I had spied off of St. Lawrence Island, that big whale lurking just below the surface, threatening to tip the boat over into the cold, cold water. Soon enough it would move on and swim away.

Most nights after practice, if I had the car with me, I would drive Doug home to his tiny apartment in Chinatown. The nights I'd left the car in Brooklyn, he and I would walk to the F train together, no ass-kicking allowed. While we waited for the bright orange F to rise in the dark subway tunnel, Doug and I talked about his old life in Seattle, how hard it was adjusting to life in New York. He had gotten a job as an architect and had moved to New York for that reason. But his real love was music.

"I always had this idea of what it would be like to live here," he said while we waited, the urine on the platform stinging our noses. "But it's so much different."

"Different how?"

"Harder." He shifted his black bass case to his other shoulder. "Like running a relay race or something, like, all the time."

"I grew up here, so I can't even imagine what it's like to come to New York for the first time as an adult. It must be so overwhelming."

"It is," he said. "At least you have Martin and your family here. That must make it easier."

I shrugged. Sometimes that made things harder, I thought. Some days I wished I lived far away from them all, away from the worries and the problems, my big family and my husband's sexual ambivalence.

"It's hard being on your own in this place," he said. "I mean, I have my friends at work and all."

"What am I, chopped liver?"

"No. The band is the best thing I got goin' right now."

I nodded. I knew exactly what he meant.

As Doug and I grew closer, Dan and Julie's harmonies grew even tighter. They started writing whole new songs together at Dan's apartment, where they would meet now and then before practice. Their best piece was a reworking of the song "Document," which Julie and I had first played way back in our Elizabethan period, the song that had the recurring lyric, "Jesus lost and found, over and over again."

Dan reworked it so that it was no longer a waltz, but was in straight 4/4 time, though it had three separate tempos for three different sections. Somehow, the first part of the song kept its lullaby quality, but in a dark, strange, *Rosemary's Baby* way, with bent, tortured guitar notes. The lyrics, "Don't forget to say your prayers. Jesus lost and found" contributed to that vibe.

In the middle section, the tempo quickened and an extra beat was dropped in, giving the song a more serious, sophisticated, but still disturbed sound. Dan could do stuff like that, give songs a dark edge, change time signatures and drop in notes. Of the four of us, he was the most disturbed, and naturally, as these things go, the best musician. And Julie knew that, which is one of the reasons she got closer to him and sucked up his knowledge. We all did.

Out of all the songs we learned that summer, "Document" was the most difficult, learned during one three-hour marathon practice. I was about to leave on a weeklong trip to Mexico City to write a story about native Mexican nouvelle cuisine, so Julie was trying to cram in as much practice time as possible before I left, to commit the new "Document" to all our memories before our break.

I spent most of the three hours trying to get the shifting rhythms down, Julie trying to come in at all the right places. By the end of the practice, I was exhausted.

"I'm pretty much done," I said to Julie. "But you're worse. You look how I feel."

"The learning process is really a bitch," she said. "I cannot learn anything on command. So all of you, get off my ass." She smiled.

"Hey, this marathon was your idea," I said.

"Yeah," Julie said. "But think of the long break you're gonna get now, honey pie."

"Are you kidding? This is gonna be playing in my head the whole time I'm in Mexico."

"Good. That's what I wanted. This has the potential to be the grand song." She swept her skinny arm up in the air.

While we were packing up to go, I could feel how stretched my muscles were and how good it felt.

"So what's Martin gonna do without you while you're in Mexico?" Julie asked as she placed her baby blue guitar in its case.

"He'll probably play music really loud." Whenever Martin came in from work, I was asleep, so he had to keep the volume down.

"He's gonna have the whole place to himself, jamming around in his underwear at top volume?"

"He probably can't wait," I laughed.

On my way to Mexico City, listening closely to our practice tapes, I noticed that our sound was changing. It was becoming tighter, richer. "Melodic pop with a beveled edge," Dan called it.

Julie was still strumming quietly on rhythm guitar and singing soft, girlish vocals. But the music around her had changed, lifting her up and thrusting her forward, like a strong setting around a small but brilliant stone. Or like a push-up bra, depending on what song we were playing.

Doug was a simpler bass player than Martin, adding a less-complicated line to the songs. Dan, however, was much more complex. His sound was dissonant at times, beautifully melodic at others. On the song "Letters," his guitar reminded me of the pretty wrought-iron gates, with swoops and swirls, that you'd see outside brownstones in New York, like the railing Martin and I had outside our apartment. Strong and heavy metal, but lattice and lightness, all at the same time. Dan's sound was a perfect foil for Julie's soft tones.

Most of all, Dan's voice was right on. When he and Julie stepped up to their mics to sing a duet, like on "Letters," they made you want to be them. It was fragile and tender and strong all in one swoop. I loved listening to "Letters" as much as playing along to it.

Because of my mounting sexual frustration, my playing really improved that summer. To compete with Dan's searing guitar solos, I had to play slightly harder and louder, something Julie wasn't always happy about. I compromised, playing softer on the vocal parts and then building up into a frenzy on the instrumental finales. Those sonic hills and valleys were becoming part of our sound.

I bought new cymbal stands, since the ones Stanley had lent me were a million years old and threatened to topple over every time I smacked them. Stanley's snare was on its way out, too, but I stopped myself from buying a new one. I didn't really have the money, and wasn't sure I should invest that much in the band.

Because sometimes, we just plain sucked.

When my foot pedal was slow in hitting its target, I dragged Doug right down with me. Julie's off notes would send Dan off-key as well. If Julie was in a bad mood, Dan would get sulky and couldn't remember his leads. When Dan and Julie's harmony was off, it was brutal. And when Doug hit a wrong bass note, it reverberated through the studio and led us all astray. But at least we knew what to strive for.

To match our new sound, the good sound on the good days, we needed a good name. I Hate Jane was too negative.

Lolligag was bantered about for a while. As was the simple and not so fitting Blue. We considered Blue Guitar. But that was too self-referential for Julie. She pitched Uber Kitty once again, but the boys wouldn't stand for it. Forget Girls, Girls, Girls.

I suggested Julie Julie Julie.

They shook their heads no.

Jane's Heir?

Too clever.

"December?" Julie asked.

"June," I countered.

"Four Heads," Doug said.

"Recliner," Dan said.

Star 69.

Speed Dial.

Bitter.

Panchino.

Gump.

Maraschino.

Tug.

Dish.

Reflector.

Stipend.

Slattern.

Slatternly.

Carmine.

Maxilla.

Shifter.

Resentful.

The Stevedores.

"How about Stepanek?" I said, Julie's last name.

"No," said Dan, bowing his head in thought. "That's not it."

We stared at him, waiting for something brilliant to spring from his mouth, like it often did from his guitar. "How about sticking an *H* in there and making it StePHonic. You know, like Stereophonic."

"Not bad," I said.

Julie sent out a demo tape, with the new band name, Stephonic, typed on a label on Side A. And we hoped that by late summer or early fall, we'd have a gig or two. We practiced hard and constantly, every other day, rather than just once or twice a week.

Every night after practice, we would all go out for a drink or two or three, sometimes four, to the Molly Wee Pub, the place where we had mapped out our imaginary "Nightlight's Glow" music video. The jukebox wasn't so great. And the drinks could have used a little more ice. The clientele wasn't hip. But we had each other's company. For the price of a drink, we engaged in band therapy. We talked about the songs we'd just played, the new songs Julie had just written. Eventually, as the empty glasses piled up, we'd move on to more personal topics.

Doug would tell us about the new girl he was after.

"She is so beautiful," he said one night about the lead singer of a band he had seen at Luna Lounge, a club on the Lower East Side. "She'll never go out with me. Do you think maybe she'll go out with me?"

"No. Probably not," I said. I had seen this girl. And she was beautiful. As long as he continued to wear that stupid baseball cap, he didn't stand a chance. "You're cute enough."

"But you need to lose the hat," Julie said, completing my thought.

Julie was still worried about Jimmy cheating on her and spent most of her pub time obsessing about it.

"So he didn't call me for two whole days," she said, while Jimmy was away on one of his film festival trips. "I know that girl Jane was there.

How much you wanna bet Jane was there? I could have sworn I saw her in the background on the E Channel. They did a pan shot of the crowd at Cannes, and I saw her."

Dan just nodded. He didn't share too many of his problems. But from what I could tell, Dan wanted to be famous and was deeply disturbed by his anonymity on the streets of New York. He was cute, talented, and smart. It was just a matter of time. So he spent most of his free time trying to dream up a gimmick for the band.

"Maybe we should all play in our underwear," he said, half joking. "Or maybe we should all wear black. Or Julie, you should wear a really short skirt. A short black skirt."

My main worry was Martin. He was now smoking a pack of Parliaments a day and started seeing a therapist because he was so depressed. I couldn't possibly get mad at him because we weren't sleeping together. Something was wrong with him.

Though I kept our faded sex life to myself, I couldn't help tell the band about a conversation Martin and I had had one day before he left for work. It was something I couldn't tell my family, because to them it would sound too awful. So I told Julie, Doug, and Dan at the pub, my alternative family.

Somehow, Martin and I had arrived on the subject of children. I wasn't exactly ready to have kids but I knew that someday, in the not-too-distant future, I would be. We were in the midst of one of those vague kid conversations that married, childless couples have at least once a year, when Martin broke down.

"I don't think I want kids," he said. It took me a minute to process the sentence.

"But when we got married you said . . ."

"I know what I said. But I changed my mind. I really don't think I want children."

I couldn't respond really. This was very big news. One of the big headlines in your life, like WAR! OR PRESIDENT SHOT. It was like finding out your husband was a cross-dresser or that you were adopted. So many feelings and thoughts rushed through my mind at once. Did I really want kids? And did I want them enough to leave Martin? Had I married Martin just to procreate? What if there came a time when we found ourselves infertile? Would I leave him? Would he leave me? Why did people even get married?

All those fears and insecurities I'd had before the wedding came flooding back. But then I remembered standing up there with him, with the God Bless You ring, vowing to love him for better or worse.

And this, I knew, was the worse. This is what had been bothering him for months.

"We don't have to have kids—" I began, but Martin cut me off.

"You should have kids," he said, all choked up. "You'd be a natural mother. Maybe you should leave me and go back with Tony. You guys would be great parents."

"I want to have them with you," I said, starting to cry myself, not believing what was coming out of his mouth. "And I'm not gonna leave you, even if you don't want them. I love you. I married you to be with you."

"You should have stayed in Alaska. You were happy there."

"I want to be here with you. I love our life," I said, laughing and crying. "I'm happy. I love what I'm doing. I love freelancing and playing in the band. If it weren't for you, I couldn't do all these things. I couldn't go to Alaska and dance with Eskimos and get paid to write about it or play the drums."

"I know," Martin said. "I know. You're right." He wiped the tears from his face.

And so Martin and I wound up crying and holding each other, until I got my breath back.

"Give it some time," I said. I was rubbing his back, still holding him. "Maybe you're just not ready to have kids. I mean, I'm not ready yet, either."

"I just feel like there's gotta be something more to my life," he said, sniffling, winding down. "I mean, you go to high school so you can get into college. And then you go to college to get a good job. And then you get the job and you find the person you want to be with. But then what? I feel like there should be something else." He waved his hands. "Something else."

That something else, I thought, was kids. But I didn't tell Martin that.

I told Julie and Doug and Dan that story. Not all the gory details, but the gist of it. Since none of them was close to being married or having kids, they didn't have much advice for me. But that was all right. All I needed was for them to listen. And to play along.

At Dan's urging we learned our only cover, a Gordon Lightfoot seventies staple. We started out quiet, slow and corny, with only Dan on guitar. "If you could read my mind, love," Julie would sing. And Dan would answer, "What a tale my thoughts could tell." They would trade lines until Julie got to the strength of the phrase "fortress strong," where we all kicked in, the band loud and clunky, very un-Lightfoot. The rest of the song was played up-tempo, mocking and laughing all the way through. It was bound to rouse the crowd at our shows. It was familiar. They would know the words, but would laugh along with us, in on the joke.

At practice, we got lost in the long buildup of a song called "Astronaut," the new band favorite. The song was about being married to an astronaut. It was Doug's favorite because it was the only one that started with a solo bass line, slow and strong. I could let loose on the drums near the end. It was Dan's favorite because his stepfather actually was an astronaut, coincidentally.

"That's so bizarre," Dan said, when Julie first played it for us. "My mother is married to an astronaut. To Charles 'Pete' Conrad. He was the commander of Apollo 12."

"Really?" Julie asked.

"Yeah. He walked on the moon back in 1969."

"Shit," Doug said. "That's really weird."

"You didn't know that when you wrote it?" I asked Julie.

"No," she said. "I had no idea."

Julie loved the song because it combined a quiet, sweet beginning to showcase her voice, tacked onto a big, dramatic flourish of a finish. But I think it was her favorite for a different reason. It was the song that cut closest to her bones. It was the song Julie had written about Jimmy, while he was away at Cannes.

"You're seven thousand million miles away from me," Julie sang plaintively as Dan and I sang harmony, wailing right along with her at the moon.

"As you breathe silently on the opposite side of the bed," she sang, and I sang, too, feeling for her. Dan's guitar notes started like radio transmissions, but built and built until the end of the last verse, when Julie would shout, "Your rockets glare," and the whole band would take off into the stratosphere, my crash cymbal propelling us into deep space. Dan's notes became like hot tongues of flame descending on you, filling you up, your pockets, your hair, your space suit, soaking your clothes in their warmth and fire.

I loved that song. And I loved being in the band. So much so that I didn't see what was playing out right in front of me, that Martin was having an affair.

• FOURTEEN •

It happened on Labor Day weekend, the same day that Princess Diana died of a broken heart in that Paris tunnel. I should have seen it coming, should have seen the signs. But I was too busy playing drums and getting ready for our first gig, I would later think, blaming myself for a split second.

I was sitting on the couch, reading, when Martin came in and laid his heavy head in my lap. His heart was pounding so hard and fast that I thought he was having a heart attack.

"What's wrong?" I asked, looking down and placing a hand on his sweaty forehead. His ears were bright red. He put his hands over his face and started to hyperventilate.

Oh my God, I thought, he's sick. He's going to tell me he's sick.

"I've been having an affair," Martin said, through his hands.

"What?"

His head was still in my lap, so I could feel the sentence, its vibration, more than I could actually hear it.

I ran the sentence through my brain.

"I've been having an affair."

I knew what each individual word meant, could understand syllable by syllable what he had said, but the whole sentence, coming out of Martin's mouth, didn't make any sense to me.

So I repeated it again to myself, diagramming it in my brain.

"I've been having an affair." *I / have been having / an affair.* I counted the syllables on my fingers. I've been having an affair. Seven. Seven syllables. I counted them over and over.

My heart started beating as fast as Martin's as the words, the syllables, the parts of speech started to string together a meaning. I've been having an affair. Martin's been having an affair.

Martin sat bolt up straight and, through his blubbering tears, blurted out facts and dates and a name and a full confession so that it was no longer an absurdity hanging in the room above our heads, a diagrammed nonsense sentence. What he told me made it all seem possible.

"It's bad," he said. "It's so bad." He shook his head and closed his eyes. "It's been going on for a year. She works with me. The friendship just grew into something more, something I thought I wanted, but something I don't want to be a part of anymore." He threw his big bass-player hands in the air. "It's something I can't get out of now."

He was still talking, but I was still on that first part. The relationship had started a year ago.

A year ago. A year ago, I thought.

I was in Alaska last July, dancing with Eskimos. And when I had come home, Martin had seemed distant, unrecognizable. I thought it was me. But it was him. The affair was the reason Martin had seemed a stranger to me that first night back, the reason he hadn't been the least bit upset about my pretending to be Rob's wife on St. Lawrence Island. He was hoping I would sleep with Rob, to make himself feel better.

"When I was in Alaska?" I asked. "Is that when it started?" He nodded and put his hands over his wet face again. The affair died after a month, Martin said, but then had jump-started again after Christmas.

Now Martin was an editor, his girlfriend was still a reporter and she was threatening him, threatening not only to tell me, but to tell his boss. He was trapped, he said, he'd been trapped for months and months and the only solution was to tell me.

"I'm sorry," he said. "But I didn't want to have to tell you. It's bad." He put his hands back over his eyes and sobbed some more. I put my arms around him and tried to transfer some of my calm to his shuddering body.

I was dumbstruck. I had heard that word used before, but had never really understood it until now. Dumbstruck. To be struck dumb. I could not speak. It was as if Martin had taken a drum paddle and had smacked me right across the middle. The words, the air, the life, seemed to be gone from my body.

Then in my shock, I told him to calm down, that everything would be all right. "It's okay," I said, not knowing what else to say. I told him that I loved him and that everything would be all right. Was it something I had read you should do in a women's magazine?

After the Affair

TEN EASY STEPS TO FIXING YOUR SHATTERED MARRIAGE

"Everything will be all right," I said, over and over, as if singing a new chorus, trying to convince myself.

She had even been in our apartment once, two years ago, at one of our parties. I remembered her, small and insignificant, not especially pretty, flirting with another guest. But I couldn't remember what she looked like. I wanted to remember her face, remember her voice, the face he was kissing, the voice that was calling him behind my back.

Everything was not going to be all right.

"She won't let me end it," he said, his face red and wet. "It's bad. It's really bad. It's so bad. I didn't want to have to tell you. I wanted to take care of it. But it's bad. It's so bad."

All I could do was nod.

"I think we should call her," he said. "To tell her I told you everything."

"Yeah." I was still dazed, still calm. "Let's call her."

"We'll end it together. Right now."

"Yes," I said. Or thought. "Right now."

I got up from the couch and followed him into the office where the phone waited for us. My maturity and serenity scared me. He dialed her number. No need to look it up in his phone book. No pause to remember a digit. Because he knew this number by heart, each dirty little digit. He knew everything about her by heart. He was carrying that fucking number around in his head for a year and I didn't know it.

He blurted into the phone, "I told her. It's over. No more. You can't do this anymore." He hadn't even said hello. How are you? I guess he knew how she would be. I hoped he didn't have the wrong number.

His tears trickled into the holes in the receiver. Was he crying for her or crying for me, for us or for them? I was so detached I wondered if the moisture from his tears would harm the phone in any way.

I grabbed the phone and was greeted by another crier. Now I was trying to calm her down.

"I just want to be friends," she said, between sobs. "I just wanted to be his friend. I'm sorry. I want to be friends still."

"You can. You can," I said, trying to smooth over the panic, the madness taking over the air in the room and bubbling over into my consciousness. I was caught between two crazy people, two crazy people in love. I felt like the only adult in this scenario, like the friar in *Romeo and Juliet.*

You crazy kids.

"I'm sorry. I'm so sorry," she said, over and over, until I couldn't stand her voice anymore. I handed the phone back to Martin and gave him the universal hand signal that said, "Let's wrap it up."

My sister and her husband were celebrating their twenty-fifth wedding anniversary that night. One of life's little chuckles in the face of despair. I wouldn't cancel on my sister, not because of this stupidity. His stupidity. And besides, I was still strangely calm.

Martin had to rush around and get ready. Find his suit and tie. I pulled on panty hose and chose a dress. It was as if I were sleepwalking. Or walking wounded. As if I had just walked away from a deadly blast, and was not physically hurt, simply in shock. Lucky to be alive, but not even aware of it yet.

This was exactly where I wanted to go on the day I found out my husband was a philandering prick—to a restaurant next to a highway in suburban New Jersey to celebrate twenty-five years of marital bliss with my mother; Paula and her husband, Maurice; Lauren; my nephew, Paul, and his girlfriend, Lori; Stanley, his wife, and their two kids, Nicole and Alex; and Maurice's sister, her husband, and their two adopted daughters from South America.

When we walked in, things were already strained. No one was talking. Maurice figured it was time to get the conversation rolling, so he asked the worst of all possible questions.

"So, Martin, how's life at the office?"

"Oh, okay," Martin said, stammering, his ears turning bright red. "It's been busy lately, very busy. Lots of news."

Lots of news.

I imagined him giving an honest answer: "Well, actually, Maurice, it's not too good. You see, I've been screwing one of my coworkers and she started threatening me, so I had to tell Helene, and now she's probably going to divorce me. But enough about me. How are you? And, by the way, happy anniversary."

We sat there for what seemed like three weeks, the traffic racing past on the highway, Maurice in his dotted yellow tie and gold tie clip, my sister in her latest outfit from the Loft, everyone teasing Martin, like they always did, about how small his appetite was. Maurice launched into his time-worn tirade about how much he hated Bill Clinton. My mother, as usual, defended the president. She thought he was cute, but she had a few choice words for Hillary.

Then Martin's beeper went off and I followed him to the restaurant pay phone, sure that it was her calling. But it was the office, with the news that Princess Di had been in a car crash. She wasn't dead, his editor said, but it didn't look so good. Her boyfriend was dead already. Martin should be ready to go in if they needed him, just in case she died, too.

So we went back to dinner and gave them the news flash and then pretended to listen to the conversation, about their opinions on Prince Charles and the rest of the royal family, about Paul returning to law school, about Lauren starting her senior year. Every time the subject of Martin's affair threatened to crawl up into my throat and swing out on my vocal cords, I ran to the ladies' room and sat in a stall and cried. I dried my tears with crumbling toilet paper and tried to get rid of the redness around my eyes so my family wouldn't know what was going on. Maybe they would think I was crying over Dodi al-Fayed.

I couldn't tell them why I was really crying. More than my mother or Paula or Stanley or anyone, I couldn't bear to tell Lauren about it. She loved Martin. He was her cool bass-playing uncle. He had been in the band. I could never bring myself to tell her what he'd been doing behind my back. Behind our backs. I was so ashamed.

On the ride home, down the FDR Drive, just past the 59th Street Bridge, we heard on the car radio that Princess Diana was dead. She had been cheated on, too, for years and years and now she was dead. And suddenly, something snapped. I calmly turned to Martin and said, "You have to pack and move tonight. Take the garment bag and fill it with as much stuff as you can." The Chrysler Building came into view as Martin started sobbing again. I hoped he would crash so I wouldn't have to feel the horror that was beginning to creep over me.

"Then tomorrow, I'll go out and you can come back and take the rest of your stuff. I don't want to see you," I said, as we passed the huddled buildings of Stuyvesant Town.

Just as we made our way onto the Brooklyn Bridge, onto the Ari Halberstam Memorial Ramp, I turned to Martin and said, "I think we should get a divorce." But I should have waited a few more miles until we were home.

"No, no. Oh God." He veered into the right-hand lane of traffic, out of control, as I reached over to steer.

When we got home, my hands started shaking, and then my whole body, as I began to look around and imagine what the apartment would be like without him there. I told him that I changed my mind, that he shouldn't leave. I wanted him here, to torture him some more. But he wasn't the one I really wanted to torture.

I went to my office, locked the door and lifted the phone receiver. I knew she would be at work, since Princess Di was a major news story. So I called her there, using the same number I used to call Martin each day. The thought of it made me nearly retch. They had the same work number.

I was transferred to her line.

When she didn't answer, I beeped her at the number she'd left on her voice mail. When she didn't call, I beeped again. And again, and again. And again, like the crazy woman I was becoming, second by second, minute by minute, losing control one peg at a time.

When she finally called back from the newsroom, she said in a quick, quiet voice, "I'm on deadline. Can I call you back?"

"No," I said angrily. "You'll talk to me now. Right now. I want you to leave him alone. Do you hear me? Leave him alone." Meaning she shouldn't tell his boss about the affair. I didn't want to say it out loud, as if his boss might be listening. "You know what I mean," I said, in a whisper. "You know what I'm talking about."

But she didn't. She thought I meant that if she didn't leave him alone, that I would hurt her. It was a good idea, hurting her, but one that hadn't occurred to me, really. Not until now. Getting a baseball bat and driving to the newsroom seemed like a very good idea. But I didn't tell her that. Maybe my sudden silence, my violent reverie, scared her.

"I'm calling security," she said.

"For what?"

But the line went dead.

I had been singing about infidelity and love lost but had not seen the real thing, right in front of me. I hadn't connected a number of recent hang-up phone calls to the apartment. Or the time Martin went out for a paper and didn't come back for three hours. Or the time my friend Beth said she saw him making a call from a pay phone around the corner from our apartment. It suddenly explained all those late nights out.

It explained why he had lost weight and looked sick. Why he was so depressed "about work."

It explained why we hadn't had sex in eight months.

It explained why he had started smoking again—and why they were Parliaments. Recessed filter, my ass. They were her brand.

It explained the time I covered the murder of Gerald Levin's son for *People* magazine and went to the precinct to report on the story and Martin told me not to tell any of the other reporters who I was. That someone might think it was a conflict of interest that I was covering a story that the *News* was covering as well. It seemed odd to me at the time, but I never questioned it. I trusted him.

She was there that afternoon, covering the same story at the same precinct, and Martin was afraid she would find me and tell me everything.

It explained why he got upset that time I called him at work and, instead of using my name, told the city desk clerk that it was his wife calling.

"It's your wife," the clerk yelled.

She was in the newsroom and had heard, too. And had gotten upset at the reminder that he did, indeed, have a wife. He was reminded, too, that I was his wife. His wife.

He'd been cheating on his wife.

My husband had been cheating on his wife. Martin had been cheating on me.

That motherfucker.

What hurt more than those missed glimpses into reality was the reality I had been living. All those practices we had together, all the time in the studio and out, him knowing what was going on. Remembering the good stuff, the good things that had happened over the past year, was more painful somehow. And all night long, those memories replayed in my brain: me thanking him for not being jealous when I was on St. Lawrence Island. Going to Mexico City and thinking he'd be playing loud music in our apartment, enjoying his solitude in his boxer shorts. Recording our songs and Martin giving me his pep talk about preserving the sounds forever. The sushi in the car that freezing night before the first gig. The smile he gave me before our show began. The night of the CB's gig, thinking it was the band that had given Martin his glow. The times he had come to the studio to see Stephonic practice. Those nights he came in late from work and I hugged him. Consoling him about not wanting kids. The nights I did the Aubrey dog dance, from couch to armchair to coffee table. How could he stand there and watch me do that? It was all tainted. Every single second of it. Every thought, every memory from the past year. And every time I remembered something, good or bad, incriminating or not, it caused a pain.

And pain had no meaning, no beauty, except in songs.

In real life, pain simply hurt. And it hurt to think. I suddenly realized what it would be like to have had a painful childhood. Every memory, every reference point to your life, would be painful to recall. Life would be too painful to live. And I imagined that that's what it would be like from now on. Every thought of Martin would be contaminated with pain. With loss.

The only person I could really turn to to stop the pain, the only one who understood how horrible all this was, was Martin. So we slept in the same bed that night. We held each other and cried and kissed and made love for the first time in eight months, a new jolt of sadness to the Tilt-a-Whirl spin.

• FIFTEEN •

Martin got out of working that first night, but he had to be at the office at dawn the next morning. I stayed home alone, watching television. It was as if we were on a crying tag team. He couldn't cry anymore, since he had to edit stories about crying Brits. So I started crying instead.

My crying would come in waves, sometimes mixed with nausea, surging from my gut whenever I thought of them together. The thought of them having sex wasn't as awful as the little things I imagined. The small intimacies and conversations, every day, over a whole year, was what made me sick. Holding hands. Whispering to each other. Her touching his arm. Him touching her face. Her running her hands over my favorite paisley shirt. Him pulling on his Converse high-tops in her apartment.

Between news reports of Diana's death, video memorials, and interviews with sobbing royal subjects, I finally lost it. I paced the living room floor and pulled at my hair as they showed the dozens of bouquets left near Buckingham Palace, as they showed that horribly mangled car. It was all so surreal. Diana, the victim of infidelity, had died the same day I had fallen victim. The same day my marriage was given its last rites. The world was in mourning, and so was I. I cried right along with the hundreds of crying faces that flashed across the TV screen. It seemed the whole world was crying. At least I had company.

My mind started to unravel. When I couldn't watch any more television, I wandered the neighborhood, wiping tears from my face as passersby looked at me, slightly concerned, always sympathetic. Should they talk to me and try to help, or avoid me? I bought the newspaper at the corner deli, to read my horoscope, to see if it said something like, "Today is a good day to leave your husband," but before I could even flip back to the horoscope page, I saw her name, right there, her byline, on page 3. I ran back to the apartment and paced again, tore the pages from the paper and threw them on the floor and stepped on them. I paced more, practically running from room to room, like a rabid animal. When I couldn't stand to be inside anymore, I went back out into the street and walked to Manhattan. I would walk all the way to their office and make a scene, right there in the newsroom, so they would both get fired.

On the Brooklyn Bridge, I took my wedding ring off and looked inside at the God Bless You. Fuck you, I said back to it, and suspended it above the churning water. But at the last second, I snatched it back and stuck it in my pocket.

"I'll hock it," I thought. "I'll hock it and use the money to buy a gun." I wondered how hard it was to actually buy a gun in New York City. I was starting to really scare myself.

I called Martin from a pay phone on Chambers Street and told him, between sobs, that he should come straight home after work. It was the first time I'd ever said that to him.

So I went home and waited for Martin, like I had night after night after night. I grabbed the scissors as the lock clicked open.

"Sit down." I pointed to the couch with the scissors. "I want you to watch this."

And he did. He sat on the couch and waited nervously to see what I planned to do.

I went into the other room, into his closet, and took out the suit he had worn the day we got married, the double-breasted, custom suit that he had made just for our wedding. I brought it into the living room and started with the crotch, sticking the scissors in and working my way out to each pant leg. I systematically destroyed the blazer, cutting off each sleeve, then working my way down to the breast pocket, the same pocket where he had carried my wedding ring on our wedding day. Martin sat there and watched and cried. He didn't try to stop me.

I took the story from that day's paper, the one with her byline on it, and crumpled it in his face. I threw his favorite CDs, *Imperial Bedroom* and *This Year's Model,* with the yellow Post-it notes from our wedding still attached, and smashed their plastic cases. I threw pictures of us and destroyed their Lucite frames.

I took a black, cast-iron 1940s-style fan that he had bought, lifted it up to eye level, and just let it go, headfirst. It crumpled under its own weight.

I wasn't the only one throwing things after a while. Martin took a colorfully painted bowl I had bought in Spain and threw it against the wall like a Frisbee. It exploded into a hundred ceramic shards and left a large gouge in the living room wall that the super had to replaster the following weekend. I took the vintage Burt Bacharach *Promises, Promises* album I had bought him for his birthday and threw it at him. He ducked and it shattered.

Martin took a small wooden box decorated with palm trees that I had bought him, and smashed that to pieces. Later that night, after calming down, we tried to repair it with Crazy Glue.

The next day, in a burst of strength I didn't know he possessed, Martin ripped the bedroom door off its hinges after I locked myself inside.

I smacked him in the face, spit on him, kicked him when he was down on the ground, and screamed and cried, as if making up for that cool streak the first day.

It was as though I had acquired some type of Betrayed Wife Tourette's Syndrome. I started saying the strangest things, unprompted, without any idea they were coming. One night, to break an awkward silence, I looked at him and shouted:

"So did you have to wash that pussy smell off your hands when you came home at night?"

Martin looked genuinely pained. "Jesus, honey," he said. "Please!"

As if extracting a series of molars, I got Martin to tell me detail after detail about their affair. I wanted his and her memories to be dragged out and left to die, to become horrible memories for Martin and me. I got him to tell me how she had lived in the West Village on the same street as our favorite video store. I could never go in there again. But it was somehow worth it. Every story and every bit he told me was that much more poison I was able to squeeze out of our life. The details were horrible to hear, but I couldn't help myself. I wanted her to no longer exist—in any positive light—in his memory. Every story, every place, was now attached to my screaming and ranting.

I made Martin tell me how they had met there, in her apartment, to have sex. I made him tell me the places they'd gone. Hogs and Heifers. The Monkey Bar. Places that were safe because they were places I didn't like. And now wanted to firebomb; it was as if every waiter who took their order, every bartender who made them a drink, every busboy who cleared their plates, was an accomplice to their conspiracy.

I did to Martin and his possessions what I really wanted to do to her. I couldn't remember her face and was worried she might be stalking me. What bothered me more, though, was knowing that Martin knew her face so well. My husband knew another woman's face so well, the lines, the freckles, the features. He had gazed at them, touched them, memorized them. I wanted to memorize them, too.

After he told me during one of my interrogations where she'd gone to college, I took a subway up to Columbia University and looked her up in the yearbook. When I saw her smiling, smug young face, I considered ripping the page out of the yearbook and stepping on it, smashing it into the library carpet. I looked around for a librarian and for a split second thought I could get away with it. I considered photocopying the picture, and pondered the many things I could do with her face. I could write TRAMP across the top, make more copies, and, on my way to band practice, glue dozens of them to the buildings in the neighborhood where they worked.

More than the page, I wanted to remove that smile from her face, her real face, to remove it forever. Who was she to smile? Even in a yearbook photo taken three years earlier. Three years! She was only twenty-four. Fucking chippy. What did she know about marriage? She should be suffering like me. Like Martin and me.

Martin, who saw her most days at work, assured me that she was in pain. But I couldn't imagine anyone in more pain than I was. And I wanted to spread the pain around. "Like a corkscrew to my heart," Bob Dylan had sung on *Blood on the Tracks.*

Finally, I understood the lyric.

I avoided the kitchen during our fights because I was worried I would grab a corkscrew, or worse, a carving knife. I was worried, actually worried, I would plunge the knife deep into Martin's heart. Forget metaphors and song lyrics.

I cried when he was home, and cried when he went to work. I called him forty, fifty times a day to make sure he wasn't speaking to her and to harass him, to push him to the edge of acceptable newsroom behavior.

"But I need to talk to her," he whispered. "We work together."

"Then quit!"

I left and went to stay with a friend at the Jersey shore, then came home and kicked Martin out.

The apartment was hell when he was there, but it was worse somehow when he was gone. So I made him come back.

I sobbed so much that I stopped wearing eyeliner, since it was bound to wash off. When they asked if I'd been crying, I told friends that I had allergies. To those who knew, I ranted and cried so much that I scared them. They had no words of advice, no words big enough to comfort.

Finally, I told my family.

"Martin's been having an affair," I said to my mother over the phone one morning.

"Oh." She sounded relieved. I had already told her about his depression. She had noticed his weight loss herself. I might have even mentioned our stalled sex life. "We thought maybe he was gay or sick or on drugs or something."

In those weeks and months that followed, the band became my security blanket. My night-light, really. That something kept glowing in the dark to help guide me to safety. One of our first shows was just five days after the horror broke. We had played two summer shows while most of our friends were away, practice shows to get us used to the lights and the sound system. Our September gig was to be our coming-out party.

"You can't come," I said to Martin at home one afternoon. "I don't want you there." He looked like I had punched him in the stomach, deflated, sick, pained, even. That hurt him more than the kicking and screaming and hitting and tearing of clothes. I knew it would. I knew it was one of the things he'd been really looking forward to, one of the few bright spots in the depressing, secret life he'd been living for months and months, why he'd come to some of our practices.

Stephonic was the offspring of I Hate Jane, the family we hadn't yet had. Would never have, now. "I don't want you there," I said again, staring straight into his eyes.

The studio was a tiny bit of calm in the horror show my life had become. I had no office to retreat to, no coworkers to complain to. All I had was the band. I shared the news at one of our practices that first week. Doug and Dan were barely old enough to be married, never mind have an extramarital affair, so I wasn't sure how they'd react. I wasn't sure how to say it. So I just went ahead and said it like Martin had.

"Martin's been having an affair," I blurted out, almost laughing, since saying it aloud seemed so absurd.

"Jesus fucking Christ," Julie said. Doug looked at me with a blank stare, his jaw hanging.

Dan stopped playing his guitar. He could talk, eat, walk, do anything while playing his guitar. But this made him stop. He smiled a perverse half smile. "What? With who?" he asked, his fingers frozen.

So I told them. Told the story over and over to them and to most people I knew until I got tired of hearing it, until there was no more relief from sharing the horror. People were shocked at first, and then deeply shaken, not so much for Martin and me, but for themselves. Because if it could happen to us, it could happen to them, too.

"But you were such a great couple," they would say, slightly dazed. "You had such a great wedding."

When people called the house, they didn't know whether to mention Martin's name, afraid I might fly into a rage. When Martin's friends called for him, and I answered, they apologized, as if a close relative of mine had died.

"How are you doing?" Bob, his friend from work, asked one afternoon.

"Well, you know," I said.

"Well, that's life at the top," he said. I wasn't exactly sure what he was talking about. Who was at the top? Martin? And was this what life was like up there? People cheating on one another?

"Yeah." I laughed. "I guess so."

All I had was banging those drums. I considered Xeroxing a photo of Martin and placing his face on each skin. Or better yet, her photo, the smiling face from the Columbia yearbook. But I didn't have to. I just imagined them there, alternately. Not photos, but the real thing. And I hit them over and over again, until my forearms were massive, my chops were amazing, my drumming better than I ever imagined it could be.

While playing "Document" in the studio, I built and built to the intense crashing crescendo, using all my strength and pounding away so hard that my hands hurt, so hard that when the song was through, Dan, Doug, and Julie all turned around, mouths open, to see the new drummer who had replaced me midsong.

• SIXTEEN •

Our first show was at Luna Lounge on the Lower East Side, a couple of doors down from Katz's Deli. I loved Katz's pastrami sandwiches, which Stanley had introduced me to when I was ten. They were too thick to wrap your mouth around, the rye bread soft and smeared with mustard. Katz's pastrami sandwich was one of the fringe benefits of putting up with New York City.

The century-old Katz's was where Harry met Sally for that orgasmic sandwich, where Joe Torre, Rudy Giuliani, and Spike Lee went for a hot dog. They had dozens of celebrity testimonial photos on their walls, musicians like Buster Poindexter, the guys from Wu Tang Clan, and Björk, who I would have assumed was a vegetarian. Maybe she had ordered a knish. There were bands I'd never heard of, like Zelig. The Katz's people, who had probably never heard of them either, wrote "German rock group," next to their name. Model Milla Jovovich, after playing a rock and roll set at a nearby club, had her picture taken at

Katz's. She didn't look like she ate much, never mind pastrami sandwiches.

Katz's had a mail-order counter in the back decorated with a neon outline of the USA and a New York rhyme: "Send a salami/To your boy in the army." The salamis floated around the sign like big meat torpedoes.

Katz's was more like an amusement park ride than a restaurant. A Sensurround experience. You had to walk past the salamis hanging in the window, then take a ticket at the front counter, which you handed to one of the deli guys. After you placed your order, he'd scribble something illegible on the ticket, and when you were done eating, you'd bring it back to the front counter and pay your bill.

I couldn't bring myself to eat at Katz's before the September show. It wasn't stage fright; my body was humming from all the fighting I had been doing that week—sick and nauseous, but my head strangely clear. I had waited too long for this show, had invested too much time and practice to screw it up. I had married these three other people in this band, maybe to the detriment of my own real marriage. This was our honeymoon. The moment of consummation.

Presiding over the ceremony was the club owner, Rob. He was slightly tubby, with a gut and a strange haircut or follicle problem, I wasn't sure which. One side of his head was shaved, but only from the middle of his head, not from the sideburn. Not in a punk way. It looked like someone had slipped with a razor. Or maybe it had simply fallen out in some weird pattern baldness. Julie treated him like he was the best-looking guy in the room, the same way she treated everyone. So Rob was smitten with Julie from the first.

Luna had once been a Chinese herb warehouse, which may have accounted for the healing power it had over me. Beneath Luna's cool veneer was a friendliness and a feeling of belonging. If you belonged, that is. Though there was no cover charge, there was a bouncer, a tall, muscular guy named Valentino who wore black leather and dreads and kept out the under-age, the drunkards, and the assholes. Valentino not only let us in each night, but said hello to us when he passed us on the street. This, to me, was a revelation. I had always hated clubs, the ones that gave you a hard time about getting in. But suddenly, I was a VIP. The velvet ropes parted for me.

Rob kept the place immaculate and had one of his bartenders scrub the floor with bleach in the early evening, just as we were loading our equipment in. If you walked past with your eyes closed, you could find Luna by the clean smell wafting out onto the street.

It was still light out when I pulled up to the metal-edged curb in the borrowed red station wagon that first night. The sun was starting to set behind Luna, and as I brought each drum inside, the light turned warmer and redder, its glow spot-lighting the tops of the tenements across the street. It was my favorite time of day now, the beginning of night.

Lauren pretended to be a roadie, carrying my cymbals and snare drum so she could sneak past the bouncer. We slipped past the foosball table, a few cozy booths, and lit, fifties kitschy landscape "paintings" on the walls, past the well-stocked jukebox at the back of the front room, beneath the long blackboard with the month's schedule written neatly in chalk. Black light illuminated us as we made our way into that back room, picking up bits of lint, smiles, and the whites of our eyes. Strings of brightly colored Christmas lights hung year-round over the bar and above the back-room stage.

Rob gave us two poker chips to trade for free drinks. We shoved them in our pockets for later, then drifted across the street to Max Fish, a smaller place with an S-shaped bar. It had once been a sundry where an old guy named Max Fisch had sold just about everything to people in the neighborhood. Painted above the yellow-tinted windows of its front doors were still the words, "Over 30 years on block."

By 1989, the hipsters had taken over and dropped the C from the name. The place had a funhouse feel, but in a mellow way. There was the curving bar, a disco ball, candy-colored stools, a couple of pinball machines, sparkly purple booths, a mechanical horse, and a red-topped pool table whose sides were covered in band stickers from the likes of Scum, Chicken, and Supreme Stamina. A mirror painting of

Julio Iglesias, like the kind you win at carnival wheels, caught my eye. But half his face was melted off. "Julio Is Moving In!" the mirror said.

One night I watched a girl on heroin slowly fall from one of the sparkly booths onto the floor. It was the first and only time I had ever seen someone slowly fall. And I knew right away it was smack. She just looked so happy to be falling, as if she wanted to draw it out as long as possible.

My only drug before the show was a scotch on the rocks, to remove any jitters. We sat and smoked at Max Fish as people filtered into Luna's big back room. We watched it from a distance, seeing the place come to life little by little, like stars appearing one at a time in the night sky, until it was filled with clusters and constellations. We could name them all.

When enough people had gathered, we'd drift back across the street and socialize. Playing at Luna was like having your own party, where your friends, and sometimes your relatives, came to sing your praises. Drummers from other bands waiting their turn to play came up to me and complimented me on my drums—on Stanley's drums.

"Where did you get them?" one of them asked, stroking the now antique wooden Ludwigs. "They're classic."

"My brother. He was a drummer. He taught me how to play." I searched for Stanley's face in the Luna crowd.

Julie's boyfriend, Jimmy, came to that first show, and to every show that followed. He stood in the center of the large crowd, right up front, with his hands clasped behind his back, his legs spread wide, and his eyes taking everything in. I held out a secret hope that Martin might disobey me and show up. I searched the room for him while waiting for Julie to give me the nod to start, Stanley's old snare drum rattling from the indie pop that Rob played in the background for the crowd.

The stage was black and scuffed and about two feet off the ground, complete with microphones hooked to a big soundboard that Rob controlled at the front of the room. Ratty old couches and armchairs provided seats. People from the television show *Friends* came to the club: In one star-studded night I saw Phoebe's cop boyfriend and Ross.

I felt like I had fallen into some bizarre sitcom alternate universe. Another night, we saw Natalie Merchant, Janeane Garofalo, and some Guess model who Doug tried, unsuccessfully, to engage in conversation.

But the best celebrity sighting was Elliott Smith. He had recently moved to Brooklyn from the West Coast. Now, here he was, at Luna. Doug had just played one of his songs on the jukebox, then went to sit at the bar to find his idol on the next bar stool. Doug looked right at him, pointed a thumb at the jukebox, and said, "Hey. Thanks." Elliott Smith just nodded.

That September night at Luna, and most nights after that, we opened the show with "Nightlight's Glow." You needed one of the best to catch people's attention. The crowd—the lint on their shirts, wide smiles, and eyeballs aglow—was having such a good time that they could forget there was a band onstage.

I could never understand that, not just in our case, but in the case of any musical act. Why did people bother coming to hear music if they were going to talk through it? Neil Young once actually stopped playing at the Beacon Theater and threatened to leave the stage if the sloping-forehead crew didn't stop yelling through his set.

Once I went to see Bob Dylan at Roseland in Hell's Kitchen. It was standing only, in order to cram as many people in there as possible. As usual, the tallest and widest man in the crowd came and stood directly in front of my five-foot frame, blocking the entire stage. When I asked him politely if he could nudge over a little, he looked down and laughed at me. When I moved slightly over to the left, I was greeted by a tripped-out hippie chick, dancing and swinging her hair, which kept hitting me in the face and filling my mouth.

Dylan was great that night. Some nights he could be a real downer, refusing to play old songs that people wanted to hear. Or badly rewriting songs on the spot to confuse and annoy everyone. But this night he was chatting with the crowd and even smiling. Even the rewrites were great. The crowd grew drunker and drunker and more and more unbearable. There was a group of teenagers talking loudly right behind us about their new tattoos. After the first encore, I insisted Martin and I leave. I just couldn't take it anymore. Martin asked twice if I was sure. With the hippie hair in my mouth one last time, I nodded. I was sure.

The next morning, Tony, my ex, called from Nashville. He had known I was going to the Dylan concert and called to congratulate me for having tickets.

"I can't believe you were there last night."

"Yeah. It was a good show."

"A good show? Wasn't it great?"

"Well, to tell you the truth, the crowd was really annoying, so I didn't stay—"

He cut me off. "Tell me you didn't leave before the final encore."

"Why?"

There was a long pause.

"I don't think I can even tell you."

"Well you have to tell me now."

Silence.

"What happened?"

Silence.

"Just tell me."

"Are you sure?" Tony asked.

"Tell me."

"Springsteen and Neil Young got onstage with him and played," he blurted out as quickly as he could, as if pulling a Band-Aid off a cut.

This must be a practical joke, I thought. Like Lies About the Beatles.

"You're kidding," I said. "This isn't like some Lies About Bob Dylan thing, is it?"

"I wish it was."

"Oh God." All I could think of was that stupid hippie broad and the tattooed teenagers and that really tall guy and how much they must have enjoyed the holy musical trinity converging onstage—Springsteen, Young, and Dylan.

"Nightlight's Glow" shut the crowd up and was bound to grab the attention of everyone, kids with tattoos, their mothers and fathers, old hippie chicks. That "Mom and Dad are dead" chorus could quiet the worst of them.

"Hi. We're Stephonic," Julie said when we were done with that first song, while tuning her guitar.

"Not to be confused with Stereophonic," Dan ad-libbed. We had just discovered there was a band with that name, too close for comfort, really.

"No. We're not Stereophonic," Julie said. "They're all boys."

"But they're cute," Doug said.

This was the quality of our onstage banter. While Julie was tuning again, Doug threatened to recite poetry to the audience.

"But I don't really know any," he announced.

"Thank God," I said.

We made our first band rule that night: no more banter. We all agreed to just shut up and let Julie tune to the chatty roar of the crowd.

By the time we played "Document," though, the crowd was ours. The song was turning into a powerful number. It was our longest song, nearly five minutes, and was by far the most complicated. But it always ended with a bang. It wasn't the lyrics so much that transcended the moment. It was the music. During the "Jesus lost and found"s Dan would launch into his most scorching guitar solo. Even Julie got in on the action, strumming that blue guitar so hard that I thought it might bleed. I matched their intensity, coming frighteningly close to the edge of an actual drum solo. But each time we played the song, I would stop just short, ending when Dan and I couldn't play any more, when my muscles ached, when his fingers were close to bleeding, when he would look up and give me the weary eye.

"Document," loud, dark, and out of control, was exactly how I was feeling. But it would end abruptly, with me hitting the crash as hard as I could, then grabbing it into silence, the crowd hanging on to that last loud chord and falling, falling, headfirst, into the hush.

• SEVENTEEN •

Back in the apartment, Martin and I continued to throw things at each other. Or I threw things. Martin ducked.

Most of my rages were based on what had already happened. I simply replayed the same old ugly facts in my head like some badly lit porno movie that I really didn't want to watch again. Just when the images would start to get erased in my mind, there were new images to replace them.

One afternoon, Martin said he had come up with an idea, an idea that showed just how he had completely lost his mind. We were sitting at our red-and-white Formica kitchen table in silence when he said,

"You know, I'd like to stay friends with her."

"What?" I said, squinting.

"I don't want to turn my back on her," he said. "I mean, who knows, maybe someday we can all do things together, like go to the movies, go to dinner even." He said this in all seriousness, without a touch of irony, and then waited for my response.

I stood up slowly, calmly, then said, one hand on my waist, one hand in the air, my finger pointed at him, "Fuck you, you fucking son of a bitch, if you think you're going to spend so much as one more fucking second with your fucking whore anyplace but in fucking hell."

I stretched "whore" out to two syllables. *Ho-wah.*

He never brought up the friend thing again. But she did.

She tried, over the phone, to convince me that it was okay for them to be friends.

"I'll decide when it's okay for you to be friends," I yelled. "Do you understand?"

"Well," she said, "maybe you and I could get together sometime and talk about things."

"I don't want to *get together* with you. I never want to see you, ever. Just reading your byline makes me sick."

"I'm not the one who did anything wrong here." She actually chuckled. "I mean, I'm not the one who broke any vows."

"Listen. You don't have to be married to commit adultery. Ad-ultery. Get it? Because that's what you've done. You've committed adultery. Adultery with my husband. My fucking husband." I hung up.

That fall, I was working freelance for *People* magazine, reporting stories for the New York bureau. The bureau chief, Maria, faced with an open reporter's position, asked me if I might be interested in a "real" job there. I thought it might be a good idea to get a full-time job, in case Martin and I got divorced and I needed health insurance. So I agreed to work for a week, to feel it out. The offices were on the twenty-ninth floor of the Time-Life building on Sixth Avenue, right across from Radio City, and had an amazing view of New York. Even the lowliest reporters had windows in their offices. There was a great cafeteria downstairs, and stock options and discounts on all Warner Bros. CDs, if I decided to stay on full-time. But it would mean the end of the band, since reporters at *People* worked long hours.

Torn between the job and the band, I talked to my sister's friend and psychic. Anna read my palm and told me I should take the job, but beware of a woman with red hair who I worked with. That she would betray me and that I shouldn't trust her.

"I don't think there's anyone with red hair at *People,*" I said, trying to picture the staff.

Anna shrugged.

"Maybe it's someone my husband works with," I said.

I thought back to the Columbia picture. I had thought for some reason that her hair had been light brown. But maybe she was a redhead. The picture was black-and-white, wasn't it? It was impossible to tell what color a person's hair was in a black-and-white photograph.

When Martin came home that night, as soon as he came through the door, I shouted, "What color is her hair?"

"Whose hair?"

"The fucking queen of England," I said, my arms folded across my chest. "You know who."

"Why do you need to know?" he asked, turning pale.

"Because I need to, that's all. Just tell me." I felt like one of those hostage interrogators. *Don't ask me any questions. Just answer mine.*

"She has brown hair," he said, cringing, not knowing what color would set me off. "Light brown hair." I just stared at him. "But she dyed it red once."

That was all I needed to hear. Her pleas to be "friends" were bullshit.

So I launched my attack. "I talked to a psychic today and she told me to beware of a redhead. Don't you see?" I shook my hands in the air. "You need to stay away from her. You need to stop talking to her. She's no good."

"A psychic?" he said. "You went to a psychic?"

"She's Paula's friend," I said, shrugging and looking away.

"You can't plan your life around what a psychic says. And she works in the same office as me. What am I supposed to do?"

I didn't tell Maria about Martin before going to work at *People,* but maybe she could sense what was wrong. I got serious sympathy vibes from her when I walked into the office that first morning.

And not just from Maria, but from the other reporters in the office. Maybe they had heard a rumor from someone over at the *Daily News*. The journalism world was pretty tight.

Whatever the reason, whether coincidence or sympathy, Maria gave me top-notch assignments. I interviewed Barenaked Ladies and Blondie, then went to Pennsylvania to cover a murder. Some woman, away with her husband on one of those murder-mystery weekend packages, set him on fire as he slept at their bed-and-breakfast. They were there for a little make-believe whodunit action, but this woman broke out the real thing. I wondered if maybe he'd been cheating, too.

The distraction of other people's horrors, and of the daily grind of a full-time job, really worked wonders on my psyche. It was great to talk to people and socialize with the other reporters. One afternoon one of them, a guy named Charlie, invited me into his office. "You wanna do lunch tomorrow?" he asked. "Maybe we can get a couple of other people to come, too. Julia. Sue." I nodded enthusiastically.

Suddenly, he got very serious.

"So how's it going?" He put on a concerned look and went over to shut his door.

"Um," I said, embarrassed. "Things are okay." I hardly knew Charlie. We had worked on a story together once, that Levin murder story. Charlie and I had gone to the police precinct to watch them bring the murderer out. But we were hardly pals. Maybe he had seen Martin's girlfriend there that day. Maybe he knew everything.

"How are things with you and Martin?" he asked.

"So you know?" I asked. He nodded and shrugged as if it were no big deal.

"How did you find out?" I asked.

"I saw the item in the *Post*." He shrugged again.

I looked at him blankly. "What item in the *Post*?"

His eyes grew wide and frightened. "You mean you didn't know about the thing in the *Post*?"

"No," I said, growing panicky. "What thing in the *Post*?"

"Page Six," he said, just as panicky. "Oh shit. I'm such a big mouth. I can't believe this. I can't believe you didn't know about it. I . . ." Before he could finish the sentence I was out the door, then at my desk, dialing Martin at work.

I didn't even say hello.

"There was an item in the *Post*?" I whispered, as threateningly as I could.

Martin said: "Uh."

"Some guy in the office here said there was an item. What's he talking about?" I could see Charlie lurking in the hallway, pacing like a nervous father. He had given life to my latest bout of insanity.

There was a long silence.

"What's he talking about?" I said again.

"Remember that night you beeped her at work?" Martin began.

"Mm-hmm." I got up to shut my door and gave Charlie a dirty look.

"Well, uh, well, I guess I should just read it to you," Martin said. I waited, my right hand on my forehead, my elbow on the desk. Over the phone, I heard Martin's desk drawer slide open. I heard the clicking of computer keys in the background, reporters—her included—on deadline. I heard Martin breathing. And then I heard the crinkle of a newspaper unfolding. He began reading.

"Which daily newspaper editor (male) carried on a torrid romance with a twentysomething reporter (female) for a year until his wife found out and started phoning the young woman in the newsroom while she was on deadline? Soon everyone knew. The affair ended—"

"But that's not right," I said, cutting him off. "That's not what happened."

"I know, I know," he whispered. "Somebody in the newsroom overheard that conversation on her end and put two and two together and called the *Post*."

"But that's not how it happened," I said. "I already knew about the affair. You told me." I paused a beat. "That's how I found out. You ended it. Not me. I *should* have fucking gone down there with a baseball bat. That would have been a nice little Page Six item."

Martin sat silent on the other end.

"Our names weren't in there?" I asked, my voice quiet again.

"No, no. It was a blind item. It's part of the *Post*'s campaign to give the *News* a hard time. We shouldn't take it personally, really, because—"

"But everybody figured it out. Right? Everybody knew who it was."

There was a downbeat.

"Yeah," he said, finally.

"So I shouldn't take it personally?"

"People love to gossip, honey," he said, trying to calm me down.

I knew. I knew all too well. And here I was, writing stories about people who didn't want to be written about. What was I doing here? I felt very dirty all of a sudden. I needed a shower. But Martin was still talking.

"The morning it was in the paper, I bought all the copies from the corner and all the stores in our neighborhood and threw them all away." I imagined him at the deli on the corner and at all the Korean grocers on Court Street, with that panicked look on his face, scooping up all those papers and then dumping them in the Gowanus Canal. "I didn't want you to see it," he said.

But he didn't have to bother. I never read the *Post.* And now I never would again. "You should have told me. You're such a fucking coward. How could you let me find out about it from someone else? Did you think I'd never find out? I'm a fucking reporter for Christ's sake."

I started piecing together some unusual looks and conversations I had had over the last few weeks. There was the call from my friend Kelly, who somehow knew about Martin cheating. A mutual acquaintance, Nick, had gossiped it to her, she said. I wondered how he knew. Then there was that call from Martin's friend Bob about life at the top. That's what he was talking about. Being mentioned on Page Six. That was life at the top. That's how everyone knew. Page Six.

"Why didn't you tell me?"

"The item was in right after I told you everything. You were already out of your mind. Do you remember the scissors? And my suit? You would have killed me. Or you would have left me."

"Well, it's not too late for that," I said, and slammed down the phone.

I decided not to take the *People* job. Instead, I left Martin.

Julie felt betrayed by Martin's affair almost as much as I did. Having played with him in the band, hearing and seeing him day in and day out, she, too, felt like she had been made a fool of, cheated on. When Julie and I were together, which was nearly all the time now, it felt like us against him.

So we decided to leave him together. For a few days at least. It seemed the perfect time for a road trip. Elvis Costello was playing at a small club in Nashville called Café Milano, which had recently been voted the best club in America.

Tony, my ex-boyfriend, got us tickets. We had had a few phone conversations about what was happening with Martin and me. But I needed to see him in person. He was my twin, after all. My older twin; maybe he could help guide me through what was about to happen in life.

And besides, my seeing Elvis with Tony might cause Martin a bit of pain. And that's what I wanted most, to cause him as much pain as he had caused me, short of sticking a pencil in his eye.

Elvis was one of many acts on the bill, which included Steve Earle, whom Tony had met a bunch of times in the bars of Nashville. The show was a tribute to the gospel quintet the Fairfield Four, who would be performing as backup for most of the other musicians.

Julie and I decided to drive straight through to Nashville, since we didn't have money to book a flight on such short notice, and since we didn't have any Stephonic shows. We would drive in, see the show, then drive out the next morning and make it back to New York in time for practice. It was a musical suicide mission.

We rented a Lincoln Town Car with a backseat big enough so we could stretch out between turns driving. Because Julie still had a Missouri license, she rented the car. It was cheaper to rent a car in New York if you were not from New York, a little factoid that amazed me and which I turned into another travel magazine article.

Before we left, Julie went to the library and checked out several books on tape, including *Into Thin Air* and the audio version of Ken Burns's *Civil War.* She also brought Elliott Smith's complete body of music.

We started out after rush hour, around seven P.M., heading out on the New Jersey Turnpike. The last wisps of a sunset were setting behind the oil refineries and factory smokestacks. For a while, we both listened to the radio. The old classic "Brandy" came on some easy-listening station. The song was a favorite of mine.

I turned the volume up. "Maybe we should think about doing a cover of this."

Julie nodded and sang along for a little while. "Brandy, you're a fine girl. What a good wife you would be . . ."

As it grew darker, Julie got into the backseat and I put on some old, driving Springsteen. It was a homemade tape Tony had given me years before, recorded from the vinyl version of *The River.* Tony had been a devout Springsteen fan and was shocked to learn when we started going out that I never listened to him. He spent several years bringing me over to the other side.

Say what you will about Bruce, but when driving had to be done, particularly all-night driving, he was the man. And there was no album better suited to driving than *The River.* As Julie drifted off in that big backseat, I listened to *The River,* with its ten songs about driving. Not just driving, but all-night driving. Dangerous driving. Salvation driving. Driving until the highway ends or you just can't bear to drive any more.

1. "Sherry Darling," which starts with the nightmare of being stuck in traffic on 53rd Street with your mother-in-law, but soon becomes a celebration of the open road. "Well, I got some beer and the highway's free, and I got you and, baby, you've got me."

2. "Hungry Heart." "Got a wife and kids in Baltimore, Jack. I went out for a ride and I never went back."

3. "The River." "I remember us riding in my brother's car, her body tan and wet down at the reservoir."

4. "Cadillac Ranch." "Hey little girlie in the blue jeans so tight, driving alone through the Wisconsin night."

5. "I'm a Rocker." "I got a Batmobile so I can reach ya in a fast shake."

6. "Stolen Car." "I ride by night and I travel in fear, that in this darkness I will disappear."

7. "Ramrod." "She's a hot stepping hemi with a four on the floor." I knew what "four on the floor" meant. But what the hell was a hemi?

8. "The Price You Pay." "In one last breath they built the roads they'd ride to their deaths. Driving on through the night . . ." Which segues nicely into

9. "Drive All Night," which is all about why you're listening to the album in the first place, and is particularly good in dangerous driving conditions. "Through the wind. Through the rain. The snow, the wind, the rain."

Until finally,

10. "Wreck on the Highway."

That last song was the antidote to the rest. Almost every song before it got you pumped up and rarin' to drive. By the time "Cadillac Ranch" came on, you were sure you could drive for seventeen days straight and not even stop to pee. But "Wreck on the Highway" made you want to pull over to a rest stop and call your loved ones.

Which is exactly what I did.

I called Martin at work, but he wasn't there. "He stepped out," the city-room clerk said.

"Thanks." I hung up the receiver and wondered just where he had stepped out to. Had he stepped out to her apartment? To Hogs and Heifers for a late-night beer and a cheap feel? I considered calling his beeper and tracking him down, but then remembered that I had thrown it at the living room wall during our last fight and had broken it into a hundred pieces. I swallowed my anger and headed back to the Town Car.

Julie and I switched places, and I lay down as Julie listened to the *Civil War* tapes. I stared up at the ceiling for two hours, watching the lights of the passing cars morph into shapes like frightened animals above me, skittering away one after another, until, somehow, I dozed off. When I awoke, Julie was still driving, but crying over a letter a war bride had gotten from her husband who died right after writing it. I thought about Martin, and worried that maybe he was dead. What was I doing in a Town Car on the way to Nashville to visit my ex-boyfriend?

Hadn't my previous adventures caused this whole problem in the first place? If I had never gone off to Alaska, Martin never would have cheated. We wouldn't be in the mess we were in now. On the verge of divorce.

I decided to tell Julie to turn the car around. I tried to calculate how many miles we'd driven, and how many hours it would take to get back. But then I saw the sign. The sign for Tennessee. We were already in Tennessee.

Julie popped in Elliott Smith, his sweet voice filling even the tiniest crevices of the Town Car. And as the stars faded and the sun came up, Elliott Smith ushered us into Music City.

• EIGHTEEN •

Seeing Tony again was like going home. I had been able to talk to him over the past few weeks in a way I hadn't been able to talk to my family. But he was family, in a strange sort of way. Kind of like an ex-husband, more than an ex-boyfriend. He was one of the few people in my life who I could just pick up with immediately, no catching up necessary, no awkward period. I thought guiltily of Martin wanting to be friends like that with her. I understood. But I just couldn't stand it.

When Julie and I got there, Tony was heating up a big tray of baked ziti that he had made. It was the ultimate Italian comfort food. The macaroni and cheese of Italy.

Julie and Tony hit it off right way. They had heard so much about each other over the past couple of years that they felt they already knew each other.

After a short nap, the three of us got dressed for our big night. When Tony came out of his bedroom, he was wearing a dress shirt I had never seen, and a pair of khaki pants I had never seen either. Even after all these years, it still freaked me out a little, these little things.

There had been a time when I was intimate with all of Tony's clothes, knew how they smelled and where he had bought them, had worn some of them myself. But those clothes were long gone, worn out or given to the local thrift shop. He had a whole new wardrobe, without me.

We went downtown to have a drink before the show. On Broadway, Steve Earle came walking toward us, carrying his guitar case. His manager was with him.

"Hi, Tony," he said as we passed.

"How ya doin'?" Tony said.

Julie and I just stared as Earle walked past, our mouths agape. Tony laughed.

"You really do know him," I said.

"I told you. Do I ever lie?"

In Nashville, musicians mingled with musicians and with regular folks. Word of mouth there traveled fast. And the buzz on the Fairfield Four show was pretty deafening. It was a small miracle Tony even got tickets.

Over at Café Milano, Elvis was in the building. John Prine, Bela Fleck, and Trisha Yearwood were in the crowd. Cait O'Riordan, Elvis's wife and former bass player for the Pogues, was there as well.

There were lots of country acts on the bill, people I had never heard of. Kathy Mattea sang an a cappella gospel tune. Steve Earle, wearing the same outfit he'd been wearing on the street, got up onstage and sang a song that Tony had put on a mix tape for me years ago but that I had forgotten all about. It was called "Valentine's Day," a sweet, sad song that held special meaning for us, since that was the day Tony and I had broken up.

Breakups are long, drawn-out affairs, so the end had been coming for a long time. The stress of the Hallmark holiday had just pushed us—or me—over the edge. I had worked a long shift at the newspaper that Valentine's Day, doing a story about kids who had had open-heart surgery. It was my newspaper's idea of a Valentine's Day story. Get it? Valentine's Day? Hearts?

By the time I got done, I was a wreck.

Since it was Tony's brother's birthday, we had no plans to go out to a romantic dinner alone. But that was okay. I was tired anyway. We were supposed to have dinner at his mom's and a cake for his brother, like we did every year.

When I got done with work around seven, I called Tony from my desk and told him I was heading over. Before I hung up, he blurted, "By the way, I didn't get you a present."

I had bought him a book about baseball and physics, two of his favorite subjects. Not much, but it was something. But all I said was, "That's okay." When I got to his mom's, they had already eaten. They had ordered Chinese food, and had not left me any. Oh, there was an egg roll. A single egg roll. And some packets of sweet-and-sour sauce and hot mustard. They had had the birthday cake without me, too. The remnants were left in a mess on the kitchen table.

There was no offer to go out for some more Chinese food. No offer to go get a slice of pizza. "Let's go back to my apartment" was all Tony could muster. It was as if Tony was daring me to break up with him—seeing just how far he could push me before I finally snapped. I could just see the *GQ* cover line:

> **How Many Inconsiderate Things Can You Do to Your Girlfriend on Valentine's Day Before She Finally Leaves Your Ass?**

We left his mother's house and headed over to Tony's in silence. I remember feeling strangely calm. I wasn't mad, really. But somehow I knew that that was the last straw. A single egg roll had done it. In the balance between love and indifference, that's all it took to tip the scales.

When we got to his apartment, I didn't even take my coat off. I gave him his present. He gave me a card, at least. It was a homemade card, with some pictures of us on the front. And for a moment, I considered forgiving him. But then I thought of the egg roll. I put my gloves on and motioned toward the door. "You know, I'm really tired. I'm gonna go home. I'll call you in the morning." I kissed him good night. I knew I was leaving for the last time. As his girlfriend anyway. And suddenly, I wasn't angry anymore. Just sad.

We broke up—later that night—for the last time, over the phone.

The next day, Martin invited me to the movies.

Steve Earle's song "Valentine's Day" summed up Tony's whole alibi. In a slow lullaby, Earle picked at his acoustic guitar and sang, "I come to you with empty hands. I guess I just forgot again."

I looked across the table at Tony, who tried to smile. He shrugged, as if to say, "I'm sorry," once again, for not getting that gift. But I had long ago forgiven him. And he had forgiven me for leaving over an egg roll. We both knew that love, or your brother's birthday cake—or what was left of it—just wasn't enough sometimes.

There, in the club, with Steve Earle singing, I almost burst out crying. I could only handle one breakup at a time, thank you very much. But Steve Earle kept right on singing.

All the sadness of the breakup came rushing back, not the fights that followed, the crying, the pleading, the refusals, the yelling, the accusations and cursing. That wasn't what was left. That all washed away with time. What you were left with was a warm, sad ember of the end.

I felt like it was happening all over again. With Martin. The feeling was the same—that hollow, fated feeling that it was coming to a close. And that I would have to walk away. That I would bump into Martin again a year from now and he would have on a shirt I didn't recognize. Pants I had never seen.

Elvis Costello got onstage. Had he not come on, I might have started sobbing and would have had to be taken out on a stretcher. But the mood in the room changed; you could feel the molecules in the air morph. It was that gift, that gift that Julie had a bit of, the one shared by Bruce Springsteen and great Nashville legends like the Carters and Cashes. It drifted over the stage, down to the crowd and gripped us all in its fist.

Elvis Costello was the only performer eloquent enough to explain his debt to the Fairfield Four. "As you can imagine," he said, "I didn't grow up with this music." Twenty years ago he had come to the United States and found a Fairfield Four album in a record shop. "To find myself standing on the stage with these gentlemen is completely unbelievable to me. We've heard some fantastic music, but what you're going to hear now is the real thing."

The Fairfield Four, actually five guys, were the guests of honor, because their music had had such an influence on popular American music and had even been recorded by the Library of Congress. Dressed in tuxedo jackets on top of overalls, as a reminder of their sharecropper days, they sang a cappella on the gospel standard "Noah."

With "Swing Low, Sweet Chariot," they proved you didn't need new threads, new tunes, guitar, bass, and drums to rock. Isaac Freeman's stand-up bass of a voice and an occasional thigh slap were more than enough of a rhythm section.

As they harmonized and clapped, calling out now and then for a witness, Elvis watched, smiling, from the wings. He shushed some people in the audience to pay close attention to the real thing.

When they were through, Elvis lit up the stage again and sang "Don't Let Me Be Misunderstood." The words were almost too much for me to handle. It was as if he were singing directly to me, on Martin's behalf, as if Martin were whispering in his ear all the way from New York.

"Don't you know no one in life can always be an angel . . . Sometimes I lie awake long regretting some foolish thing, some sinful thing I've done."

How could Elvis know what was happening in my life?

I looked around at the other faces in the crowd and saw that Elvis was talking to them, too. They were in a trance. We were all spellbound, trapped in Elvis's orbit, in the gravitational pull of It.

He and the Fairfield Four then launched into "That Day Is Done," which Elvis had written with Paul McCartney. It felt like the flip side of "Days," the song that Martin and I had heard that magic night in SoHo, the night we watched the lights of the Empire State Building flip off.

Days. That Day Is Done.

It was all ending. Even Elvis was telling me so.

Now there was no place for the show to go. It would take an all-star finale to top Elvis. And so that's what followed. Everybody climbed onstage and sang "Jesus Is on the Main Line." And we all got to our feet.

Late that night, when we got back to his house, Tony pulled out some old photo albums and showed Julie pictures of me as a twenty-one-year-old, when I used to answer Elvis's calls to *Musician* magazine. He pulled out more photo albums, older and older, he and I growing younger and younger with each volume. There I was as a longhaired nineteen-year-old, back when he and I first met. "Look at all that hair." Julie laughed. "Both of you." Tony had lost a little since then.

We laughed at pictures of me on the beach. Pictures of Tony at college in Omaha. Then his high school years, when I wasn't yet in the pictures.

While Julie went in the other room to call Jimmy, Tony and I got down to business.

"So how's it going?" he asked.

I told him the Page Six story. I had saved it for this one-on-one, in-person sit-down. He sat there, all right, without saying a word, his mouth hanging open like Sleepy Steve's.

"I just don't know if I can do it," I said. "I don't know if I can work through this. It's too big."

He nodded and thought for a while.

"Well, if you decide you want to, you can," he said, finally. "You're capable of it. I mean, there aren't many people who would wanna face it and work through it, but if you want to, you can do it."

Tony was the first—the only—person to say these words to me. They sounded insane.

"You think?"

He nodded.

I rubbed my forehead. "I can't get any perspective. I'm in the middle of the whole mess and I can't see what's right anymore. Maybe we need to just walk away from the whole thing."

"You're married, though, remember?"

I knew what he meant. Because we were married, we had vowed to give it a chance, long before anything went wrong. You made those vows at the best of times, in preparation for the worst of times.

"I feel sometimes like this is karma for me, for cheating on you while I was in Italy that time."

"Don't say that. That's just dumb. That has nothing to do with this."

But in a way, it did. I had told Martin about my cheating on Tony. I had almost bragged about it. As if it were just another adventure, that time in Italy. A badge of independence. Maybe I had set him a road map.

I remember actually telling Martin that cheating wasn't the worst thing you could do in a relationship. We were sitting on a beach, at the Jersey shore, I remember, and I went on and on about it. That there were worse betrayals. Ignoring the person you loved was worse than loving two people at the same time. Or being indifferent. Or abusing them, psychologically or physically abusing them.

But cheating on them *was* abusing them. It was a sign of being indifferent. I hadn't been on the other side, so I had no idea. I hadn't been cheated on since freshman year in high school when John Menke kissed the slutty girl across the street right in front of me while I sat on my front porch and played my acoustic guitar. I had dropped my pick into the guitar hole, I was so shook up.

It had been so long since I had been cheated on that I said cheating was forgivable. I said it because I thought it was true. Because Tony had forgiven me.

• NINETEEN •

When we got back to New York, Julie landed us a gig at a club called Spiral on Houston Street. Their sign was a big black-and-white spiral projected onto the sidewalk out front.

Though we were still fresh on the club scene, we were the headliners that night, playing after Vitamin X and Talking to Lois. At the better clubs, the bigger your following and the better your sound, the better placement you had on the billing. But at Spiral, there was no rhyme or reason to your placement in the lineup. I think they just threw the names of the bands in a hat and took it from there. Vitamin X, Talking to Lois, Stephonic. It didn't matter. Because another night at Spiral, we were the first of seven bands. There was nothing like being the opening act for six unknown bands.

That first night, though, we were the stars. And it was Doug's birthday. Since he was so far from home, he made sure everyone knew in advance so that he wouldn't spend the entire day without someone making a big stink about it. I bought him a chocolate birthday cake in a bakery in Brooklyn, on my way to our show, and placed it gently in the backseat, next to my bass drum. I snuck the cake into Spiral without Doug seeing, and hid it behind the bar.

All our friends were there: Sara; Pam Marla, the nurse; her husband, Smash Mouth Tony; Dan's girlfriend, Pauline; Jimmy; Laura; Doug's friends from work, Dwayne and John, the rollerblader. And Doug's platonic friend Audrey. Julie's friends Dave and Mary from Philadelphia drove up for a show now and then. There were the usual drunks gathered at the bar. But no Martin. Though we still lived in the same apartment, sometimes sleeping in the same bed, my show moratorium was firmly in place.

Playing in Spiral's long, narrow space made you feel like you were playing to an empty room. So everyone moved up closer to the stage to make us feel less lonesome. Front and center, holding a large yellow shopping bag in one hand, was a small Asian woman with a big grin on her face. She stood a few feet in front of our other friends, even in front of Jimmy. She had a pixie haircut under a fuzzy brown knit hat, with a wide-spread seventies collared shirt and big platform boots.

Though I had no idea who she was, I recognized the look on her face as we played. It was the look I had the night we heard Elvis in Nashville. In a musical trance, she swayed to the beat, putting her shopping bag down between songs to clap loudly. Especially after "Letters."

Letters in a box
Tied with packing string
Back in my closet among the other things I saved.
I should have thrown them away.

"Do you know her?" I mouthed to Julie, between verses, nodding my head toward the woman.

Julie shrugged.

I summoned Doug over with an idle drumstick.

"Who is she?"

"Beats the hell out of me. But she sure is cute. You sure she's not my birthday present?"

I gave him a look that said, "You're a pig."

After we'd packed up our equipment, Julie and I went up to the woman to introduce ourselves.

"Hi. I'm Julie."

"Yoko," the girl said, pointing to her chest. "No good English." She shook her head vigorously. "Japanese."

I thought of our friend Laura, who had lived in Tokyo for a year and was fluent in Japanese. We grabbed her from the bar and dragged her over.

Laura began talking quickly in Japanese with Yoko, laughing and clapping her hands, then falling into a long, deep, solemn discussion.

"What's she saying?" Julie screeched impatiently.

Through Laura's translation, we learned that Yoko had come to New York as part of her annual American music tour.

"Concerts in Japan are prohibitively expensive," Laura told us, as if translating for the UN Security Council. "Around eighty dollars a ticket, so Yoko has to come to the United States to fill her quota every year."

Yoko chattered some more and Laura nodded. "She loves bands so much that she pays the plane fare and travels from city to city to meet the musicians and bring their new demos with her back to Osaka to the record store where she works."

"Hanky Panky," Yoko shouted, pointing to her big yellow shopping bag. Hanky Panky, the name of the store, was apparently written in Japanese on the bag. Yoko was very excited.

To help finance her trips, she also worked in her grandfather's drugstore. She had a third job as well.

"But she doesn't know the word," Laura said.

Yoko mumbled something over and over in Japanese. Finally, she shook an imaginary cocktail mixer between her hands.

"You're a bartender!" I yelled.

"Yes, yes," she said, satisfied. "Bah-tenda." She nodded and repeated it a few more times, to commit the word to memory. "Bah-tenda. Bah-tenda."

Yoko visited Minneapolis, Nashville, Los Angeles, Seattle, Chicago, anyplace with a good indie scene, she said. She was only twenty-two, but had been here twice already.

Her first trip had been two springs ago and only included Philadelphia and Baltimore. But the second trip, this time around, she hung out with Jon Spencer Blues Explosion and was invited to a sound check. She clapped her hands as Laura relayed the story to us.

New York was her last stop. Earlier in the day, in a record shop window, she had seen one of our band flyers that Doug had made on his computer at work. "You," I said loudly, as if Yoko were deaf, "are our first international fan."

Julie introduced Yoko around as I snuck behind the bar to grab Doug's surprise birthday cake.

"Nice hat," Doug said to Yoko, poking at the brown yarn. While he struggled to talk to her, I stuck a few candles into the top of his cake, lit them with the bartender's lighter, asked him to turn down the house music and then paraded out with the cake, its candles lighting up the dank club.

When Doug saw the cake, he blushed deep red. "Did you do this?"

I smiled, as Laura, Jimmy, Dave and Mary, Sara, Pauline, Pam Marla, Smash Mouth Tony, Doug's friends, and the collection of drunks at the bar launched into a flat rendition of the birthday song. It was a bitch of a song to sing. Julie and Dan sang their sweet harmony, though. Even Yoko knew the words.

With only one international fan, it was easy to give her special treatment. We made plans to take our Yoko to dinner a few nights later. We went for *shabu-shabu,* Japanese barbecue, at an Upper East Side place that Laura said was very authentic. Julie, Laura, and I were the only westerners there. But Yoko seemed slightly uncomfortable, as if she'd rather be out eating a hamburger or pizza. Yoko didn't look like the other people in the restaurant. She was a hipster, or whatever the Japanese version of a hipster was.

During dinner, Yoko excitedly talked to Laura, who translated for us as much as she could. "She wants us to come downtown with her to see Ron Sexsmith," Laura said. Yoko nodded.

"She saw him play last night at the Westbeth, and went backstage to meet him. She loved him so much, she's going to go and see him again tonight," Laura translated. "She would love for us to join her on this endeavor."

I had heard Ron Sexsmith when he had once opened for Elvis Costello in Philadelphia. I knew he had played at Arlene Grocery, a club around the corner from Luna. They had a poster of him on one of their walls.

"We should go," I said. I was in no rush to get home to the battlefield.

"I'm in," Julie said.

We took a cab down to the Westbeth, but by the time we got there, the show was sold out. Yoko took Laura's hand and motioned for us all to follow. The man at the door waved us past. "Any friends of Yoko's are friends of mine," he said, parting the velvet rope.

Who was this woman?

We took seats at the back of the theater just as Sexsmith was taking the stage. From the first fingerings on his acoustic guitar, I knew we were in for a treat. His voice was soft but powerful, like his guitar work. Matching the music's gentle melodies were even more gentle lyrics, painting intimate sketches of episodes in Sexsmith's life.

One was a heartbreaking but uplifting song about a strawberry blonde he once knew as a boy. Like a great short story, the song had a beginning, a middle, and an ending that brought it all home. I wished the song were a story in a book, so I could go back to page one and start it all over again. "Strawberry Blonde." Just like Julie.

About halfway through the set, I looked up and saw a familiar face. Bill Flanagan, my former editor at *Musician,* was running down a middle cut in the audience. Though I had spoken to him on the phone a few times over the years, I hadn't seen him since the late eighties, at a Lucinda Williams show at the Hoboken club Maxwell's. Bill hadn't changed a bit. I looked to see if his wife, Susan, was trailing behind him. But no, it wasn't Susan. It was a man. A man with his head bowed. With a receding hairline, in a black raincoat and black-rimmed glasses.

Elvis Costello.

Julie squeezed my leg as they flew past us. "Did you see?" she began. But I cut her off with,

"And I know the guy he's with."

"Oh my God," Julie said.

The groupie tables had turned.

I turned to look at Yoko, who was so engrossed in the music, she hadn't even noticed Elvis. Then, as if to say he was with us, on our wavelength, Sexsmith announced he'd now play a Gordon Lightfoot cover. Not the one we performed night after night. But his very own. "Sundown."

"By a fellow Canadian," said Sexsmith, blushing a little. He launched into the pretty guitar line and started singing, "Sundown, you better take care."

Julie and I searched the crowd for Elvis and Bill, trying not to stand up completely in our seats. We spotted them, about ten rows ahead of us, to the right, as Sexsmith sang, "I can see her lookin' fast in her faded jeans."

I broke my own rule and started talking over Sexsmith's singing. In hushed whispers, Julie and I made a plan.

"As soon as he's finished, we need to just run straight for them," I whispered. Julie nodded. As much as we enjoyed Sexsmith, now we couldn't wait for him to shut the hell up and get off the stage.

"Sundown, you better take care, if I find you been sneakin' round my back stair." All right already, I thought. All right, all right. Wrap it up.

As Sexsmith took a bow, thankfully his final bow, we made a beeline, with Yoko and Laura in tow, straight for Bill Flanagan.

"Bill!" I waved my arms as the house lights came up. "It's Helene. Hi. How ya doing?"

"Helene!" he shouted. I went over and hugged him.

"Have you met Elvis?" Bill asked.

"No."

"Helene was our first intern at *Musician,*" Bill said. "We didn't even know a magazine could have an intern before Helene called us, begging for a job."

"Very nice to meet you," Elvis said, shaking my hand.

"You used to call Bill at the office all the time," I said, not letting go of his hand. "I'm the one who transferred you." He raised an eyebrow, trying hard to look impressed. I couldn't stop myself. "You were the highlight of my workday."

Elvis blushed now.

"How's the Burt Bacharach thing going?" I said. According to the official Elvis Costello website, he was recording a full album of songs with Burt Bacharach. As Elvis gabbed on about how great Bacharach was, Julie nudged me. I'd forgotten she, Laura, and Yoko were even standing there. When Elvis came up for air, I introduced them.

"This is my bandmate, Julie. I'm in a band now," I said to Bill, as an aside. "And this is our friend Laura. And our only groupie, Yoko." Yoko smiled and shook Elvis's hand. She had no idea what I had just said.

"Well, we should probably get going." Bill put his hand on Elvis's back. "It was great seeing you again. Good luck with everything. With the band and everything. What's the name of the band?"

"Stephonic," Julie and I said in unison.

"Well, I'll keep my eyes open with the music listings. I'll come and see you guys sometime."

Then, as quickly as they had appeared, Bill and Elvis vaporized into the night. With a determined step, Yoko led us across the theater, into the same crowd into which they had disappeared. She led us behind a door, and up some stairs. "Come, come," she said, pulling Julie's hand.

"Where are we going?" Laura asked in Japanese.

"Follow me," she said in English.

At the top of the stairs was a tall man guarding the backstage door. "Yoko! So good to see you again. Come right in."

There, before us, was Elvis once again. And Bill. And Ron Sexsmith. And Susan, Bill's model wife from the Cars video, and Elvis's sometime keyboard player and producer, Mitchell Froom.

Yoko beamed.

"I can't believe this," I said, looking at Julie. "Do you believe this?"

The inner sanctum.

Julie just shook her head, as free drinks were thrust into our hands. Yoko worked the room, in her broken English, until we sidled up next to Bill again.

"You remember Susan, my wife," he said. I had ridden a train to Gloucester, Massachusetts, with Susan years ago on our way to the *Musician* Christmas party. We had chatted on that long ride to Gloucester, the only women in a large group of rock journalists.

Susan had been the first model I had ever met, and I was astounded—not just by how smart she was, but by how stupid I had been for assuming she would be dumb just because she was so pretty.

Meeting her again, I had a vivid flashback of that party, down to the very clothes I had worn: tight jeans, a white cowl-neck sweater, and beige suede boots with cowboy fringe on them. What had I been thinking? Susan and I had stuck together that weekend in Gloucester while the boys played. The *Musician* editors formed their own band and got up at the Christmas party to perform a set of covers.

Jock (*Jock!*) played keyboards, since he was, after all, the expert on MIDI. His brother, Gordon, played drums. Sort of. I wanted to knock him off his throne. But he probably would have fired me. The former guitar salesman played guitar, of course. Peter, the only real musician in the group, sang.

The *Musician* band helped prove my theory that all writers were frustrated musicians deep down inside. Bill had told me that the *Rolling Stone* editors had had their own band as well, called the Dry Heaves.

I had ridden back from that *Musician* Christmas party in the backseat of a car, between the rock critics Timothy White and Charles M. Young. White, who was the editor of *Billboard* magazine, had told me I should get a job at AP, like he had, to learn how to write. Chuck told me to hitchhike to Nicaragua and see as much of the world as I could. The two of them argued over me, as if I weren't even there.

"Gloucester, right?" Susan said, shaking my hand, jolting me back to the present.

"Yeah," I said. "What a party." I meant the Christmas party, so long ago, but Bill thought I meant this party.

"I didn't realize you were headed back here," he said. "We would have waited for you."

"Well, I didn't know either. But Yoko seems to know everybody."

We caught up on the guys who used to work at *Musician,* where they were now. Peter, the guy who had hired me, the only other guy besides Bill that I really liked, wound up working down in Nashville for Madonna's record company.

"He's married, with a kid," Bill said, his eyebrows high on his forehead.

"Good for him," I said.

"They're all married, all those guys."

"Did they marry each other?"

Bill laughed. And changed the subject.

"I'm over at VH1 now. I'm a producer."

When Julie heard that, she looked like she might go into cardiac arrest. I imagined having to pound on her chest, right there in the middle of the party.

"You should really try and come see us sometime," I said. "We play Luna a lot. And Spiral. But we're trying to get a gig at Brownies. That's our goal."

While we made more small talk, Julie slowly made her way across the room toward Elvis. Before long, she was chatting with him. Yoko pulled out a small Instamatic camera. And Julie posed for a photo with Yoko. It was the photo Yoko would send us a few weeks later, from Japan:

Julie, Yoko, and, between the two of them, surreal as could be, Elvis Costello.

• TWENTY •

Martin and I made some progress that fall, thanks to Elvis. And thanks to Tony. Martin was so excited about my brush with Elvis that it helped bring us a little closer for a few days. Though I was still angry, not only about the cheating, but about the *Post* item, I couldn't help telling Martin every detail of my Elvis encounter. Martin wasn't the least bit envious, as usual.

"I'm glad I wasn't with you, actually," he said. "I don't think I would have been able to handle it." Just the thought of hanging out with Elvis made his ears turn red.

Tony called after my trip to Nashville and, uncharacteristically, asked to speak to Martin. I shrugged and handed the phone over. "Tony wants to talk to you."

"Me?"

I nodded.

Martin didn't do much talking; he just said "Mm-hmm" a lot.

When he finally hung up the phone, after about ten minutes, I asked, "So what did he say?"

"He just wanted to give me some advice."

"Like what?"

"Well, basically, he said, 'You just have to take whatever she dishes out.' "

Between airborne records, CDs, and picture frames, Martin and I started talking again, talking like friends instead of crazy lovers. I even went so far as to buy him a Christmas present, an impulse buy on something I'd seen in a shop window. Something I'd seen him admire once.

"So did you really love her?" I asked him one December day, not in an accusing way, but like a person who actually wanted to know.

"Do you know how you and Tony feel about each other?" he asked. "How you always felt like he was your twin?"

I nodded.

"Well, that's what I felt like with her." He said that whenever she had insomnia, which I hoped was often, she would watch from her Carmine Street window as the *Daily News* and the *Post* were dropped off at the deli across the way, and then read the big headlines from three flights up. He assured me he had never witnessed this in person.

She loved newspapers as much as Martin did. She was a history major, and an expert on the Bataan Death March, which Martin found infinitely fascinating.

We both laughed. It was one of the things Martin and I didn't have in common: that fascination with troops marching through Poland, Berlin rallies, ships exploding at sea, the Japanese bombing Pearl Harbor, and of course, the Bataan Death March.

"Did she watch the Hitler Channel, too?" I asked. He nodded. We both laughed again. I couldn't believe I was laughing. With Martin.

"I mean, I had never met that person before," he said.

"Do you think you should be with her, then?" I asked, like a friend.

"No, no. It was just like what happened with you and Tony. We just couldn't get along. The reason I went back to her was that I wanted to be sure. But right away I knew it wasn't going to work out." He hung his head. "It was my fault for going back."

I hadn't wanted to understand anything he was saying. Anything he had been feeling. But now I was starting to.

"I told you about it all because I wanted to be with you. I wanted you to forgive me," he said. "But I know that's too much to ask. I know you'll never be able to forgive me." I wanted to contradict him, but I was afraid he was right.

"But that's okay," he said. "You don't have to forgive me. I'm willing to live that way."

"No. I think I do have to forgive you. But I don't know if I can. I really don't know if I can. It's so big. Just too big. You know what I mean? It was a whole year. You were cheating on me for a whole year."

The horror started to descend once more, gripping my insides and making me want to double up onto the floor or go lie down on the couch or throw an old vinyl record at his head. It was like a wave, hitting the shore. It would go out for a short while, but the tide would bring the next wave in, guaranteed. As long as the moon stayed in the sky, the tide would come back in.

Though the horror would come less frequently, when it did come, it was just as intense as that first day. There was a line in "That Day Is Done" that I remembered from the concert. "I thought at once my heart would burst / Still every time is like the first." And that's what it was like.

"A whole year. How could you have cheated for a whole year?"

"I know. I know. I'm sorry. I'm so sorry. You have no idea how sorry I am."

I did understand how sorry he was. And I understood, even more now, how he wanted to be friends with her. But I couldn't handle it. Martin tried bringing the subject up again, but I still couldn't imagine them hanging out together—not without me chasing them down the street with a hatchet.

"I'm with you now," Martin said. "We're together and she's alone. I can't just turn my back on her. And besides, you told us that first day that we could be friends."

I think it was the "us" in that sentence that got me going more than anything else.

"Well I changed my fucking mind."

"But I can't just ignore her."

"Yes you can."

"But I can't."

"You can and you will," I screamed.

"But there's no reason for it. You don't get it. I'm with you."

"No, no." The anger was rising. "I get it. You're the one who's not getting it. It's either her or me."

He walked away from me, but I followed him into the next room. "Remember when we got married?" I shouted, sticking my finger in his face. "Remember the forsaking all others part? Well, it means more than just not sleeping with someone else." I darted into my closet and pulled out his Christmas present, which wasn't wrapped yet. It was still in its shopping bag. I pulled it out and ruined the surprise.

"You have to choose," I said, holding the new suitcase I had just bought—a forties-style hard-cased leather number with rounded corners. It was turning out to be a wise purchase. "Until you choose, you can get the fuck out." I threw the suitcase at his feet. "Merry fucking Christmas."

So Martin left. He packed the new suitcase I had bought him and left. But not before giving me my Christmas present, too. It was hidden in his closet. It was wrapped already.

When he handed it to me, I refused to unwrap it, not out of malice but because I knew the sight of it would start me crying. I was so tired of crying. I waited until he left the apartment before I tore the wrapping paper off.

It was what I thought it was, better than a make-up diamond ring, better than 1,000 bouquets of roses.

It was a brand-new snare drum.

...

For our Christmas show at Luna, the plan was to learn two new covers. One was the tune from *The Grinch Who Stole Christmas,* the "bahoo doray" song that the whole town of Whoville sings at the end of the cartoon, except with a driving beat and a tambourine, which we pretended was sleigh bells. For his guitar part, Dan played the "bahoo doray" part over and over, but then, for his solo at the end, resorted to "Dreidel, dreidel, dreidel." I hadn't even known Dan was Jewish.

"What is that?" Doug asked.

"It's a Hanukkah song about a dreidel," I explained.

"What's a dreidel?"

"I'm not really sure."

Our other cover was from Rob, the club owner, who was really into us by the winter, and had sent our tape to a record label in California. To showcase Julie's soft, fragile voice and her simple guitar playing, Rob suggested the new cover tune, "Just Like Honey," a pretty, melodic song by the Jesus and Mary Chain. He chose it, no doubt, because he wanted to hear Julie sing the line "I'll be your plastic toy."

My favorite line was "Eating up the scum is the hardest thing that I could do." During practice one afternoon, we kept losing the thread just at that lyric. "Let's take it from 'Eating up the scum,' " Julie said every time we stopped.

No one seemed to notice, caught up in the mechanics of the song, but then Dan heard what Julie was actually saying and crooned, "Eating up the scum, dum de dum de dum." Every time Julie sang the line, Dan would echo it back earnestly, "Eeeating up the scummmmm," until we were all laughing, Julie giggling over her lyrics, missing a beat, then throwing me off, which in turn threw Doug off, until we had to stop altogether.

Regardless of the "scum" line, the song was a good pick, since we worked out the three-part round-robin harmony within it. On the chorus, "Just like honey," which gets repeated about 20,000 times, I would start, and then Dan and then Julie would join in, just like "Row, Row, Row Your Boat," and we would repeat it over and over until it built up into a wonderfully sweet crescendo. I was not only amazed I was able to sing and play the drums at the same time, but that I could build up the loudness and the energy while still staying in tune. Just as we reached a high point, we'd bring it back down and work it to a whisper.

One practice, after a particularly successful round of harmony, Dan got all excited, which was unusual.

"Well, that little round robin rocked," he said, smiling. "Suddenly, we're a pop band. We're ashamed to admit we like it."

"We're like ABBA." Julie laughed.

"It's fucking good," Doug said.

"Fucking good?" Julie asked.

"Just like honey," I said.

"That fade was wonderful," Doug said. "We just faded and then we came back. That was totally us. We just made that an us song."

There was one line I tried to ignore every time we played that song, the one that went, "Walking back to you is the hardest thing that I can do."

Not every practice went as well as that one. Julie wrote us a new song called "Sorry." We practiced it for hours and hours, until we were all sick of hearing it. But no matter how much we played it, we could never get it right. Julie tried rewriting it, but it didn't matter. "I don't want to play this song anymore," Doug announced.

"So then," Julie said, "what do you want to work on, Mr. I-Can't-Bear-to-Work-on-Something-New?"

"Yeah, Mr. Lazy Bones," Dan said, going into his little old man voice. "In my day we would do a song for four hours, in the snow, barefoot."

At our next practice, Julie took out the very word the song was based around—"sorry." She changed it to "I bite my nails." It was like replacing the Beatles' "Yesterday" with "Last Thursday Afternoon."

"I changed the vocals," Julie announced, "because it was sounding too much like a Michael Bolton song. It was too sappy."

"But I really liked the words before," Doug said.

"Sorry," Dan sang.

"I liked it, though," Doug said. "I don't care if it's sappy."

"You know, Michael Bolton just cut his hair," I said.

"So it's okay now to sound like Michael Bolton? Is that what you're saying?" Julie asked.

"That's not what I'm saying."

"You wanna rename it the Martin Song?" she asked.

"Sorry, Martin, you're out!" Doug laughed.

"Is he out?" Dan asked. I nodded. "What's the latest?"

"The latest," I said, "is that I was home on Sunday morning working and the phone rang and it's a hang-up and the phone rings again, just once, and then stops. Of course with my new suspicious mind, I call him at work and say, 'What the fuck is going on?' He starts getting all panicky, saying, 'It's her. It's her. She's calling you.' Then he said someone at work told her that he had been bragging about the band, about how we keep getting better and better gigs, and she got mad."

"What?" Dan asked.

"Whack job," I said. "So then she called him back and wanted to have lunch with him and he said no and she got upset and that's when she tried to call me and say she wanted to have lunch with him. That I should let him have lunch with her. But she never actually spoke to me. She hung up."

"So, let me get this straight," Dan said. "She's mad because people were talking about the band?"

"That *he* was talking about it," I said. "He's getting better, and seems happier now, I guess."

"Happy being with her or being with you?"

"Not being with her," I said. It was true. Though I hadn't seen him all that much, Martin sounded all right on the phone when he called from his mother's or from work. His girlfriend, or, by this point, his ex-girlfriend, had no idea he was not living with me.

The few times I did see him, he was gaining weight back and seemed peaceful almost, even though he was homeless. He was happy the affair was over. And happy I was no longer throwing vintage vinyl at his head.

"Wow," Dan said.

"The life of a rock star." Julie laughed.

For weeks, I put up with his girlfriend calling the house in an effort to "be my friend" so that I would let them "be friends." But she hung up just as I picked up the receiver. I knew it was her. I could smell her through the line.

"How can you put up with that insanity?" my friend Sara asked one night over drinks. "Why don't you just leave him once and for all?" The question made me feel weak and pathetic. I had thrown him out, but couldn't face the idea of divorce. My stomach turned at just the sound of the word. But why didn't I just cut him loose once and for all? Why was I such a sucker?

Some days I wished that I had found them out, that I had found Martin and his girlfriend in bed together, or in one of their bars having a drink together, or walking down the street holding hands. Then it would have been much easier to just hate him and walk away.

But it wasn't like that. He had told me. He had confided in me and had asked my forgiveness. I didn't say any of this to Sara. The territory had already been covered, in dozens of previous conversations.

"I mean, you don't have kids and you don't own any real estate together or anything," she said. "If you're gonna leave him for good, you should probably do it now."

"I've tried," I said. "I've tried leaving. It's not for lack of trying. But then I sit there and have to look at his favorite chair or the rug his mother gave us or the bed we bought together or the couch . . ."

"Give him all that stuff," she said. "Or better yet, burn all your furniture."

We were quiet for a minute while I contemplated that idea. Would I drag it outside on the breezeway and douse it with gasoline, or just set it alight right there in the apartment? There was an awkward silence as we both sipped our beer. We both stared down at our hands. But then it dawned on me. The answer. The answer to Sara's question. Why didn't I leave and stay away? Or kick him out and not let him back in?

"I think it's because I still love him," I said. I wasn't sure if I had just thought it or had actually spoken it. But then I saw Sara flinch, and knew that it had come out of my mouth.

"Oh," Sara said, nodding, looking up at me.

"Oh," she said again. The weight of the answer was still settling on her brain. And on mine.

"Well, that makes sense," she said finally. I thought about it myself, this revelation—that I somehow still loved him. Was still in love with him.

"There's not much you can do about it if you still love him," she said.

Love was the only excuse you needed for acting like an idiot.

One morning soon after, I was cleaning out the closets and decided to rifle through the pockets of the coats and jackets Martin had left behind. I came upon a ticket stub to a concert. When I looked at it to see which show it was that we had seen, I noticed that it was not a show we had seen. It was a show they had seen, last Christmas, a classical concert at Trinity Church in lower Manhattan.

I imagined them in their sweaters and winter coats trudging down there in the middle of the afternoon—before Martin had to go to work, when he was supposed to be having lunch with me. Holding hands, her in her mittens, him in his black leather gloves, the gloves I had bought him. That motherfucker. And the horror descended again, in full force. I decided to call him at work and terrorize him.

"It was her idea to go to that concert," he said. "She was into classical music."

"Oh *really*?"

"She was a cellist."

"A cellist? I love the cello. Now I hate the cello! See what you've done? You've made me hate the fucking cello."

"What are you talking about? You never told me you loved the cello."

I slammed the phone down.

That night, at practice, I thought about their precious Christmas concert and the cello, and knocked the shit out of my drums.

As if to harness my energy and make the most of it, Stephonic went back to Night Owl and recorded another demo. Paul couldn't believe how much better my drumming had gotten. I couldn't tell him that Martin's face and the face of his girlfriend were mentally planted on each drum skin and had made me a killer, or at least an angrier drummer.

For the cover of our demo, a CD this time, Martin's friend Ben took some pictures of us. It was his way of showing he was on my side in the battle with Martin. The photo we used for the back cover had us all looking down at his lens, with a painted blue-and-white sky behind us, clouds floating by. For the front cover, we used a black-and-white shot of us huddling together in the rain, outside Ben's studio.

Doug continued to make flyers for each show, scanning in clip art of robots, fat ladies at the beauty parlor, or Richard Nixon jumping up in the air. Each announced a different show, another night when I could get lost in the rhythm of the drums, get caught in the wave, the amusement park ride, and forget, sometimes, for a few seconds maybe, what was happening in my life. I looked forward to the calm and the utter escape, like that girl slowly sliding from her sparkling booth at Max Fish whacked out on smack.

I loved driving with my backseat and front seat full of drums, up onto the Brooklyn-Queens Expressway on my way to the Manhattan Bridge. The lights of New York would be just starting to flicker on. The view swept from Liberty Island—the soft green glow of the statue—over to the Empire State Building, its lights the color of the current holiday. Purple for AIDS Awareness Week; green and red for Christmas; red, white, and blue for Presidents Day.

From the bridge I could see night actually arrive. My only comfort. The best thing about the Manhattan Bridge was its view of the Brooklyn Bridge, which, night after night, would somehow stretch its heavy Gothic arches across the deep-blue river toward the buildings of lower Manhattan. The night was just beginning to swallow everything whole. But for a few brief moments, the Woolworth tower, World Trade Center, and the smaller buildings crowded around them reflected the last bits of orange light from the day, giving the world back its glow.

• TWENTY-ONE •

Over the next month, we played more than a dozen shows, all under the cover of darkness. The hardest shows to play were the ones closest to the West Village, because they were so near to where Little Miss Bataan Death March lived. Where she had gazed out her window at the deli on those sleepless nights, reading the headlines from that window. Which window was it? And which deli?

Though I tried to stop myself, before the shows I would wander over to Carmine Street and gaze up at the apartment windows. Which window had they stood behind, undressing each other? Which window was the bedroom window? And the horror would rise, as fresh and as awful as that first day.

We played one gig at the Elbow Room, a cavernous club on Bleecker Street, which had long ago been lost to the legions of Jersey and Staten Island clowns. Around two A.M. on weekends, you could almost hear the ferryman call, "Last boat leaving." But the Elbow Room had its charms. It was where the Bleecker Street Cinema had once been, an art house that held particularly fond memories for me. I had seen *Wings of Desire* there with Tony, with its plot of fallen angels and love. Life was painful, the story went, but without pain, there was no beauty.

The Elbow Room was also next door to Kim's Underground, one of the best video stores in the city. While waiting to play our set, I wandered down there and flipped through the videos, making a list in my head of the movies I really had to make a point of renting someday soon, films that would make me a better person: *Fellini Satyricon, Fanny and Alexander,* and that other Bergman movie where the guy plays chess with death. What was the name of that one? I had to get that one someday. Martin had never wanted to rent it, so I never did. But now I could rent whatever the hell I wanted, whenever I wanted. I could listen to whatever music I wanted on our stereo. My stereo. I could listen to G. Love and Special Sauce anytime I pleased, over and over, until I couldn't stand his retarded voice anymore.

And suddenly I spiraled down into another pit of sadness that would take fistfuls of anger, and a hundred hits of the snare drum, that snare drum, to climb out of.

I realized I was the only one in the band with a history in New York. Doug still had to think twice before he pronounced Houston Street. For every place we played, every restaurant we ate in, every street we walked down, I had a memory, usually attached to Martin.

Julie, Dan, and Doug were all newcomers. Every place we played, I brought baggage. As the drummer, I carried the heaviest equipment. And now I had that new snare drum to lug around wherever I went.

Upstairs in the Elbow Room, Dan was anxiously waiting for our gig to begin. His mother was in town from California, and he was nervous all night because she said she was coming to see us play. Out of all of us, Dan's crew made up the smallest part of our audience at each gig. We had only met one friend of his, and his girlfriend, Pauline, who came to all the shows.

He got all excited about his mother's impending visit, scanning the vestibule for her every few minutes and telling us stories about her. Dan loved his mother, but he told us that she was kind of a crackpot.

"She eats everything with chopsticks," he said.

"Is she Chinese?" Doug asked.

"No," I sneered. "Dan's not Chinese."

There was a pause.

"You're not, are you?" I asked Dan.

"No. She carries around this pair of chopsticks in a special box in her purse. She eats everything with them."

"Even soup?" Doug asked. Dan didn't even answer him.

I loved meeting my friends' parents. It filled in the reasons why they were the way they were, made you understand their personality tics and appreciate them a little better.

We waited and waited, disappointed every time another friend showed up instead of Dan's mom. One of them was Martin's friend Matt from the Zones, who was still the bass player for the Toasters. He had traveled all over the world with them during the last decade. He had been through two wives already. He wasn't even thirty yet.

Matt had been in the music business so long that he'd seen many unknown bands blossom into the biggest acts in the country, and then sometimes become unknown again. You never could guess. He loved to tell the story of the day when he was exhausted after weeks on tour, a day when nothing had gone right, and he had taken it out on the younger kids in the ska band opening up for the Toasters. The band, with a cute, blond female singer, had nicely asked if they could change their order in the lineup so they wouldn't have to break down their equipment. Matt told them to get lost.

The girl singer was Gwen Stefani, the band No Doubt, and they went on to sell like a billion records.

"Is Martin coming?" Matt asked, while we stood at the bar, while I waited to go on.

He didn't know what was happening between us. Martin hadn't seen him in months because Matt had been on the road playing in places like Ljubljana in Slovenia. ("Good night, Ljubljana!")

I wasn't about to break the bad news to him. That his old friend was a cheating sack of shit. That he wasn't allowed to come to my shows.

"No," I said. "He can't make it tonight."

While we were up there onstage, playing our loudest songs, Dan kept throwing glances at the club door. He played louder than he ever had that night, and I followed along, our anger and disappointment propelling the band to new heights. But his mom never showed up.

I knew how Dan felt. I hadn't stopped searching the doorways and crowds for Stanley. I still had hope he'd show up sooner or later. And now I had Martin to watch for as well.

Gig after gig that winter, it felt like the band was drawing closer and closer to something, some core or source or heart of it all. Though I wasn't sure what *it* was. Maybe it was a musical community, or fame. Probably not fortune. Whatever it was, we were on the brink of it.

We were not only getting along, but our friends were starting to mix, like in a marriage. Relationships were crossing over, so that I could have a drink with one of Doug's friends and vice versa. Our regulars became tight-knit, and our shows became the highlight of everybody's week. My girlfriends developed crushes on Julie's friends. Doug's friends hit on some of my friends. It was all incestuous and wonderful.

At one show at Luna, a friend of mine named Katrina started chatting with a guy who just happened to be at the bar. He didn't know our band, but had just wandered in because of the music. Soon after, Katrina and Rodney started living together, and wound up getting married.

Our band marriage had become more than just the union of four people, just like my and Martin's marriage had been more than just our own business. We were starting to affect the people around us, to touch other lives, just by existing.

Some nights, before a Luna show, we'd eat at either Katz's or a place on Ludlow called Standard Notions. Sometimes it was just us, the band, and sometimes it was our extended family of friends. Standard

Notions was an old sewing shop, which had been transformed into a bar and restaurant by Mason Reese, the trollish redheaded kid who had done commercials in the seventies. Over dinner, we'd review our set list and talk about what problems to avoid: my tendency to miss the chorus on one song or Julie and Dan's tendency to go flat on the Gordon Lightfoot cover.

The neighborhood was really turning into our own. I knew the hardware stores and the candy wholesale place around the corner, the Jewish hagglers who sold underwear, the Spanish restaurants, and the pickle barrels at Russ and Daughters, with its cool pink and green neon. We were also making friends with the other local bands, including one group called the Rosenbergs, who we played with a few times at Luna. Right after we met them, one of their songs was featured in the show *Dawson's Creek.* For a few weeks, that became Julie's new goal: to get one of our songs featured on *Dawson's Creek.*

One night we went to see Smash Mouth, our friends who had lent Martin the bass amp for that I Hate Jane show 20 million years ago. Smash Mouth's show was at Spiral. They played there all the time, in the way we often played at Luna. Little did we know that the night we went to see them—Valentine's night—would be their last together. Trouble had been brewing for months. John, the drummer, got a girlfriend, and the band was no longer allowed to practice in the fortress of solitude. Female kryptonite had arrived.

But there were other pressures. Bigger pressures. Every band's nightmare. One day at St. Vincent's Hospital, where Smash Mouth Tony held a day job as a respiratory therapist, a nurse from Neurological ICU came running up to him and yelled, "I heard your band last night on the radio!"

"You heard my band on the radio?"

"It was the end of the song and they announced your name. Smash Mouth. Right?"

"Yeah," Tony said. "That's us."

Soon, the mystery deepened when the guy from the T-shirt store in

Manhattan, which had printed their encephalitic baby head shirts, called Tony and left a message on his answering machine congratulating him on his band's success.

Beep. "Dude, congratulations on your hit single. If you need any more T-shirts, just let me know. Ciao." Beep.

Finally, Tony saw a video on MTV. There, before him, was another band called Smash Mouth, singing their new hit, "Walking on the Sun."

"It was very bittersweet," Tony said. "Because I really liked that song."

Tony considered renaming his band My Three Sons of Bitches. But that name was already taken, too. Instead, he called the T-shirt guy back and told him to run off a gross more—and charge it to Smash Mouth's label, Elektra Records.

At Spiral that Valentine's night, we didn't need to move up and fill the space for Smash Mouth. Because of the other Smash Mouth's success, the place was packed. The crowd was in for a surprise.

There would be no "Walking on the Sun" tonight. Just the other, very angry, very disappointed Smash Mouth with its usual power punk standards: "Arthur Kill Road," "Buried Up to Your Neck," and "Useless" (a tribute to Tony's boss). Halfway through the set, Tony took the mic.

"Happy Valentine's Day," he deadpanned. "We're Smash Mouth. The other Smash Mouth." We cheered. "I'd like to welcome the members of Stephonic, who are here tonight in the audience. At this time, I'd like to invite their drummer, Helene, up onstage to sing a duet with me."

As the crowd applauded, I bounded up to the stage. Tony swung his bass onto his back and bent down to offer me his hand. He pulled me up, and the band flew into my favorite of all their songs, "The Joe Pesci Song."

When the chorus came around, I poked my head in next to Tony's at the mic and yelled, "Don't fuck with me, you fucking fuck." Another warm, cathartic, Lower East Side Valentine's Day moment. Exactly what I needed, and exactly what I needed to say.

• TWENTY-TWO •

Martin started spending the night now and then, until eventually, he moved back in. There had been some good news: my cello-playing nemesis moved away. It had been in the works for some time, I guess. But I had not gotten wind of it. I was, again, the last to know. She took a job at a newspaper in another city. And was suddenly out of our lives.

I started teaching a writing class at New York University that spring semester, and, at Martin's suggestion, took the students to the *Daily News* one night for a tour to show them what a real newsroom looked like. It was the first time I'd been there since she had worked there, and was a little nervous about seeing everyone, since they all knew the terrible secrets of my love life, thanks to the *New York Post.*

Martin's colleagues were great, though. They greeted me as if nothing had ever happened. They welcomed my students, showed them how the paper was edited and laid out on a computer screen. They chatted with me about the band and promised to come and see us.

It was a wonderful visit. So great that she got wind of it. I suppose she thought of it as their newsroom. The site of their love. When she called the house one last time to cause trouble, I told her, "He's my damn husband and I'll visit him at work anytime I please." Maybe I would get a job at the *Daily News* just to spite her.

She started to tell me that they had slept together one more time after the horror. But I cut her off.

"I don't believe you." I wasn't sure of that, but that's what I wanted her to believe. When I mumbled to Martin what she had said, he grabbed the phone and started screaming at her, calling her a liar, a desperate freak. And then he said the words I'd been waiting for him to say for months.

"I don't want you to ever call here again. I don't want to ever see you or talk to you again."

Part of me believed him when he told me they hadn't slept together again. But a big part of me didn't. Part of me believed it was just her last stab at getting back at him, or maybe getting him back. But the other part of me believed she just wanted to let me know what was going on. A sister speaking the truth.

"You motherfucker," I said to him, when he slammed down the phone. "All this time you're telling me you want to make things better, and you go and fuck her again?" Things deteriorated from there.

I started throwing CDs and anything else I could grab.

"She's lying," he said, his hands in front of his face.

I ran over and punched him in the head. "No. You're the liar." Punch. "You're the cheat." Punch.

"Stop it. Please. Stop it. I can't take it anymore." He tried to run toward the front door, but I wouldn't let him leave.

"Where are you going? What, are you gonna go run back to her? Take the shuttle for one last farewell fuck?" When he couldn't get past me, he turned and ran into the bedroom, but I chased him, cursing and screaming the whole way. He tried to escape to the office. But I followed him in there as well. He pulled open the office window, the one that looked down at the trees in the courtyard, trees that were still bare from winter.

"What are you doing?" I yelled, as a gush of cold air flooded in.

"Getting away from you," he yelled. He stepped up onto the windowsill, then squatted out onto the fire escape, but I grabbed his left arm and dragged him back in, onto the windowsill. Was he jumping or simply escaping?

"I'm sorry. I'm sorry," I said. "Please. Come back in. I'll stop. I'll stop."

I let go of his arm, and left him standing there, his shoulder resting on the cold glass of the upper window. "I'm sorry." I sat on the floor and hugged my knees to my chest. The thought of his body falling six flights made me nauseous. "Please. Please come back in."

He stepped down into the office. I rose and touched his arm. We were silent for a minute or two as we walked calmly into the living room. But the horror was rising once more inside my chest.

"How could you do that? How could you sleep with her again?"

"I didn't," he screamed, grabbing my arm and squeezing it until it hurt. "I didn't sleep with her again. Do you hear me?" He shook me.

"Don't fucking grab me like that." I was on him, pummeling him as he held his arms over his head. He made a break for the front door, and before I could understand what he was doing, he was on the breezeway. I was afraid to look out there, afraid he was throwing a leg over the beautiful wrought-iron railing out on our front balcony, about to jump from our fairy-tale apartment with its pointed towers.

"Stop!" I screamed, from inside the doorway. So loud and so frightening that the next-door neighbor opened her own door and peeked out. So loud and so frightening that Martin did. He stopped. Stopped running. Stopped leaving. Stopped doing whatever he planned to do out there.

When I looked out, reluctantly, both Martin's feet were firmly inside the breezeway.

"Please." I put my arm around him. "Come inside. I'll stop. I swear. I'll stop. I'm sorry."

I took his hand and led him into the living room. I sat on the velour couch, Martin on the green chair, where Aubrey had once done her little dog dance. Where I had done mine.

Suddenly, there was a bang on the door. It was 3:30 in the morning. "Who the hell is that?" I thought. But Martin knew.

He put his face in his hands and mumbled, "It's the cops."

Another bang. Then, "Police! Open up."

Our neighbor had called 911.

Martin took a breath and walked over and turned the doorknob. He looked over at me again. I looked away.

"What's going on in here?" one officer asked, as he made his way into the living room, surveying the damage. Furniture was overturned, CD cases were scattered and broken.

"Whoa," the other cop said.

"I'm sorry, officer. Everything's all right," Martin said, calmly.

"Is it?" he said, giving Martin a dirty look. The window in the office was still wide open. Despite the fact that I had punched Martin that night, over and over, had done a majority of the screaming and had actually started the fight, despite the fact that Martin had been the one on the fire escape, the cops came down on him. I guess they always grilled the man in these cases.

They questioned me, too, but in a kind way. One of the two officers took me into the back room and closed the door. It was freezing in there. I turned and shut the window.

"Are you really all right?" the cop asked. I nodded and looked away, so embarrassed. So guilty. My arm hurt where Martin had grabbed it and shook it. But I didn't mention it to the cop. I didn't mention the fire escape either.

"He didn't try and hit you or hurt you in any way?"

"No," I said, shaking my head.

"Do you feel like you're in danger? Because we'll take him in right now. We can arrest him, and he won't be able to come anywhere near you."

The idea was so absurd, me being afraid of him, when I was the attacker, that I almost laughed at the question. "No. You don't have to do that."

When he was satisfied I wasn't being abused, that I had no black eyes and no bruises, he pulled out a police report, a domestic abuse form, and asked me to sign it, to declare that I was not a battered woman.

I signed it and he opened the door to the rest of the destruction, to Martin. The officers headed for the front door. “You really need to keep it down in here,” the other cop said. “People are trying to sleep, you know.”

“Take it easy on each other,” my cop said, sensing Martin might not be the culprit.

That night, the NYPD put an end to the horror. We were so mortified, so humiliated by the fact that our neighbor had called the cops, so embarrassed that they had come to our home, that we didn’t fight again. Not like that at least. Because Martin packed his forties-style suitcase, put on his coat and left one last time, this time on his own.

• TWENTY-THREE •

Our relationship and the band relationship seemed to work at an inverse proportion. The worse things were with Martin, the better we seemed to play. Happiness made for boring music.

We played a great show at a place called the Baggot Inn, a small basement club on West Fourth Street, down the block from the famous jazz club the Blue Note, and across from where Edgar Allan Poe had once lived. The Poe House had been a fraternity back when I had gone to NYU; I drank from a beer ball in there. Which was fitting, really, since Poe had been such a drunk. But since my NYU days, the university had kicked out the frat house crowd and handed the building over to the law school students. So long, beer balls.

If you were a law student who wanted a drink these days you had to head across the street to the Baggot Inn, a quiet bar with very few patrons. The place was named after a famous Dublin bar where all the up-and-coming Irish musicians had played. And it was there, in the

American version—featuring, the sign said, "$2 McSorley pints!"—that we played one of our best, most scarcely attended shows.

It was billed in *The Village Voice* under the heading "Divas and Damsels! A Showcase of Women Artists." I'm sure Doug and Dan were thrilled, sandwiched between the girl bands Wendress and Princess. The *Voice* didn't even get our name right. Stephonie, it said.

But we rocked to an empty room. It was kind of like the proverbial tree falling in the forest. If you played a great show for no one, was it still a great show?

Joey Ramone showed up at another show at a place called Coney Island High on St. Marks Place, a once-cool strip now plagued with novelty shops for the kids from Jersey, places with belly-button rings and T-shirts that said things like WELCOME TO NEW YORK. NOW GO HOME. Or REHAB IS FOR QUITTERS. Or, my own personal favorite, DO I LOOK LIKE A FUCKING PEOPLE PERSON?

Coney Island High had several floors and a sign with a cartoon head with a big grin, the logo from one of the amusement parks at the real Coney Island in Brooklyn. The club was next door to where comedian Lenny Bruce once lived and was just a few doors down from what used to be the Dom, home to Andy Warhol's Exploding Plastic Inevitable, the psychedelic, pre-disco light and sound extravaganza, where the Velvet Underground had regularly played. In a strange, karmic twist, the club was now a drug rehab drop-in center.

Ramone was as tall and as ugly as the pictures I'd seen of him twenty years ago. Maybe even taller, and uglier. He barely saw us play, but made a break for the manager's office, where he sat with his impossibly long legs propped up on the desk. You could see him through a crack in the door. Julie sang a little louder that night, hoping he might hear us through that crack. Later, as the evening's headliners, Astrochicken, took the stage, I told Julie to slip through that crack and give Ramone one of our tapes.

"You've got nothing to lose," I said. "You're irresistible. He'll love you." But she was too frightened. And to be honest, so was I. Joey Ramone was a legend. A very scary-looking legend.

Julie did get the courage to send some tapes out to newspapers and magazines, though. So in issue number 62 of a fanzine called *Jersey Beat* (a pun on the name "Mersey Beat"), there appeared:

> TAPE REVIEW
>
> STEPHONIC . . . Two gals, two guys, three songs. Pretty romantic, lilting tunes with those breathy girl vocals heard everywhere in indie-rock these days. Shifting dynamics, ringing guitars, and a thick, full sound let you wrap yourself up in these tunes as snuggly as a woolen blanket on a cold night. —Jim Testa

Not bad—though the "heard everywhere" made me a little nervous. The review gave Julie enough confidence to send our demo to Arlene Grocery, where Ron Sexsmith had once played. Arlene was an old grocery store that had held on to its red-and-yellow bodega awning and flashing colored bulbs. Some bands boycotted Arlene because they didn't pay anything. But they didn't have a cover charge and had a great sound system that attracted some established acts every now and then. Local legend had it that Mick Jagger and David Bowie had even shown up at Arlene one night when Milla Jovovich sang with her band, Plastic Has Memory (after her pastrami pit stop at Katz's, I suppose).

Though I loved Luna, Arlene was the coolest place in the neighborhood, and within a few weeks, we had our first show there. Brownies was still Julie's goal, but Arlene was a step in the right direction. The place was really cozy, with exposed brick walls and homemade-looking wooden shelves behind the bar.

We opened for a band called Professor and Maryann. I had heard about them, but had never actually heard them play. We played a good, solid set, and when we were through, the Maryann of the group came up to Julie.

"You guys were great."

"Thanks," Julie said, bending down to pack her guitar away. "We can't wait to hear you play. We've heard a lot about you."

Maryann smiled shyly.

"Good things," Julie said.

When we were done moving our equipment, we all settled onto bar stools with our free drinks. I sat next to Doug and sipped my second scotch of the evening. Dan made a toast, tapping the rim of his beer bottle against his girlfriend's cleavage. "Cheers," he said. Pauline blushed.

Doug and I watched this little interaction from a distance. "Oooh," Doug said to me. "Erotic."

From the first chord, I forgot I even had a drink in my hand. And once Maryann started singing, my ice cubes started melting at a much faster rate.

I can feel your heart beatin'
Like a tropical rain.

Maryann had a husky but fragile singing voice, a sexy, throaty whisper. And she loved singing so much, she looked like she would tongue kiss the microphone any second. She sang with her eyes closed and drew you right into her passion, and made you want to be her, or kiss her, or something. Like Julie and Dan on their best nights, she definitely had It. But she had It on every single song she sang.

The Professor played acoustic guitar. He had glasses and a short haircut and a shirt and tie, and sang on some of the songs, too. He seemed to be watching Maryann's every move, and looked her in the eye whenever she happened to open her eyes. Which was not very often.

The most beautiful song they sang was about being on top of the world, the stars and the lights of the city shining up. There wasn't a sound in the club, except for the soft music and Maryann's voice. We were all in a trance, completely in the moment, deeply lost in those quiet lyrics and chords. For a moment I was high above the city, back in the Rainbow Room, circa 1994, Martin and I dancing to this song instead of "Stardust," the lights of the city shining up at us.

When the song was through, I was shocked to look around Arlene and see there were people surrounding me, that others had shared the moment. I had forgotten where I was for a half hour. The ice had completely melted in my drink, pushing the scotch level dangerously close to the rim. I turned to look at who was sitting next to me.

"Wow," Doug said, his eyebrows at the top of his forehead.

After we all regained our composure, we whooped and whistled. The Professor and Maryann stepped down and joined us for a jittery drink, and for those few minutes, I felt part of a bigger whole, part of a community that, until four months ago, I hadn't even known existed.

"You were fantastic," I said, as Maryann stepped up to the bar.

"Oh thanks," she said, waving her hand.

"No, really," Julie said. "That was an amazing set. I'm Julie, by the way," she said, extending her hand.

"I'm Danielle," said Maryann.

"And this is Ken." She pointed to the Professor. He nodded.

We all sat together and talked about our music, about our bands, about their record label and Julie's quest for one. They were like upperclassmen, giving us the lowdown on what to expect senior year.

Danielle and Ken had been in a larger band and had played around a while before realizing they should go out on their own as a duet, she said. They had been living on Staten Island and had played a lot of bars out there before hitting Manhattan. They were discovered by the Hoboken label Bar None on their third gig, at CBGB, opening for Freedy Johnston.

Ken had been working as a professor and she as a beautician. But now they were just musicians. And here they were, at Arlene Grocery, with us.

And at that moment, looking at all the familiar faces around me, my friends, my band, this other band, I felt that there was no place I would rather be than here, now. It was nearly—just nearly—perfect.

• TWENTY-FOUR •

We landed a Friday night gig at Brownies, opening for a band called the Problems. Our music life was about to hit its dream point. Or at least Julie's dream point.

Brownies, where Julie had seen Pork so long ago, where she had decided to start a band, was a step above the other places we'd been playing. Real bands played there all the time. Bands with record contracts. Bands that got written about in the *Voice.* Though we were listed in the *Voice,* we weren't good enough yet—or popular enough—for a real write-up.

Brownies paid, unlike most clubs. They had a stiff cover charge, usually about $7, which you exchanged for a bracelet so that you could drink. It looked like a hospital bracelet, but without a name or sickness scribbled on it.

Our show was a little on the early side—eight P.M., early for the rock world. I had a faculty meeting that night at NYU, so I had to drop my drums off at Brownies early, before the meeting. Either that, or I had to lug them to the meeting with me. Lugging the drums around was starting to get to me. It was really a pain in the ass to carry all that equipment to every show. Places like Brownies had amplifiers, so all the other band members had to carry with them were their guitars. But I had the bass drum, the tom-tom, the hi-hat, the floor tom, the cymbals, the cymbal stands. And of course, that snare drum.

My back hurt most nights after a gig from carrying everything. Doug usually helped. But I did most of the lugging. Into the car, out of the car, back into the car, then out of the car again to lock the drums in the storage space under our building. My knee was starting to go, too. My hi-hat knee, from repetitive stress syndrome. At most shows now, I wore an elastic brace.

But this was Brownies. It was that smoky club on the Lower East Side, that cool, off-the-beaten-path type place with a long copper-topped bar and ripped pleather stools. There was a band room down in the basement with a disgusting couch upon which we were supposed to relax before our gig. But the room looked like some maniac's torture chamber, with dirty walls and a cement floor and an exposed lightbulb hanging from the ceiling. Even the bathroom—covered in band stickers like RAT FACE and my favorite, ENDANGERED FECES, on the lid of the nonflushing toilet—was nicer than this room.

Despite the meager surroundings, there was a crowd of fans gathering upstairs. The club was a little too smoky, a little too crowded. But it was crowded with people I loved. And some I didn't even know.

There was my sister. And my boss, Maria, from *People,* with a bunch of the reporters I had worked with. Without nosy Charlie. There was Pam Marla, the nurse, and Tony, formerly of Smash Mouth. Laura, our Japanese translator, and Ben, who had taken our photos. And Sara. My mother was there. Stanley still wasn't there, but that was okay. Lauren was there, with a fake ID I had helped her buy a week earlier.

She helped me carry my equipment to the stage from the back of the room, where I had stored it earlier in the night. While moving the drums, my snare came down off a shelf where I had shoved it and hit

Lauren in the head. But I caught it, breaking the fall just as it came crashing down. That fucking snare drum.

"I'm fine," she said, waving it off and laughing. "Really. Go. Go and play."

Before we went on, I downed my usual scotch—free of charge—to calm my nerves and loosen up my muscles. My upper arm, where Martin had grabbed me during our fight, had healed. We climbed up onto the stage and took our places, instruments tuning, humming, rattling.

Julie stepped up to the microphone with her blue guitar, smiling out at the audience while I counted off in the background. One, two, one, two, three, four. And off we go. Julie strumming away. Dan launching into a searing guitar solo. Doug giving me a smile and a nod.

I'm sweating, not just from pounding away, but because of the stage lights. Blue and green and red and yellow bathing me and my bandmates in a rainbow glow that says, "Look at us. And listen."

And the audience does.

We've played these songs dozens, maybe hundreds of times, but the energy coming from the crowd, and from the music itself, is so overpowering that it transforms the moment, as if the songs are being played for the first time. There's the low down underwater sound of "Nightlight's Glow," with its obnoxious chorus. And "Letters," with Dan and Julie's bittersweet harmony. "Document," with my mantra, "Jesus lost and found," with that crescendo and abrupt finish, with the cymbal crash and catch. There are our covers, "Just Like Honey" and the Gordon Lightfoot song: "If you could read my mind, love, what a tale my thoughts would tell."

But our last song is our best song, the one that Julie had written while sleeping alone in her bed, with Jimmy off at Cannes.

"Astronaut."

I had always loved the song, but now it seems different somehow, deeper and sadder, since all that's passed. All of our songs' lyrics are hard to take, but maybe because of the music that goes with it, "Astronaut" is the hardest.

Instead of singing along with Julie, feeling her pain, I'm singing for myself now, licking my own wounds. Because Martin's gone now, on his own, for good.

The song starts off just as it always has, with Doug's insistent, simple bass line. "I hold faith," Julie sings, "that you drift in space. I'm watching the big black sky. A girl could go to rot, married to an astronaut."

And all of a sudden, it becomes my song, not Julie's song. "As you breathe silently on the opposite side of the bed," Julie sings, but I mouth the words. For the seven thousand millionth time, I think about the nights he came in late, so late, saying he'd worked overtime and then had gone for a drink with the guys. Those nights when he would come in and I would turn toward his cold side of the bed and hug him, no questions asked.

But then the chords change and the music surges and I'm swept up in the sadness of it all, ducking my head down behind my tom-tom to hide the sorrow on my face. The music is swelling and so is my chest, the tears fighting their way to the surface of the moon as the band surges on, with me in its gravitational pull, playing the soundtrack to my screwed-up marriage, a prisoner in some corny, tragic music video that is not playing just in my head, but is real, right here, unfolding in front of me, in front of everyone I know.

I try to just concentrate on the music and draw myself, my whole body, into the beat. But the body is already lost to the beat. It's my head that's the problem. The lyrics aren't important, I tell myself, not to a drummer. Concentrate. But the lyrics are there, wrenching and piercing like that metaphorical corkscrew to the heart.

I'm gonna watch and wait
For you to return someday.

When I look up again, out at the crowd, there's Martin, standing in the center, looking as sad as I feel. For a second I think I'm dreaming, but everything around me is too real. He's real. And right there. He's in the distance, but close enough so I can make out his face, half smiling and half looking like he's about to cry, so proud of me, and so tired. Tired of fighting and yelling and waiting for me to forgive him. But getting it. Getting every second of it. Getting every lyric.

"You're seven thousand million miles awaaay from me."

And suddenly, I want to put the drumsticks down and fly up over the drums and above the crowd and drift right over and hug him, take him in my strong drummer's arms and tell him what I told him that first day, that day that Diana died, that day he told me everything. I want to tell him that everything will be all right. It really will be. It really is. Everything's all right. It's all right. It's all right.

And the chorus explodes with Julie's words, "Your rockets glare," and we're off and in space, and I'm no longer drifting, drifting, but shot out into the stratosphere, part of the music filling the space over our heads and inside them, the air vibrating around us, and Martin sees me through the noise, through the crowd, through the cigarette smoke and the three other thrashing bodies onstage, and for that one moment, that long, drawn-out, 7,000-million-mile music video moment, we connect.

And it is. It is all right.

• TWENTY-FIVE •

To celebrate, Martin made a party reservation for my birthday at Lansky Lounge, a restaurant and speakeasy-type music club on the Lower East Side. It was named for the Jewish mobster Meyer Lansky, who used to drink there back in the thirties when it really was a speakeasy. The front of the place was a kosher Jewish restaurant called Ratner's, which had been there since 1918. But at night, when the restaurant was closed, the whole place became Lansky Lounge.

Ratner's entrance was on Delancey Street, under an orange neon sign in cursive handwriting, but that door was closed at night. You entered Lansky's by its original speakeasy back door on Norfolk Street. There was no sign outside, just a fedoraed wiseguy-wannabe bouncer stationed in front of the secret entrance. He gave you a wink as you descended down the grimy back stairs to an even grimier alleyway.

When it rained, which seemed to be every time you went to Lansky's, the staff would lay down big boards in the alley because of the giant cesspool that would gather there. You'd climb across the boards, then up a set of rickety metal stairs to—finally—the velvet-curtained entrance.

The place was dark and mysterious, just like you'd expect a speakeasy to be. There were cozy booths and lamps on all the tables and a long bar and a menu full of things like potato latkes and smoked salmon and pierogi. It was comfort food for me, the food my mother and grandmother had cooked. Food that stuck to your hips.

Fortunately, the club featured big bands most nights, with dancing in the front—in Ratner's—on Saturday nights, so you could work off the peasant food. The whole place was closed on Friday night, the Sabbath.

But on Saturday night, the place was packed by girls with bangs in forties-style vintage dresses and ankle-strapped, impossibly high heels walking around arm in arm with guys in pin-striped suits. You half expected Robert Mitchum to walk in and start slapping around some dame. It was quite a scene.

The thrill, though, came from simply knowing the place existed. No one had written about it yet. It was all through word of mouth, being able to find that secret, dirty passageway as if you were really on to something. Which is what the owners wanted you to think, of course. In the end, it was just another nightclub, trying anything to get your business. But for a few short months, it was our nightclub, our secret place.

Martin reserved a booth for us, and when we walked in, I thought it would be just us. But a small crowd of my friends was waiting.

"Happy birthday!" they yelled.

"Happy birthday, honey," Martin said, giving me a kiss. He was slightly nervous with everyone looking on, still hating him, using their dirty looks to machine-gun him down. I realized how much courage it took for him to call each and every one of these people and invite them, the awkward silence that must have followed the "Hi, it's Martin." The conversation that followed, longer than anyone wanted, because of the complicated directions on how to find the place. But he had done it. He had brought them all together.

My favorite gift came from Julie. It was probably the least expensive, but it meant the most. It was an iron-on decal of Mighty Mouse, whooshing through the sky with his arm outstretched, his little fist in your face. "That's you," Julie said. "Mighty Mouse." She gave me a jab in my muscled forearm.

We ordered latkes and lox and martinis and Rob Roys and toasted until we were drunk, at which point Laura pretended to be a rock journalist and interview me and Julie.

"So what are your goals for the band?" She stuck her microphone, a fork smeared with sour cream, in Julie's face.

"A record contract," Julie answered matter-of-factly. "With a major label. World tour. Stardom. Piles of money." We all laughed.

"And what about you?" Laura asked, sticking the fork in my face.

"My goal for the band?"

Laura nodded.

"Well, I've already surpassed my goal," I said, slurring drunkenly. "All I ever wanted to do was to play in a band, really. Play out a few times. And we've already done that. Done way more than that." I waved my hands and looked over at Julie for confirmation.

"I mean, your dream was to play Brownies, right?" I said. "And we've already done that. I mean, I never thought we'd even get that far."

Julie looked a little green to me, probably due to the grease from the latkes mixed with all that birthday alcohol.

At our next show, opening for a band called Shine Ola, Julie announced to the crowd that we wouldn't be playing out again until April 1. "April Fool's Day," I echoed into my microphone. We had no shows scheduled at all for March.

But we had plenty of practices. Dan tried spiffing up the songs with some of his jokes. Instead of "Jesus lost and found" on the "Document" finale, he started singing, "Jesus in my fish bowl swimming round and round / Jesus in my toilet, should I flush him down?"

We moved to another studio, one that didn't smell like Magic

Marker or burning amps or whatever the hell that smell was at Night Owl, to a slightly more expensive space in the same building, a few floors down. It was Ultra Sound, where I Hate Jane had practiced.

But the change was a mistake. Maybe it was the old I Hate Jane vibes flitting around the place, the spirit of Sleepy Steve, or the resin of Martin's lies caught in the atoms in the air. Or maybe it was the noise from other bands bleeding through the poorly insulated walls. One afternoon we were tortured by a band that sounded like it was fronted by the comedian Gilbert Gottfried. Another time, a country band next door kept throwing us off our beat.

"Is that Johnny Cash?" Doug asked, leaning into the offending wall.

"No," Julie said, annoyed. "It's just some guy—"

"Not Johnny Cash himself. The song, I mean."

I nodded. " 'I Walk the Line.' "

Whatever the reason, ambient noise or ghosts or failure to play out, our songs were lackluster. Doug started listening to the bands next door, staring up at the ceiling. He'd daydream and miss his part. And then Julie would yell at him. And then he'd get mad and sulk. During one bumpy rehearsal, he announced that he'd drunk several cups of tea before arriving. "I have to really pee."

"You're excused," I said.

As he shut the door behind him to head to the hallway bathroom, Julie started whispering. "Was he being snotty to me or is it my imagination?"

I didn't answer.

"Was I being snotty to him?" she grilled me.

"He's always snotty. He's snotty to everybody. He's a giant snothead."

I laughed, but Julie and Dan didn't.

When Doug walked back in, we started playing again. Doug suggested I place a drumroll and a single hit in the break before the bridge on the song "Stop Me." Julie flipped out.

"No, no, no. I'm putting my foot down," she yelled.

"Yeah," Dan agreed. "That doesn't work."

"I like the idea of filling up that void, though," Doug said.

"You never liked that void," Julie said. It was a strangely Zen comment.

" 'Cause it's all robotic," Doug said. "It's all stiff."

"But that's the point," she shot back.

I had to jump in.

"I propose we don't make any major changes until after the next show. I'm not against change. I just don't want to play the wrong thing onstage." Everyone nodded. "Why don't we play a different song? How 'bout Gordo?" Gordon Lightfoot, or Gordo, as we now called him, always cheered people up, especially at our shows.

"I don't want to do Gordo," Julie said.

"Why not?"

She shrugged. But I knew what she was thinking. Julie didn't like singing someone else's lyrics, lyrics to a song that had actually been played on the radio, a song that people in the audience readily recognized. It wasn't that Gordo was better than Julie. It was just that people knew his songs. That was all. But I guess that's what annoyed her. We had a long way to go before we were ever played on the radio. We existed in that shadowy netherworld with thousands of other bands floating between obscurity and fame. And that's what bothered Julie.

"We're not doing that song," she announced. "We can't do that song at every show."

"We haven't had a conference about it," Doug said. He was under the impression that this was a democracy, when in reality, this band, and every band, was a dictatorship. Julie just didn't have a little mustache.

"I think we should do that song," I said.

"Rock and roll, Helene," Dan said. Gordo had originally been his idea, after all.

"What's wrong with that song?" Dan asked. "People like it. It's fun."

"Why can't we have another fun song?" Julie asked.

"You wanna learn one now?" Dan asked, annoyed.

"No," Julie said, sulking. "Not now."

Doug chose the wrong moment to try and come to Julie's aid, to get on her good side. "I think since we're expecting a big crowd at our next show, we should be gutsy and not do the song and they'll know not to expect it," Doug said.

Now everyone was baffled.

"Oh, stop," I said.

"What's gutsy about making them unhappy?" Dan asked.

"It's gutsy to not play a song people want to hear," Doug said.

"Why is that gutsy?" Dan asked. "We're not fucking Guns N' Roses, where we have a fan base or anything."

"Julie doesn't like the song," Doug said.

"We're not doing it at the next show," Julie said.

"I'm outa here," I said, half joking and standing up to leave.

"You and me," Dan said. "We're takin' it on the road." We both headed for the door, and everyone started laughing, even Julie.

"Come on, Julie," Dan said. "One for the Gipper."

Julie started strumming, a frown stretching across her face.

"Now it's like you're in the ice capades and you're not smiling," Dan said. "People notice, you know."

"Fuck off," Julie said.

At our next practice, she came equipped with a new cover for us. It was "Brandy," the song we had heard on the radio on our way to Nashville. I had pointed it out to her in the car, so there was no chance of me saying I didn't want to play it. Doug was still kissing her ass. But Dan took it as a personal affront that Julie was replacing Gordo with another seventies pop hit. I saw no reason why we couldn't alternate Gordo with "Brandy."

Dan placed a layer of feedback over "Brandy" to lessen its cheesy patina. When the feedback worked, "Brandy" sounded pretty in a Yo La Tengo/Sonic Youth kind of way. But when the feedback got away from Dan, which it did more often than not, the song was a complete disaster, which was probably his goal.

That long month of March, Julie got to writing some new songs. She was a sponge, soaking up the daily movements and emotions that were flowing through our practice door. One, called "Gone Away," started out with a description of the flickering Christmas lights hung in the living room of a man who had just lost his love. It was as if Julie had been watching Martin and me all winter, had saved up the emotions and waited till spring for the song to bloom, its cutting lyrics now fresh and painful.

While I was playing the song one day, my right arm started to really act up because of the hi-hat action. I worried it was psychosomatic, brought on by Julie's lyrics. I sat it out at practice that afternoon. Every now and then I banged on the snare with one stick. "I'm like that one-armed drummer," I joked, trying to relieve the tension in the studio. "What band is that?"

"Def Leppard," Doug answered. But no one was laughing.

When my arm got better, Julie brought up the topic of drum lessons. Not only that. She suggested that Doug and I rent rehearsal space and work on our rhythm section. "You guys should get together and mix it up a little," she said. "Like Dan and me." She and Dan still met every week at his apartment to work on harmony and to write new songs.

I didn't think it was such a bad idea, actually. Doug and I could always use some extra practice. But when I tried to work it out with Doug, he changed the subject. He never out-and-out refused, but he never agreed to a practice time.

Over dinner one night at Standard Notions, he accused Dan and Julie of screwing up one of our last gigs with their lousy vocals. They were off, but we all were, some nights.

Suddenly, across the table, the band was us and them. Me and Doug versus Julie and Dan. I tried to bridge the gap; despite my Mighty Mouse biceps, I wasn't nearly big enough.

• TWENTY-SIX •

It rained on April Fool's Day. Not just rain, really. It was more like a monsoon. This was a problem for three reasons.

Number one, no one would come out for our Arlene show. To celebrate our first show in over a month, I had bought a clean, new white Fruit of the Loom T-shirt just for the Mighty Mouse decal Julie had given me. But now no one would even be there for his debut.

Second, the car, with my drums inside, nearly floated away on the floodwaters.

And last, but certainly not least, Julie claimed that the rain made her guitar go out of tune more easily.

Not being a scientist, I wasn't sure if moisture could actually cause her strings to come loose. But it didn't matter. Julie, in her heart, believed that it did. So every three minutes, between each and every song, Julie retuned every string on her guitar, even more so than usual. I think she tuned every string two or three times. E-E-E-E-E.

A-A-A-A-A-A. Back to E-E-E-E-E. A-A-A-A-A. E-E-E-E-E-E. A-A-A-A-A-A.

Then the next string A-A-A-A-A-A. D-D-D-D-D-D. Back to A-A-A-A-A-A. Back to . . .

Julie also had a terrible cold. "I want to thank everyone for coming out in the rain," she said, finally in tune, to the tiny crowd. "I've been taking Sudafed and everything's a little hazy. It feels kinda good. I've been taking Nyquil at night and Sudafed in the day."

"Woo-hoo!" someone screamed.

Thankfully, the taking of over-the-counter drugs helped Julie's onstage persona. She sounded just like Rudolph the Red-Nosed Reindeer, the animated version, before he ditched the fake nose, but she was much less nervous than usual. Despite the epic guitar tunings between songs, we sounded all right. Better than all right, really.

"Maybe she should take Sudafed before every show," I whispered to Doug, after a stunning version of "Letters."

"That one shakes the Nyquil slumber that I was in," said Julie, retuning her guitar. The drug fan yelled back his approval once more. "Woo-hoo!"

"At this point I'm not making any sense," Julie said. "But everybody seems to agree with me."

"I don't agree with you," bantered Dan.

"Well, you're wrong," I said to Dan.

"And you?" Julie asked Doug, trying to pick an onstage fight.

He didn't answer. So Julie tuned her guitar again. E-E-E-E-E-E. A-A-A-A-A-A. E-E-E-E-E-E. A-A-A-A-A.

We ended with "Astronaut," not our best version, 7,000 million miles away from each other on that Arlene Grocery stage.

For Easter, I invited everyone in the band to my mother's house for dinner. Doug was the only one who accepted. He brought his roommate, Brad, with him. It had been months since they'd had a good meal. Between the two of them, they put away so much ham I thought I might have to drive them to the Jersey City Medical Center.

Easter night, we had practice. So I brought Julie a ham sandwich.

"This is the best ham I ever ate."

"Can I have a bite?" Dan asked.

"No," she said. "Get your own." She was serious.

I felt really bad. "I would have brought you one," I said. "But—"

"But you thought, since I'm Jewish, right?" Dan said, joking, but not really.

"No. No, that wasn't it at all."

We stopped talking and started playing "Stringbean Boy," a song Julie had written for Doug. The bass line was strong and up front, but the lyrics were a backhanded insult, "You're the king of the castle, your castle your head. I suggest you spend the day in bed."

Doug took it as a compliment that Julie had written him a song. Despite the lyrics, it was a great little rocker, which caused Doug to jump vertically forty inches off the stage during each performance.

Sometimes his enthusiasm was contagious. Sometimes it was not.

"That was a mess," Dan announced, after playing "Stringbean" at another practice.

"I had the most fun on that one at the last show," Doug said, jumping in the air.

"At least it gave the audience something to look at," Julie said.

"You guys were all like . . ." Doug was rooting around for the right adjective.

"Despondent?" I said, throwing him a vocabulary word.

"You were the one who told people near the end of the show that we'd only bother them with a few more," Julie said to me.

"When I'm upset or nervous I come across as being bored or disinterested," I explained. "I admit it's a problem. It's a problem in my life. In my relationships and everything. I seem nonchalant—"

"When in fact there's a fire inside you?" Dan said.

"I think people thought we just weren't having fun," I said.

"We weren't," Julie and Dan said together.

"But we have to look like we're having a good time even if we sound like crap," Dan said.

Julie agreed. "It's those times when we do sound like crap that we have to entertain in other ways."

"You should do back handsprings," I said.

Before our next show, Dan tried to cheer us all up with a Sylvester Stallone hand puppet. It was Rocky dressed in his boxing regalia and was meant to be our new mascot. Dan made us all gather around Rocky in a huddle and then delivered some pep talk that I cannot remember, thankfully. We were all very embarrassed for him.

Dan also suggested that Julie and I go shopping for tight-fitting T-shirts. "A little bit of sexy can't hurt. We need to maximize the fact that we've got two women among us."

Doug nodded.

So Julie and I went T-shirt shopping at the new boutiques on the Lower East Side, stores with overpriced Keith Haring tees and other designer hipster wear. I bought a baby blue tee with a cartoon deejay spinning a record inside a bottle. CLUB SODA, it said. It was stupid, but clingy. My boobs were sure to bounce on that "Document" finale.

Though the band was in a temporary slump, my freelance life was improving. Weeks earlier, I had pitched a story about Yoko, our international fan. I thought it would be fun to follow her around on her next United States tour and write a feature about it. I had sent a pitch letter to one of my favorite editors. When I didn't hear back from her, I decided to follow up.

"It'll be great," I told my editor, Susan, at *Request.* "I could write about all the bands she comes in contact with, about the music scene in the city she's in. Maybe I can even nail it down as a trend. Japanese fans coming to the U.S. to make a musical pilgrimage. Like that couple in the movie *Mystery Train.* What do you think?"

"I don't think so," Susan said. "Do you have any other ideas?"

This happened all the time with editors. You had to have a list in front of you every time you spoke to an editor, in preparation for just this very question.

"Well, Elvis Costello is working on a new album with Burt Bacharach," I said. "I grew up listening to Bacharach as a kid. And you know how I feel about Elvis."

"I like that. See if you can get an interview with both of them."

According to the Elvis fan website, the two were working mostly by phone and fax machine between Dublin and Los Angeles. Every few months, though, they would get together in a hotel room in some major city and work together.

Elvis, I knew, would be much harder to nail down than Bacharach, so I started with his publicist. She never called me back, of course. That's what publicists did, for the most part: They formed a barrier between you and your subject. I tried again, and again. Then I had a revelation.

"Can I speak to Bill Flanagan?" I said, after dialing VH1's offices.

Bill picked up when he heard it was me. Maybe he felt guilty about my crummy internship, or about not coming to see me and Julie play one of our recent shows. Or maybe he picked up just because he was a really decent guy.

"Hey, Helene. What's up?"

"I'm trying to get an interview with Elvis," I said, not wanting to waste his time with small talk. "But his people won't call me back."

"Take down this number," he said, without missing a beat.

"Let me grab a pen," I said. "Okay."

"That's his personal assistant," Bill said. "Let her know I gave you the number and that you're a friend of mine."

The next morning, while I was on the phone with my friend Sara, call waiting beeped in.

"Hold on," I said to Sara. "It's probably some moron selling something. Hang on."

"Hello?" I said, clicking over, sounding annoyed.

"Hello," the voice on the other end said. The voice with the British accent. The voice that used to call *Musician* magazine all the time.

"Can I speak with Helene Stapinski, please?" the voice said.

"This is Helene."

"This is Elvis Costello."

"Can you hold on a minute?" I asked, my voice hardly getting past my frozen vocal cords.

I clicked back to Sara.

"It's Elvis!"

"Elvis Presley?"

"No, no, no. Elvis Costello!"

"Oh," Sara said. "Oh my God!"

"Gotta go," I said, and hung up on her.

"Sorry," I said, clicking back to Elvis. "I had to hang up on my best friend."

"Oh, I'm sorry. You could have called me back. I'm calling from Dublin. . . ."

"No, no, it's fine."

Martin wandered into my office and shrugged, wanting to know what was going on. ELVIS, I wrote on a piece of notebook paper.

He turned very pale and looked like he might fall on the floor. I waved him out of the room. A few seconds later, I heard the front door swing closed, as he walked out onto the breezeway, probably to smoke.

Elvis was quite chatty, talking excitedly about his Bacharach project and about his love of all music. He was the most chatty interview subject I'd ever had, in fact, and at times, I considered interrupting him when he went off the subject. But each and every time, he came right back to answer the original question I'd asked, like a jazz musician returning to the main musical theme after going off on a riff.

We talked like excited new friends about our shared love of Burt Bacharach. I told him about hearing my first Bacharach song, "I'll Never Fall in Love Again," as a six-year-old, and relating to the line, "What do you get when you fall in love? You get enough germs to catch pneumonia."

"I had pneumonia when I was six," I said excitedly. "So I remember hearing that and feeling like it was written for me."

"That's a great song. I just bought the album that the song is from, the *Promises, Promises* soundtrack."

"I just bought that album, too."

"Vinyl?"

"Yeah. Oh, yeah. Of course."

I failed to tell him that I had bought the album for my husband over a year ago as a gift, and had since smashed it, throwing it like a deadly Frisbee at Martin's head.

Elvis told me about how he had heard "Anyone Who Had a Heart" on the radio when he was a kid. He remembered feeling a tugging in his chest, not knowing why exactly, but feeling a deep sadness he'd never really felt before. And something else, too.

"I was only nine or ten, so I was way too young to understand what the song was about. But I knew it always made me feel really strange. It was really erotic, back when I didn't know what erotic was. You just know it makes you feel peculiar."

We talked about Tin Pan Alley and the history of songwriting, the Beatles, and anything else that popped up. It felt like we were on a first date. Phone sex was sure to follow. Then I asked him about the Attractions and when they might get together again.

It was the only time he was quiet. And that's when he said, "In rock and roll, you get in a groove and let it fly. It's either magic or it's boring. When you get it right, it's the most fantastic feeling."

I knew that feeling. In *clave.* The groove. The moment when it all comes together with the melody and harmony and rhythm, really happening, in a room packed with all your best friends, your lover and strangers, having them clap and love you because of what they've just heard. Or walking down a SoHo Street, the same song playing in both your heads, both catching the Empire State Building snap off at midnight.

In *clave.*

We talked about Bacharach and what it was like writing songs with him. "There's a virtue to the darker melodies," he said, "the ones that wrench a little bit more. They have a beautiful melody but also a mystery." Writing with Bacharach was all about finding a common ground, he said.

"They wouldn't be an attractive bunch of songs if we were pushing to the extremes of our musical personas. A hybrid of 'Pump It Up' and 'What's New, Pussycat' would just be punk with a quirky musical stage tune."

When the interview was finally over, he told me he'd be in New York and that we should get together for a face-to-face.

"Sure," I said, trying my best to sound cool.

Before my sit-down with Elvis, his publicist sent me a demo tape of the new Bacharach album. I listened harder to that album than I'd ever listened to anything before. Martin and I listened to it together, over and over, joined by our headphones, just like in our I Hate Jane days.

According to this new record, it seemed Elvis had experienced some of the very same horrors we'd just gone through. It made us feel less cursed, in a way. If Elvis was having similar problems and lived to tell about them, maybe we would, too. If he and Cait hadn't gotten divorced, maybe we could survive this, too.

The new album was much sadder than any of Elvis's other records. There were no overly clever lyrics or any angry-young-man posturing. These were songs of love and loss. About cheating and leaving and loneliness. Grown-up songs about grown-up subjects that I was now all too familiar with.

I noted every emotion, every oboe, every glockenspiel. I knew every line backward and forward and could tell, easily, which ones were more Elvis's songs and which were more Bacharach's.

The interview took place on the West Side in midtown, just a few blocks from Julie's apartment, in the record company offices. I was incredibly nervous. I had barely been able to contain myself on the phone interview. I might not survive a face-to-face.

I made a long list of questions, an unusual move for me. I usually flew freestyle, worrying about touchdown once I got airborne. But this time I had over two dozen interview questions, most about the songs on the new record. What would the first single be? Was that glockenspiel or xylophone? What would the album be called?

When I was ushered into the conference room for the interview,

Elvis was already seated at the long wooden table, a porkpie hat on his head, thick glasses and a gap-toothed grin on his face.

He was just as polite in person as he'd been on the phone, and rose as I entered the room.

"Nice to meet you," he said, shaking my hand. He obviously didn't recognize me.

I didn't mention seeing him in Nashville or at the Sexsmith show. I thought he might think I was some obsessive, crazed fan. Which I was.

I stuck to the music. The new music. The song about cheating. The song about leaving. The song about an empty, dark house and longing for the one you love to walk through the door.

"You know, you and Martin really belong together," Elvis said. "I've been thinking about you two and I think you really should be together."

What?

"I've been through the same exact thing as you two and I can honestly say, you need to work it out. Marriage is sacred, really. I mean, I know I was divorced once, but I was married at a very young age, you know. But this time around, with me and Cait, things are different. Very different. It's a more mature relationship, really. A real marriage of minds. And one of the things about marriage is forgiveness. You have to find it in your heart to forgive the one you love. Especially if they ask for it."

I nodded, in disbelief. How did Elvis even know about Martin? Had I mentioned his name in our phone interview? Had Bill read the *Post* item and filled him in?

But Elvis rambled on.

"Martin has strayed, I know. But these things happen. We're all human, you know. We make mistakes. Some are bigger than others, of course. And I know it's hard to forgive him for this one. But you can do it." He nodded and I began to cry. But he placed an arm around my shoulders and consoled me with his words.

"The human heart is an amazing organ. It has the capacity for a great many things. And I know you have a good heart. It's big enough to forgive Martin. To welcome him—wholeheartedly—back into your life."

How could this be happening?

But it wasn't really.

Those words were there, but under the surface. They were in the lyrics, in the orchestration, in the glockenspiel and xylophone both, in the cello, even, in the rhythm, the melody, and harmony on each and every song.

• TWENTY-SEVEN •

The Elvis sit-down really did take place. He mentioned Martin, not by name, but specifically, anonymously, unknowingly, in those new songs.

We talked about "This House Is Empty Now," and how the lyric turned on a single word that belonged to two different phrases that joined them, a clever bit of writing that Elvis didn't do often. "Were you so unhappy then? You never said *so* this house is empty now." That little "so" brought the phrase together and lifted the song up to a whole other level of sophistication. Of sadness.

For the first time in his career, Elvis had written a whole album of ballads, some slightly faster than others. But all ballads. No rockers. No clever puns or biting lyrics.

"Whenever I tried to be too clever with the words, it fell right off the page after a couple of days," he said. "I felt the simpler I wrote the better. It let the music shine through a bit more."

He talked about how writing these songs was different from writing songs for the Attractions. "He's very good at delaying the killer blow," he said of Bacharach. "And maybe encouraging me to not give away everything I have vocally in the first few moments of the song. When you lead a rock band, it's like leading a cavalry charge." I nodded.

The songs, I said, heat up in the bridge. And kind of explode from there. He nodded.

Some of the strangest lyrics, I said, were the words for the song "Toledo." "Where did that come from?" I asked.

"I don't know," he said. "I think really it's just acknowledging a sort of male weakness. There's quite a lot of male weakness in here of one kind or another." We both laughed nervously. "There's a guy here who's come home, having been unfaithful. He's confessed, saying, 'It's no use saying that I love you and how that girl really didn't mean a thing to me.' "

The lines, with Elvis speaking them straight to me, cut through my brain.

"And Toledo's just his alibi," he continued. "Blaming the town you're in, it's a classic male kind of trick. 'It was the cup of coffee I had. She made me do it. It was Toledo's fault.' " We laughed. Though I wanted to spit.

"So poor old Toledo gets beaten up a bit in that song," he said. "Toledo the city in Spain is a very beautiful town. It's a citadel. I've spent a lot of time in Ohio for my sins," he laughed, "and, no disrespect, I can imagine someone sitting in an industrial part of Toledo dreaming about being in a magical city in Spain. It's kind of about the excuses we make for the wicked things we do. It just says it in a strange way."

"What's the last word of the line?" I asked. "Does anybody in Ohio dream of that Spanish city *there*?"

"It's 'citadel.' Not 'city there,' " he corrected.

"Oh, 'citadel.' Okay. I couldn't figure it out. I thought it was 'city.' "

"Oh that's a shame," Elvis said, genuinely disappointed. I was worried I had insulted him.

"I have a tape," I explained, "so it's not as clear as the CD might be."

"Oh," he said, worried. "I hope it'll be a little clearer on the CD."

Mishearing lyrics had always been a problem for me. I remembered hearing the song "What a Feeling" from the movie *Flashdance* and for years thinking the lines in the chorus, "Take your passion. Make it happen," were "Take your pants off. Make it happen."

The Police song "Spirits in the Material World," I misheard as "We are nurses in the maternity ward," of course.

And then there was Creedence Clearwater Revival's "There's a bad moon on the rise," which I, and many people I knew, misheard as "bathroom on the right."

But I mentioned none of this to Elvis. He was busy apologizing to me for not enunciating properly on the word *citadel.*

"I do sing rather softly on a lot of these songs."

To change the subject, I brought up the fact that these were darker, more emotional ballads than what he usually wrote.

"The people in these songs are still kind of fighting with themselves a lot of the time," he explained. "Like in 'I Still Have That Other Girl.' Someone wants to give in to a passionate moment but knows in the long run it's going to end in disaster."

Direct hit.

"The Toledo guy is wrestling with his conscience."

Tell me about it.

" 'My Thief' is about somebody who wants a haunting dream because it's better than no dream at all."

I nodded.

"The intention is really to make a record where you kind of enjoy the sympathy you feel for the characters," he said. "Maybe you recognize yourself in them. I know I do."

"Oh, I'm there." I laughed. "I'm definitely there." He had no idea how there I was.

"Most of these things have either happened to me or I know them really well from observation," he said. "There's a fair amount of divorced people in the world who will know what it means to say, 'Meanwhile all our friends will choose who they will favor, who they will lose.' A lot of people have had that, even if you just break up, you know what that is. That's not exactly the most optimistic thought to leave people with. So the next song is a very sad song, but we've sort of disguised it."

" 'Tears at the Birthday Party'?" He nodded. "It swings," I said.

"If every song was as dark as 'My Thief' you'd want to take the record off after five minutes."

"You'd slit your wrists or jump out the window," I said, thinking of Martin out on the breezeway that cold night.

He nodded. "You have to give people some breathing space. There are more depressing subjects to sing about than broken hearts. But people have a habit of getting overwhelmed by too many sad romantic songs back to back."

"I know what you mean."

He talked about his favorite moment of writing with Bacharach, which took place in a hotel room in Los Angeles while composing "I Still Have That Other Girl."

Elvis and Burt taped all their sessions, just like Julie did, so they wouldn't forget or overlook anything. "We kept tapes running all the time, since the music kept changing shape throughout the day," Elvis said. "That Other Girl" was really coming together in L.A., except Elvis and Burt couldn't get back to the top, for the big payoff and buildup.

"So I'm staring out the window thinking about it. And Burt starts playing. This amazing thing. And I'm going 'That's it. That's it. What's that?' And as I turn around, he's completely gone. He's not even there in the room. He's got his eyes shut and his hands are just moving and he's actually being visited by the muse there and then. And that was it. It became the introduction and the tag. It's a pretty serious piece of composition."

"Yeah," I said, knowing it well. "It's beautiful."

"It's so him. And I nearly talked over it. He came back to himself and he said, 'Did you get that?' It would have been the perfect moment for the tape not to be working." He laughed. "Apart from me going, 'That's it! That's it!' over it all, we were able to decipher it."

"That's great."

"It was really a wonderful moment. Obviously things aren't really thrilling to describe in the writing process. I'd come away really elated some days but it would be hard to describe it to someone else. It's too meticulous, the detail of getting a bar to pay off."

I told him I had seen the documentary on TNT that showed both of them working in another hotel room together, Elvis waving his arms around and mumbling about something or other. The moment of conception didn't translate, just as he feared.

"My husband and I replayed it over and over again on the tape just to laugh," I said.

"We both look like madmen," he said, laughing as well.

We talked about him using the drummer Jim Keltner rather than the Attractions drummer, Pete Thomas, and the strange time signatures he used, 3/8 thrown in from the middle of nowhere in one song. Uneven bars of 4/4 with rhythmic changes midsong.

"We ended up with not so many songs in 6/8 as I might have anticipated working with Burt," he said.

"Yeah, he's the 6/8 guy."

"I'm, if anything, more of a 6/8 guy. Certainly if you look at my catalog, I've written more songs in 6/8 and 3/4 than anybody of my generation by a country mile. That's the swing I can do. Strict 4/4 is really boring to me. I can't hear it anymore."

Had I interviewed Elvis a year ago, I might not have followed his logic as well as I could now, having played in the band with Dan, changing time signatures midsong and knowing how much stronger it could make a tune.

We moved on to the orchestration, so I wouldn't misidentify any instruments in writing my story. I correctly identified the fluegelhorn in several songs. Chimes on two pieces. Harp on a few tracks. Two oboes, including one solo. No cello solos, thankfully.

"But was that a glockenspiel or a xylophone?" I asked.

"Both a glockenspiel and marimba," he said. "No xylophone."

And on that cue—bing bing bing—the door opened and in walked the publicist to tell us our date was over. "I look forward to reading your story," Elvis said as we shook hands. And then he gave me the biggest compliment I had ever received from any man.

"Your questions," he said, "were wonderful."

• TWENTY-EIGHT •

A few days later, I got a call from an editor at *Request* named Jim Meyer whom I had met in New York during a magazine party. He had come to one of our Stephonic shows at Brownies during his trip. I was hoping he was calling to write a story about our band.

"You'll never guess who I just met," he said.

"Who?"

"Yoko."

"Yoko?" I thought of John Lennon's widow.

"Yeah, the famous Yoko," he said. "Or I should say the second famous Yoko."

"Ohhh," I said. "Our Yoko."

Jim had seen my pitch about the Yoko tour idea. It had stuck in his brain like a catchy melody. And just this week, he was at a 12 Rods show in Minneapolis and had run into Yoko herself.

"We're doing a road issue this summer, about bands on the road. Fans on the road, whatever. And I think the Yoko piece would really work."

"Is she coming to New York?"

"No, but she'll be in Minneapolis for another week. Can you come up and spend some time with her and then write about it?"

I booked a flight to Minneapolis for the following Thursday and a return for Sunday. We didn't have any shows scheduled for the weekend, only practice. I was a little worried about the trip, though, since Martin and I were planning on going down to Cape May on the Jersey shore for a couple of days. It was our first trip away together since the horror. There was no way I could cancel it. I was excited about sleeping in a big, goofy Victorian hotel under a fluffy comforter, ordering room service and having sex. Doing all the cliché couple things that couples did in an effort to make it new again, to start over. But I worried that Julie would be pissed about all my traveling. Yoko and Cape May were a bit much in one week.

Julie knew about Cape May. I decided I would lay the news about Yoko on her the next night when we played a show at Meow Mix, a lesbian bar on Houston and Suffolk streets, a couple of blocks from Luna. The bar was known locally for its weekly group viewings of *Xena, Warrior Princess.* But most people knew it from the movies, as the rock club where Ben Affleck's lesbian love interest sang in *Chasing Amy.*

Maybe because of all that was going on, I felt especially discombobulated when I got to Meow Mix. But it wasn't just me. Doug stumbled in just minutes before our show with his friend Brad, both of them lugging Doug's giant bass amp. Julie looked like she might strangle Doug.

"What the hell happened to you?" she yelled.

"I was running late, so we hopped in a cab on Houston and about six blocks away there were all those fire trucks," Doug said, trying to catch his breath. We could hear them in the distance, honking and whirring in the warm, rainy Lower East Side night.

"So Brad and I got outa the cab," Doug said, Brad nodding along, "and he helped me carry the amp. But I forgot where this place was, so we ended up carrying the damn thing way too far." He waved an arm in that direction. "We had to backtrack."

Julie gave him a dirty look and walked away.

Onstage, she couldn't get her guitar tuned right, no matter how hard she tried. Maybe it *was* the rain after all. In an attempt to entertain the audience, Doug joked, "Hey, let's do that tuning song again."

Julie gave him a look that said: Eat shit.

Dan was there with his Rocky puppet, which didn't help matters. I was wearing my tight Club Soda T-shirt and felt especially exposed. Despite another pep talk from Dan, in our football huddle, our set was awful. The band that came on after us, a group of hard-core rockers dressed as S&M nuns, gave the night a particularly surreal feel.

I considered not even telling Julie about the Yoko trip, because of the foul mood she was in. Maybe I would just go and then call her from Minneapolis. But I had to be brave. While we were packing up, before the S&M nuns started singing, I took a deep breath.

"I have bad news."

"What now?" Julie said, her arms outstretched in surrender.

"*Request* wants me to go to Minneapolis this weekend to interview Yoko. I'll only miss one practice." I clenched my teeth and waited for Julie's tirade.

She was angry, but she decided to play the uncaring lover. She avoided eye contact and said, "Just make sure you're back by next weekend. I booked us another show at Brownies."

"A Saturday night," Doug said, giving me two thumbs-up.

"Opening for Richard Lloyd," Dan said.

"Who's Richard Lloyd?" I said.

" 'Who's Richard Lloyd?' " Dan asked. He screwed his face up in mock disbelief. "He's only the founder of the seminal seventies rock band Television. You're a music writer. You should know that."

"Oh, right." I was used to Doug being snotty to me, not Dan. "I knew his name sounded familiar. I just couldn't place it."

Before I could work up a better retort, Dan left, taking his stupid hand puppet with him.

When I got home, I couldn't sleep. I was excited about my Yoko trip, but what was really keeping me awake was what Dan had said to me. It was pretty dumb of me not to know who Richard Lloyd was, I thought. I turned over and flipped my pillow. But not everyone knows who Richard Lloyd is. If you stopped a person on the street, just any person, and quizzed him, "Who is Richard Lloyd?" I mean, how many people would know who he was? Right?

I decided to give Martin a pop quiz. "Honey," I said, poking him with my elbow. "Do you know who Richard Lloyd is?"

"Wha?" he said, half asleep.

"Richard Lloyd. Do you know who he is?"

"Does he work at the paper?"

"No. Forget it. Go back to sleep."

I twisted some more and closed my eyes, but all I could hear was Dan's voice. *"You're a music writer. You should know that."*

Why hadn't I said something back to him? Something witty. Something hurtful. Who the hell did he think he was, talking to me that way? I never treated anyone like that in the band. Well, Doug. But he treated me the same way. We shared a mutual disrespect. But I never talked down to Dan.

I should have said, "First of all, I'm not a music writer really. Since you're such a loser and have so much time on your hands all day, you have nothing better to do than sit around and remember seminal rock bands from the seventies. Asshole."

The next morning, at six A.M., full of vengeance, I called Julie. I had worked myself up into a crying jag.

"I'm sorry to wake you." Julie was obviously rolling over to pick up the receiver. "But did you hear what Dan said to me last night?"

"What?" she asked groggily. "What did he say?"

"That thing about Television."

"Whose television?"

"The band. Television. Richard Lloyd. Remember?"

"Oh yeah. He's a jerk. Don't pay any attention—"

"Who the fuck does he think he is, talking to me like that. Like

I'm some piece of shit. Well, he's the piece of shit. This whole thing is bullshit. I don't need this aggravation. I'm quitting. I'm quitting the band."

"What?" Julie asked, waking up now.

"I'm too old for this shit. I've told you that before. But this time I mean it. I don't need this. This bullshit."

"Why don't you just wait a day or two and think about it a little bit. Don't do anything crazy. Go to Minneapolis, and if you still feel this way when you get back, we can talk about it."

"I'm not gonna feel any different." We were quiet for a moment. I could hear Julie breathing, wanting to go back to sleep, wanting me to shut up already. For a minute I thought maybe she had fallen back to sleep. But she was there, awake, not wanting to hang up on me.

"All right," I said, sniffling. "I'll call you from there."

I left for Minneapolis the next day, and by the time my plane touched down, I was sorry I had called Julie. Sorry I had quit. I called her as soon as I got to my hotel room.

"I'd like to rescind my resignation."

"No problem," she said, laughing. "I didn't take you seriously anyway."

"I've got my period. I was definitely premenstrual."

"Take two Midol and call me tomorrow. And don't worry. I didn't say anything to the boys."

That afternoon, I headed over to the record store where Yoko and I had arranged, via e-mail, to meet. Talking to Yoko on e-mail was a lot easier than trying to decipher her broken English, and a lot easier than me trying to speak Japanese.

"Harrine," she wrote.

> so I come to usa again, you know. this time I watched good shows many place in usa, too. I went to l.a., austin (south by south west), seattle, minneapolis. and I will go to atlanta, georgia soon.
> so we meet minneapolis, favorite record store.

The store was called Let It Be. She had chosen it, not because of the Beatles reference, but because of its wide indie selection. When I spotted her browsing behind a stack of CDs, that giant yellow Hanky Panky shopping bag was on the floor beside her. Her knit brown hat was missing. And her short hair was a new mellow purple. It had long ago been permed and was now just in the dying stages of frizzy.

Her eyes had changed to contact-lens blue, accentuated by her blue eyeliner. Her eyebrows were painted on, something I hadn't noticed last time I'd seen her, six months ago. But she was wearing the same black platform shoes as she had on the night of our show at Spiral, except now they were even more scuffed from weeks of traveling.

"Yoko!" I said, waving to her as I approached.

"Harrine!"

We hugged, and in an awkward language-barrier moment, I reached into my bag and pulled out our four-song demo CD. "This is for you. From Stephonic."

Yoko did a little jig right there in the store, practically kissed the CD case, and shoved it into her big Hanky Panky bag.

We made—or tried to make—small talk. Thankfully, she pulled a handheld pocket translator out of her bag. With the tiny computer's help, I learned that she had paid only $800 for her round-trip ticket and had landed in Los Angeles more than a month ago. When she heard about South by Southwest, though, she had taken a bus to Texas.

"I take Greyhound."

"Greyhound?" I suddenly felt very maternal. I had heard horror stories about Greyhound trips, about skanky people having sex in the backseats. About a fat woman who sat next to my friend on a six-hour ride, with her fat five-year-old son standing between her legs the whole time. About people traveling with farm animals. About one bus driver swerving off the road to get a slice of pizza. It was probably safer to hitchhike from California to Texas.

"Were the people scary?"

"Oh no, no. I always sleeping, sleeping, two days." She folded her hands next to her face. "No problem."

In Austin, a writer she had met in Japan scammed her a wristband for the South by Southwest shows. Then she took the bus back to L.A., where $200 in traveler's checks were stolen from her in a youth hostel.

"I stay with friends now." She nodded her head and looked as serious as she possibly could.

"You can stay with me at the hotel," I said. "I have a giant room. We can get a cot . . ."

"No, no, no," she said. "I stay with Velma."

"Velma? Who's Velma?"

Velma was a Minneapolis band, named, no doubt, for the smart girl in the Scooby-Doo cartoons, the brunette with the glasses who always guessed who the bad guy was before he pulled off his mask. Velma was one of those pop cultural references that twenty-something indie band members prided themselves on knowing.

Yoko was best friends with Velma's lead guitarist, Ryan, whom she'd met a week ago at the 12 Rods show, the same show where she had met Jim from *Request.* Ryan, who had been taking care of Yoko, chaperoning her to shows and introducing her to his musician friends, lived near Loring Park. We headed to his apartment in my rental car.

Ryan had promised Yoko a ride to the Matt Wilson show that night, so the plan was to leave my car near the park and go over with them, since I didn't know my way around town. Wilson, formerly of the folk-rock psychedelic Minneapolis band Trip Shakespeare, was playing songs from his new solo album at a place called the 400 Club.

Coincidentally, his brother and former Trip Shakespearean, Dan Wilson, had recently scored a nationwide hit with his own band Semisonic. In fact, I had just seen the poster for their new hit—"Closing Time"—in the Let It Be window. It was bound to be an interesting night for Matt. Was he jealous? Proud? On the verge of fratricide? I wondered if Yoko was aware of the Trip Shakespearean drama unfolding in the Minneapolis music world. I considered asking her, but it all seemed too complicated. How would I ever pantomime fratricide?

When Ryan answered the door, I was happy to see he had an honest, gentle face. He had a deep voice and a six-foot frame that didn't match his boyish looks. It was obvious, right away, that he wasn't trying to take advantage of Yoko. He invited us in and told us to make ourselves comfortable. We took a seat on the giant battered couch, his roommates barely looking up from the television, which was set to MTV. This was not a nightly news crowd.

They were deeply absorbed in the latest version of *The Real World*, lost in the lives of someone else's roommates, ignoring one another. "One of my other roommates is opening for Matt Wilson tonight," Ryan told me. Wilson had produced Velma's CD, he said. He grabbed a copy of it and handed it to me. "Take a look. I'll be right back. I gotta change my shirt."

The CD had a picture of a rocket on the front, with the title *Astronaut, I Am Not*. I flipped the CD case over in my hand and read the songs on the back. They had a song called "Astronaut."

I turned to Yoko and tried to explain the strange coincidence to her. She looked at me with eyes wide, a bit frightened. Or confused. I wasn't sure which.

While we waited for Ryan, I got her to tell me about her home life back in Osaka. Somehow, I managed to decipher that her father was a senior research chemist in the food industry. She had one nineteen-year-old sister, she said, who had very bad taste in music. "She like painted singers in Japan, like Marilyn Manson, except Japanese." She made a stink face.

Yoko had been to college, but I couldn't understand what the name of the college was. So she wrote, in straight capital letters in my notebook, MUKOGAWA WOMAN UNIVERSITY.

"In Kobe. But there was earthquake." She paused, trying to think of the right words. "My university broke."

She excitedly told me that when she was a sophomore, she had studied for four months at a college in the United States.

"Where?"

"Spokane!" she said enthusiastically. I'd been to Spokane; it did not merit such enthusiasm.

"I like American university much more. Friendly people. Japan not friendly. If you don't know me there, you don't say hello. You just walk. More free here," she said, smiling. "And many races. In Japan only one race." She held up her index finger. "In Japan everyone is too busy. Busy, busy, busy. No relax. No good. Six days a week, work. It's boring."

When Ryan reemerged, I decided it was time I explained who I was and why I was carrying a notebook around with me. How Yoko and I had met. How our band had a song called "Astronaut," too.

"Weird," he said.

"Isn't it? Anyway, I thought Yoko would make a great story, just following her around for a little while."

He nodded. "I never met anybody who's been so into music before in my life. I don't think it's hard for her to make friends. You just can't help but like Yoko. She comes off as so naïve, but she knows more about music than anybody."

Ryan and I were talking way too fast for Yoko to understand. When he realized she couldn't keep up, he stopped, then said, slowly, to her, "You make music fun again."

Yoko made a baffled face and shook her head.

"You make music fun again," he said slower. She shrugged, uncomprehendingly.

"You . . . make . . . music . . . fun . . . again," he said, loudly, as if Yoko were wearing a hearing aid.

She threw her hands up in desperation.

"You don't want to know," he said, waving her off. "Then it won't be so much fun."

Ryan called his friend Suzanna, the girlfriend of Velma's bass player, and asked her if she had room for me in her truck. She was the one driving to the 400 Club.

"You got room for three? A woman who's traveling with Yoko. She's doing a story on her." He nodded and laughed and said, "It'll be a time."

"You can come with us," he said to me as he hung up the phone. "No problem." He turned to Yoko and said, "You'll get more press than most of the bands you've seen."

Yoko nodded and smiled. She had no idea what he was talking about.

I had been in Minneapolis for less than four hours, and already I was falling for the place. There seemed to be a real music community here, where people actually knew and liked one another. I had seen a bit of that in New York, with Professor and Maryann, the Rosenbergs, and Smash Mouth, but nothing like this.

The 400 Club didn't look that much different from Luna, with Christmas lights strung up and a small black stage. A sign that said NO DRINKING ALOUD hung behind the bar. The biggest difference from Luna was the large number of big, blond people inside, their ample butts spilling over the edges of their stools.

You rarely saw blondes in New York. Natural blondes. And these girls were big-boned, not just tall like New York's models. You could tell these girls enjoyed their bratwurst and beer. Maybe it made them a happier breed of people. It was incredibly refreshing. There was a warm vibe here that you didn't feel too often in New York's clubs. People were smiling, having a good time, and admitting it to one another. Admitting that they ate brats and loved brats.

The only person at the 400 Club who didn't know Yoko was the guy at the door—the new doorman, it turned out. She flashed him her passport to prove that she was indeed over twenty-one. But once inside, Yoko was a celebrity.

"Yoko!" one of Ryan's friends yelled when he saw her. He ran over.

"I saw you sleeping the other day," he told Yoko. "But I don't really know her yet," he told me. She laughed and put her hands over her face, embarrassed.

Another guy named Max told her that next time she came to town she could stay with him if she liked. Yoko gave him the okay sign with her thumb and index finger.

A woman named Andrea came running over and gave her a

squeeze. "Good to see you again." Andrea had met Yoko in Los Angeles last time around and then had run into her at South by Southwest a few weeks ago.

When Ryan's roommate John saw Yoko, he yelled, "Hey, Yoko, what's up?"

She pulled out her Instamatic camera to take a shot of John before he went onstage. But the doorman yelled, "No pictures in here. Absolutely none."

Yoko looked like she might cry, but as soon as the doorman stepped back outside, she whipped out the camera again and started shooting.

"Oh, I almost forgot," John said, ducking behind the bar and coming out with a CD and T-shirt, which he handed to Yoko. She stamped her feet in excitement. "Ohhhh," she said, holding up the shirt, with John's band name, THE WONSERS, written on the front. "Yahhhh." She nodded her head.

"And this is for you," he said, handing me a pair of white panties. On the crotch was the Wonsers logo, written inside a red heart.

"Thanks," I said, slightly less enthusiastic than Yoko. "My husband will think I slept with the band."

"Cool," John said.

He then took the stage and launched into a series of loud pop songs. As I shoved the underpants into my bag, Yoko jumped up and down, her head bopping above the tall blond heads every two seconds, like an underclassman joyfully lost in the crush at a high school dance.

When Matt Wilson took the stage, the crowd thickened and Yoko pushed her way farther up to the front. I followed close behind, wanting to bear witness, but also wanting to protect her. "Very close," she said to me, pointing to the stage and nodding. "Good. Not in Japan. I wish I live in Minneapolis."

Seeing Wilson after Ryan's roommate was one of those musical revelations, when you can see plainly who is the star and who is not. Wilson was a professional, with thousands of stage hours behind him, with years on the road. But you could see he was born to be up there. He glowed. He had that It.

Being so close, I could see that his guitar-strumming hand was bigger than his other hand, muscled from all the playing he had done in his life. His forearm was also bulging with music-induced muscles. Wilson tuned his guitar in seconds, never looking down once, simultaneously chatting, intelligently, with the audience.

After a few songs, including a pretty potential hit called "The Sun Is Coming (to the Cold Places)," I tapped Yoko on the shoulder and motioned that I was heading back to the bar. My feet hurt.

Ryan was already there, having a beer with a guy named Brian, another local musician, from the band the Hang Ups. He had met Yoko on her last tour in Los Angeles. "We could hardly communicate then," he said. "But her English has gotten a lot better." I nodded.

"More people know Yoko than me," said Brian. "And I've lived here twelve years."

"I don't know where she gets her energy," Ryan said, watching her head pop in and out of the crowd. "She wears me out just watching her."

When Yoko came over for a break, she spotted Brian and started jumping up and down, rubbing his thigh in her excitement. Brian turned red.

At one A.M., the band played its last song and the house lights came on, temporarily blinding everyone in the place.

"What's going on?" I asked Ryan, confused, wishing I had sunglasses.

" 'Closing time . . .' " he sang.

And that, I remembered, was why I lived in New York.

Yoko and I met for lunch downtown the next day. She was dragging a bit, her contacts replaced by blue-lensed shades to cover her tired eyes. Though it was a sunny seventy degrees, Yoko was wearing her brown knit hat, the same one she had worn to our Spiral show, but it had the strange addition of green and yellow braids, which she had sewn onto either side of the hat. Now it was even more of a conversation piece.

"That's a cool hat," said one guy, stopping her on the street. "Where are you from?"

"Japan," she said, attempting to launch into an explanation of her musical pilgrimage. But he didn't get it. You either got Yoko or you didn't.

After a struggle with her pocket translator, Yoko deduced that he was a professor at the University of Minnesota. That really got her going, since that night she was planning on going to see a show on that campus.

"Modest Mouse," she said to him, naming the headliner.

He had no idea what she was talking about, and walked on.

She cheerily waved goodbye to his back and headed to the library to check her e-mail. It was her daily ritual, the first thing she did each day, no matter what city she was visiting. Today she had to file a review of Matt Wilson's show for *Popsyrock,* a magazine she wrote for for free.

Her next stop was invariably a new record store, this day a place called Garage D'Or, where she managed to scam a Sonic Youth poster from the store clerk, whom she had met the other day on the street. The clerk, Jeff, was a friend of a guy who had helped record Velma's CD. He was—surprise, surprise—also in a band.

"I have many, many poster in my home," Yoko said to Jeff. "Poster, poster, poster," she said, pretending to slap them up with both hands. "No more wall."

I pulled the new Matt Wilson CD from the display wall and placed it on the counter. "I'll take this," I said to Jeff.

Over lunch, Yoko took my notebook and scribbled a list of all of the bands she had met—and in some cases, had been photographed with—while on her tour. When she was done, she grimaced at the list and said, "Some, not all. I forget some, I think."

I turned the notebook my way and flipped back one, two, three pages and read what Yoko had written:

Little Rabbits
Flaming Lips
Sean Lennon
Elliott Smith [3X, she wrote, next to his name]
Cornelius [her favorite]
Presidents of the United States of America
Neutral Milk Hotel [whom she planned to stay with in Atlanta]
Minus Five
Matt Wilson
Fastbacks
Wave
Apples in Stereo
Optiganally Yours
Azalia Snail
Centimeters
Gravy
pee
Track Star
764-Hero
Tuatara
Elf Power
Fuck
Gerbils
Virgins
Free Design
Liquor Giants
Model Rockets
Silver Scooter [a band from Austin that Doug was friends with]
Giggles
Chika Chika
Kruddler
Bran Van 300
Toothpaste 2000
Action Plus

Red Shadow Chorus
Myriad
Shallow
Morning Star
Morcheeba
Jim White
Lifter Puller
American Paint
Brian Jonestown Massacre
Kristin Hersh
Call
Propeller
Movies
Baggers
Dead Moon
Strike Three
Muddy Frankenstein
Playmates
Sandwiches
Jon Spencer Blues Explosion
Cibo Matto [whom she was often confused with]
Roto Spasmo
Nick Lowe
Willie Wisely Trio
Seagull Screaming Kiss Her Kiss Her
The 3Ds
Autumn Leaves
Bennett
Young Fresh Fellows
Dirty Three
12 Rods
Pizzicato Five [whose lead singer she was also sometimes confused with]
High Llamas
Buffalo Daughter

Ray Wonder
The Hang Ups
The Wonsers
[And of course] *Velma*

We headed over to Hazelworks, the place where Ryan made his living silk-screening T-shirts. He brought out a big bin of rejects and told me to pick one. I gestured to Yoko to go first, but she shook her head. "Yoko has no room in her luggage for clothes," Ryan explained. "Only CDs."

I dug in and came up with a winner—a light blue extra-large music festival shirt with a list of bands on the back—Barenaked Ladies, Semisonic, the Specials, and G. Love and Special Sauce. Except on the T-shirt, it was written as G LOVE AND *the* SPECIAL SAUCE. Someone had gotten it confused, probably, with the Specials.

The Specials. G. Love and *the* Special Sauce. Because of that tiny, unnecessary article—*the*—the T-shirts had wound up in the damaged bin. *The* damaged bin. Maybe it was messed up on purpose, by someone who simply hated G. Love and Special Sauce. Someone like Martin.

The reason I chose the shirt, though, had nothing to do with G. Love and Special Sauce. *The* Special Sauce. The reason I wanted it was that the front of the shirt featured Herbie the Dentist from *Rudolph the Red-Nosed Reindeer.* Instead of a dental tool, Herbie was holding a V-shaped electric guitar. A bubble over his head read, "I want to be a rock star."

"Is there another one of these?" I asked Ryan. I wanted one for Julie, in return for Mighty Mouse. He dug around and came up with another, then handed it to me.

"Our lead singer will love this," I said.

"Julie!" Yoko squealed.

"Yeah," I said. "Julie."

That night, yet another Yoko admirer, a guy named Glen, met up with us and took us over to the Modest Mouse show at the university. While

Glen parked the car in a local garage, he told me that he was a former bass player and current Montessori schoolteacher from down south. But his claim to fame was that he had dated the actress Parker Posey as a teenager. He showed me an old picture of them together, in his car.

"Wow," I said, as enthusiastically as I could. "That's her all right."

Glen had met Yoko at a Flaming Lips show, a boom-box extravaganza that they tried, in vain, to describe to me. "They had, like, forty boom boxes, all synchronized," Glen said excitedly. Yoko chimed in, something about samples and a local jazz band.

As soon as we got to the door of the Whole, the university venue, we saw Jeff from the record store. Yoko ran over to hug him. "Every time we go somewhere I see another musician she knows," I told Glen. "I'm even beginning to recognize people."

"Well, this town is small. But it spawns so many bands. You shake a tree and fifty lead guitarists fall out of it. No drummers, though. Drummers are hard to come by."

"I play drums."

"Really?"

"Stephonic!" Yoko chimed in. "I love!"

"That's the name of our band," I said. "She saw us in the fall in New York at a place called Spiral. This little divey club downtown."

"Worse than this place?" he asked.

"No."

The Whole was possibly the worst venue ever, in a low-ceilinged basement, without windows, no air-conditioning, over eighty-five degrees easy, with the charming addition of orange-red lights glowing overhead.

"I feel like a french fry at McDonald's," Glen said, his glasses fogging up. Yoko didn't seem to mind the heat, though. She somehow kept her brown knit hat on her head and made a break for the free poster table, scooping up Modest Mouse's ad for their new album, *The Lonesome Crowded West.*

With her booty, she headed up to the front of the stage, more of a platform on the other side of the room, less than a foot high. Yoko was front and center once again. I decided to hang back with Glen and find a chair. I was starting to get tired.

Just twenty minutes into Modest Mouse's set, Yoko was already searching the crowd for us. "Not very good," she said, twisting her face while the jazzy, free-form band rambled loudly behind her.

"I agree," I said.

"Shall we move on?" Glen asked. Yoko nodded.

Rather than head back to the car, Glen took us on an epic stroll across a bridge over the Mississippi that linked the campus with the 400 Club. Run Westy Run, an old Minneapolis favorite, was back together for a reunion show. It seemed anyone not being held captive in the university dungeon was at the 400 Club for this show. It was the place to be tonight. Even the Velma gang was there.

Just as I was saying hi to Ryan, Run Westy Run took the stage and the crowd cheered. Though I knew nothing about them, I could tell from their songs that the members of Run Westy Run had lived their heyday in the late seventies and early eighties. Every original song was a tribute to bands from that era. There was the Led Zeppelin-ish song, the Billy Squier song, the David Bowie song. But it was all new to Yoko. Her hat and braids flew up in the air as she danced. "I like better," she yelled to me.

When we got back to the garage, after a late-night stop at Denny's for French toast, the parking attendant was nowhere to be found. Worse, the metal grating was pulled down. The place was deserted.

"This does not bode well," Glen said.

The three of us stood there paralyzed, not talking, for several minutes, until Glen decided finally to go off and search for someone. This, I remembered, was the downside to acting like you were still a teenager: sitting on the damp ground Indian style at two A.M., locked out for an hour, knees and hips aching.

My knees would be even more unhappy when I stood up. Glen found the parking attendant and got the car, got us back to town, but by then, my knees and hips were practically arthritic. From the dampness, from all that standing in the clubs, from sitting on the ground. I couldn't wait to lie down.

The next morning, Yoko got up earlier than usual—before noon—to help one of her musician friends move into a new apartment. Yoko took, but she gave back as well.

It was pouring rain outside, not a good day for a move. It was such a nasty day that even your closest friends would bail on you. But there was Yoko, helping Roger from Roto Plasmo move his mattress in the downpour. "I tell Roger I help," she said wearily. "So I help."

Yoko's first stop that night—her last in town—was at a party at the home of a group called the Sandwiches. On their basement walls were paper plates with names of bands that had played in that very same basement: Detroit, Grant Hart, Steel Shank, and, of course, Velma. Yoko jumped up and down, pointing at each plate and reminiscing about her own personal encounters.

Sadly, Yoko was under the impression the Sandwiches themselves would be playing that night, but she had misunderstood. One of the Sandwiches was deejaying. Yoko was not pleased.

After studying the Sandwiches' CD collection and drinking a beer, Yoko told me we should go. The Odd, a Rolling Stones parody band, was playing across town—their farewell concert. That was where everyone was headed tonight. And, sure enough, there they were. Glen and Jeff and Ryan and the gang, and even Jim Meyer, my editor from *Request,* all hugging Yoko. It was like a going-away party for Yoko instead of the band.

For the occasion, the Odd's guitarist wore a red boa. The drummer, a Kiss T-shirt. The lead singer, in a silver astronaut jacket and black shorts, with a sock in his jock, was yelling, "Can we turn up the lights? Because you all look so fucking beautiful." They flew into a song about wet, wet pussy, and when they were done, the crowd exploded, Yoko included.

"From now on," the singer said, "every gig is our last gig."

They launched into "Gonna Eat You Out," which inspired the keyboardist to pound the organ with his tongue, then pull a Jim Morrison—sort of—and stick his finger out through his fly. Yoko laughed, but seemed a little confused. Her musical cultural references didn't stretch back that far. I looked over at Ryan. He shrugged and gave me a knowing look.

We had no energy left to translate.

When I got back to New York, I was greeted by an e-mail from Yoko. The subject field read, very enthusiastically, "I'm in athens!!"

> harrine! hello! this is yoko from athens. thank you for hang out with me when i was in minneapolis. i think you must be tired. now, i stay with members of newtral milk hotel, olivia tremor control. they are all nice!! here is very small town. so when i walk on the street, i always meet friends. very funny . . . i'm excited! "mashumaro court" and more!! keep in touch!

• TWENTY-NINE •

At band practice on Monday, we did a postmortem of the Meow Mix show. It was not pretty, but at least everyone seemed to be in a much better mood than they were that night. Especially me. I was tired, but in a good way. In the way that made you miss home. I was glad to be back.

Dan charmed his way onto my good side with his jokes and guitar impersonations. "Next time we play Meow Mix," he said, "I'm gonna get one of those T-shirts that says, NO ONE KNOWS I'M A LESBIAN."

He delivered an Axl Rose rendition of "Letters" that cracked us all up, then injected the lick from the Clash's "Should I Stay or Should I Go" into every song we played. He repeated it over and over until he drove Julie over the edge.

"Go!" she said, laughing. "Just go!"

But he kept on noodling with it, playing the riff. "All those things you make fun of," Julie said, "one day you're gonna use in a song. 'He who fucks nuns will one day join the church.' You ever hear that one? That's from a Clash song, too."

We played "Brandy," and though it faltered near the end, Dan's feedback sounded very pretty. We ran through "Gone Away," which sounded good, but wasn't quite ripe enough to play out yet. We played the usual "Nightlight's Glow," "Astronaut," and "Document," which we nailed.

"Okay, chickie-poos," Julie said when we were through. "Time's up. Time to go home."

Cape May turned out to be incredibly corny, with its Victorian pointed roofs, gift shops, and another bed-and-breakfast every fifteen feet. But the room we stayed in was clean and comfortable with a big feather bed and a large desk, where I set up my laptop.

While Martin sipped drinks down on the big wraparound porch and read, I banged out the rough draft of my Yoko article upstairs. During breaks I came down and sat with him, both of us reading together in the warm May sunshine.

We had a long, relaxed seafood dinner in the hotel's dining room and then spent the rest of the night in our room, watching *Mystery Train,* which we had rented back in Brooklyn and brought with us down to Cape May. I thought there might be something from the movie that I could use in the Yoko story, something about the Japanese music tourists coming to Memphis.

When we had seen the movie years ago on one of our first dates, Martin and I had thought it was the funniest film ever made. One of the funniest lines ever was when Steve Buscemi looked at Joe Strummer and said, "You fuckin' shot me." But the movie, on second viewing, was excruciatingly long. I nearly fell asleep before it was over, burrowed into Martin's side. As soon as the credits started to roll, I passed out. Without even having sex with Martin. But it was all right. We still had the morning. And the morning after that. And the morning after that.

We lingered in bed and spent the afternoon reading and writing and talking about stupid stuff, like why we had both loved *Mystery Train.*

"I loved that movie," I said. "Remember how much we loved that movie? That Joe Strummer scene?"

Martin nodded.

"What happened?"

"Maybe we outgrew it. People change. Or maybe you were just tired."

We spent some time not talking at all. After months, the silence was no longer awkward between us. And in blissful quiet, we drove back to New York, just in time for our Brownies show.

Playing on a Saturday night guaranteed that everyone you knew would come out. It was not a school night. Everyone was there to drink beneath the bar's beehive lamps, working hard to be hung over the next morning. Brownies was packed; people were sweating. They were standing still, and sweating. So many drinks were being sold that the manager was a very happy man. We were all happy. For a little while anyway.

While we were setting up for sound check, I realized I was missing a piece of equipment. An important piece of equipment.

"I can't find my hi-hat," I said to Julie, scanning the floor in a rising panic.

"Where could it be?"

"I don't fucking know." I rifled through the stands and cymbals.

"What's wrong?" Doug said, coming over.

"My hi-hat is gone." I was growing more and more freaked out. "What the hell am I gonna do?" Did someone steal it? Had I left it in the car?

Julie went and got the soundboard guy, who came over and offered me a hi-hat they had in the back room. But it was unassembled. Ever since that first show at Pyramid, I always kept my hi-hat cymbals and their nut in place because I was so nervous about putting them together quickly enough.

"No, no," I said, waving my hands, feeling like this was a pop quiz I was about to fail. "No. I need my own hi-hat."

"Okay." The guy shrugged, confused.

I stopped for a second and thought about the last time I had seen the hi-hat. Where, where, where? Jesus lost and found. Jesus lost and found. It wasn't at home. I had scanned the floor before leaving. It wasn't in the trunk, where I thought I had left it after the last show. The last show. That was it.

"Meow Mix!" I yelled. "It's at Meow Mix."

I ran out of the club, past our friends and family members, strangers and fans, straight to the car and headed over to Meow Mix. And there it was, right near the back door, where I had left it last week. "This is mine," I said to the boyish sound-check girl, grabbing the hi-hat by the neck like a naughty runaway child.

"We were wondering who that belonged to," she said as I flew past her again.

Just in time, I arrived with my missing link, dropped it in its spot near my left foot, and we were off with "Nightlight's Glow."

Maybe it was because I was so worked up from running around, but the song sounded great. And it only got better from there. We built and built, playing a great rendition of "Astronaut," sending the audience into orbit around us, clapping and hooting and screaming our names. "Letters" was heartbreaking. And so was "Honey." We put "Document" where it was meant to be, at the end of the set. We played off of the crowd and off of one another and burned and burned until the music was so bright there was really nowhere else to go but to simply stomp out the flames. Which I did, with that sudden crash and grab.

The crowd cheered and asked for an encore, which of course we didn't have. And besides, we were way over time, the soundboard man was signaling to us. Wrap it up, his right hand said.

We drifted down into that club like rock stars, our friends and people we didn't know greeting us and thanking us. "You were amazing," Martin said. "Really." He hugged me. And my friends hugged me. Lauren hugged me. Doug hugged me. It felt an awful lot like Minneapolis. All that hugging. Except it was much better. The bar was open till three A.M.

That Tuesday, before practice, I called Julie at work to ask her what she thought about going with me to buy some more new equipment. I was ready to commit to more percussion purchases, maybe some new cymbals for my new cymbal stands.

"Maybe you should wait," she said.

"Wait? Wait for what?"

She didn't answer.

"What's the matter?" I asked.

She didn't answer.

"Is it Jimmy?" I asked.

"I can't really talk here," she said, whispering in her cubicle. "Why don't I call you when I get home?"

For the next hour, I paced the rooms of my apartment, wondering what Julie was going to say. I tried writing, but that was impossible. I paced over to the couch and turned on the television. I flipped past the news, past *The Simpsons,* the episode where Marge falls in love with her bowling instructor. I loved that one, but I was too tense to laugh. I clicked over to MTV and saw the new video from Smash Mouth—the famous Smash Mouth. Not a good omen.

Maybe it was Jimmy. Things between them seemed especially strained lately. He had talked about moving to the West Coast so that he could be closer to the movie industry. And Julie hated L.A. She told me there was no way she was moving out there if he decided to go. But he hadn't decided to go. Not yet anyway. Maybe he had today.

Maybe she was still mad that Doug and I weren't practicing on our own. While I waited for her to call, I decided to get in touch with a local drum studio I had looked up weeks ago in the phone book. I grabbed the fat Brooklyn Yellow Pages off the shelf and flipped through until I found the number. It rang twelve times, until a sleepy guy answered. I booked the studio for two hours and wrote it in my date book, for the following Monday afternoon.

Now, when Julie called back, I'd have something good to tell her. Something she wanted to hear. Something to cheer her up.

The phone rang and scared me a little. I jumped to answer it.

"Hello."

"Hey," Julie said.

"So what's going on?"

"I think Jimmy's moving to L.A.," she said.

"I knew it," I said.

"I've been trying to decide whether to go with him or not." She had never said this before.

"You're moving to L.A.? But what about the band?"

"No, I'm not moving to L.A. I've decided to stay." Then she started crying.

"I have to make this work," she said, between sobs. "I have to make this band work. If I'm gonna stay behind, I have to have something to show for it. I can't just keep fucking around."

"Okay," I said, trying to calm her down.

But she started crying harder. "You're not gonna kick me out of the band, are you?" I said, just joking, to cheer her up a little.

She didn't answer.

"Julie?" I asked.

"Yes."

"What?" I asked.

"Yes."

"Yes what?" I asked.

"Yes. I think you should leave."

"Leave?"

"Leave the band."

I was silent. Like eight months earlier, in this very same room, with Martin on this very same phone, I was speechless. I was growing numb, limb by limb, the numbness radiating out from my solar plexus. I was numb, like just a few months ago when his girlfriend had called on this very same phone to tell me they had slept together again. I hated this phone. I needed a new phone.

"You're kicking me out of the band?"

told me, that a redhead I worked with would betray me. Julie was that redhead, the strawberry blonde. I thought about my trip to see Yoko in Minneapolis, how it had been our Alaska, my time to give Julie and Dan their chance to plot behind my back, to meet in secret, to line up a new drummer. Yoko had done us in. Just like the Beatles. We had even met at Let It Be records. Maybe if I hadn't gone to Minneapolis, this wouldn't be happening. Maybe if I hadn't quit the band after Dan's Television comment. Maybe if I hadn't said that thing at Lansky Lounge about already surpassing my stupid "band goals." Maybe if I had taken lessons with Andy White.

I remembered our last practice, where Dan had played "Should I Stay or Should I Go" over and over again. He was so passive-aggressive that whatever he was thinking came spilling out of his guitar. Should I stay or should I go? Was that his code to Julie?

". . . So I just went back in there," Doug was saying, "got my stuff and wished the new guy lots of luck. Then I checked my messages 'cause I figured you would be—"

"She knew," I said, cutting him off. "She fucking knew ahead of time. She'd already hired a drummer."

"I bet she has a new bass player, too."

"I can't believe this," I said, the tears rising in my throat now. "I can't believe she would do this to us."

"I know. I know."

I pushed the tears back, thinking about those stupid "Letters" lyrics, the lyrics Yoko had loved so much.

This is how the news arrives . . .
My tongue was tied and I saw stars,
But I didn't cry. No, I didn't cry.

Martin hugged me as I began to crumble. "I bet this was Jimmy's idea," he said.

"No. I think it was her and Dan." I waved a limp arm.

Afraid I would break down in the bar, I told Martin I wanted to go

"I guess I am. I'm sorry. I'm so sorry."

How can this be happening? I thought. Or maybe I said it.

"Dan has been pressuring me." She blew her nose. "He's threatening to quit the band. I have to make some changes. I'm sorry. I can't lose him. He's too important."

She was right. She needed Dan more than she needed me. But I didn't say that.

"But I'll take lessons." I was the desperate lover all of a sudden. "Doug will, too. I actually called this place today. The guy said I could—"

She cut me off.

"No," she said. "Forget it."

Somehow, I wasn't in tears. Somehow, I understood what she was saying. Even though I couldn't feel my hands or feet. And somehow, I started consoling her, just as I had consoled Martin and his girlfriend that first day.

"Don't cry. It's okay. I understand."

But that made her cry even harder.

"I always told you that you should find a real drummer," I said, laughing a little.

"It's partly my fault," she said. "I should have encouraged you a long time ago to take your lessons. But I held you back. You wanted to be a stronger player, but I made you play so soft all the time."

That's true, I thought. But I really wanted her to stop crying. "It's okay," I said.

"I'm sorry. I'm so sorry."

I was so sick of hearing people say they were sorry.

"So I guess I won't need to come to practice tonight," I said, a pain slowly starting to make its way into my head. I thought of the empty evenings stretching out in front of me, in my life and in my calendar book. What would I do with myself, now that I wasn't in the band? Who would I complain to, day after day? Who would I joke with and laugh with, who would I get to do Axl Rose imitations for me? Who would call me chickie-poo?

Would I ever see Dan again? Or Doug? I realized I had never seen Sleepy Steve after I Hate Jane broke up. After all that time we spent together. Now I'd never see those guys.

And now Stanley would never get to see us play.

I considered asking Julie if we could play one more time, one more gig, just so I would know it would be my last. Just one last fling. Our rooftop *Let It Be* farewell. But I didn't want to seem pathetic. I didn't want to grovel.

So Julie and I said goodbye. I knew it wasn't the last time I would talk to her. We had become too good friends for that. Even if I never saw Dan and Doug again, even if Stanley never got to see us play out, I knew I'd see Julie again.

I kept the receiver in one hand and used the other to press the button down to get a new dial tone. I punched in Doug's number and let it ring and ring until the answering machine picked up. He had already left for practice. I wanted to let him know myself that I wouldn't be there and to warn him that Julie might be dropping a bomb on him as well.

When the machine beeped, I left him a message to call me right away. Maybe he would check his messages before going to the studio. "It's an emergency," I said.

When I called Martin at work, he decided to come home early. He didn't even wait to hear the whole story.

"I'll be right there," he said. He cabbed it and arrived less than twenty minutes later, out of breath from taking the spiral staircase two at a time. He was barely through the door, and I began to tell him everything that had happened. I wasn't crying, for some reason. I was still numb, except for my head, which was pounding now.

"I think I need a drink," I said. So Martin and I headed to the West Village to the Corner Bistro. I left another message for Doug to let him know where we would be. The Corner Bistro was one of those comfort spots in New York—with dark wood, snug booths, a great jukebox, and a menu with grilled cheese sandwiches and burgers. And in the musty front-room tavern, the mugs of beer were only $2 a pop.

As I was ordering my second of the night, Doug walked throu door, looking very strung out.

"Are you okay?" I asked him.

"Fuck," he said, choked up.

"It'll be okay," I said calmly, touching his arm.

"Fuck," he said again, his voice cracking. "They had a new drumr there."

"What?"

I felt that familiar pain, the same one I had had when Martin ha told me about the affair. That stabbing, followed by a breathlessnes and a sudden desire to lie down on the barroom floor.

"What do you mean? How could they have gotten someone on such short notice?" I asked, in a trance, not wanting to understand.

But I knew. I knew it the way that everything suddenly becomes clear and you fit all the pieces together and the horror is there, unbelievably staring you in the face. I knew it the way I knew it with Martin, the way everything started to make sense as soon as he confessed, the hang-ups to the apartment, the beeper going off all the time, the late nights.

"I showed up for practice and I'm setting up and then all of a sudden, this guy shows up and sits behind the drums," Doug said. "Like nobody says anything to me. So Julie takes me out in the hall." He took a deep breath. "She told me she kicked you out of the band. And I was like, what? I told her I thought it was a bad decision, that it should have been a band decision, and she told me that if I didn't like it, it was too bad. And that I should just concentrate on being the best bass player I could be. Or else I'd be the next one to go." He laughed a nervous laugh, an unbelieving laugh. More of a "huh" than a laugh, really.

I couldn't speak. My head was filled with so many ideas. I was grateful that Doug had stood up for me. But I was still sorting it all out. Had Julie set Doug up? Had she not told him about the new drummer so that he'd get mad and then quit?

Then I started to think back. I remembered what that psychic had

home. I didn't want to cry in public. So I hugged Doug goodbye, and Martin and I headed home to Brooklyn.

"Call her right now," Martin said as soon as we walked in the door, his face and ears turning bright red. "I want to talk to her."

"But she's still at practice." I thought of that other drummer there, in my place. He was probably so much better than I was. He could probably screw on a hi-hat nut in his sleep, and knew how to do a proper drumroll. He probably had more than one tom-tom. He definitely had more than one tom-tom. I started crying.

For the next hour I watched the minutes click by on the red digital cable clock above the TV and cried. The TV was on, but I wasn't watching it. When ten P.M. rolled around, the time practice was scheduled to end, I started calling Julie's apartment. I'd let it ring and ring, until the machine picked up. Then I'd hang up and call back, like a madwoman. Just like that first night, on Labor Day weekend, when I'd freaked out Martin's girlfriend at the newspaper.

When Julie finally answered, I started crying into the receiver, tears falling into the mouthpiece holes. "How could you do this? How could you replace me just like that? I wasn't mad before. I really wasn't. But this, this is different," I said, starting to get hiccuppy again. "You had this all planned. You . . . and . . . Dan," I hiccupped, "have . . . been . . . planning . . . behind . . . our . . . backs. All . . . the . . . while. . ."

"No," she said, not a trace of tears in her voice now. Maybe she had made herself cry earlier to get off the hook, knowing I would console her and not yell at her. What an actress.

"No," she said. "No. No. I called Dan and told him what happened right before practice and he called his friend, this guy. I don't even know him, but he was around so he showed up—"

"You're lying," I said. "You're a liar. I don't believe anything you say."

"Give me the phone," Martin screamed, wresting the phone from my hand. Now he was the one defending me. Julie and Martin had traded places.

"No," I said, pulling it back. "Let me yell at her."

"It's Jimmy," he yelled into the receiver, over my shoulder. "Isn't it? Jimmy put you up to this."

And he was right. In a way, Martin was right.

Now it was us versus Julie. It was as if, in some superbalanced universe, I couldn't have both the band and Martin at the same time. I thought about it and concluded, rationalized, really, that to make it in music, you had to give everything up, like Julie had. Let the boyfriend go to L.A. and bet it all on red. You couldn't stay in a bed-and-breakfast in quaint little towns and have croissants and strawberry jam delivered to your room. You had to live on a bus and play and play until your hands became as monstrous and as muscular as Matt Wilson's, the Trip Shakespeare guy. You had to be willing to take your drum paddle and willow stick into your skin boat just like those guys in Alaska, and make your way around the coast of an island in the middle of the Bering Sea, miles and miles, to a gig in a crummy high school gym, just so you could sing songs that you'd sung hundreds, thousands, maybe hundreds of thousands of times before. You had to work three jobs like Yoko so you could have money to fly across the planet and ride Greyhound, so you could sleep on strangers' floors, just to hear musicians sing lyrics in a language you couldn't understand, lyrics to melodies you knew by heart. You had to stay in $20-a-night rooms in Ljubljana like Matt from the Toasters. You couldn't even have a home really. Or a wife. You had to play with that bass player you hated, like Elvis Costello, just because he was the best bass player in the world and you couldn't help yourself really, even if you couldn't stand him anymore. You had to get up in front of people all alone and sing your songs, like Elliott Smith, even though you suffered from horrible stage fright. You had no choice. You were allowed one passion per life. That had to be it. And now I had Martin, finally, for better or worse.

He coached me through the breakup. He never brought up the band, only if I did first, for fear I would get angry and fly into a fresh rage, which I did from time to time. Sometimes I still got mad about what had happened with me and Martin, but those fits became fewer and farther between until they all but evaporated and were replaced entirely by my band rage. I could only handle one rage at a time.

Martin would hold me when I cried, which I did more often than I would ever admit to Julie. Sometimes I cried for us, but most of the time I cried for the band. Somehow, the band breakup took an even harder toll than the breakup with Martin. I couldn't understand it at first. But then I figured out why.

I had never completely lost Martin. After he had cheated, he had stayed and fitted the pieces of my heart back together. But the band was gone. The band was gone for good.

Doug moved to Seattle a few months later. I knew it really was over. We'd never get back together. There would be no makeups, no reunion practices or shows. No one would fit those pieces back together. I never got to give Julie that Herbie the Dentist Rock Star T-shirt.

I stayed away from Luna and Arlene and Meow Mix and Brownies, like the haunts of an ex-lover, worried that I would bump into Julie. I couldn't go to any more shows or even stand to read the band listings in the *Voice* for fear I would come across Julie and Dan's new band, Calamine.

Some nights, I forgot that Calamine existed and I would dream about us being together again, playing at Brownies, working ourselves up into a euphoric frenzy with "Document," Julie thrashing around onstage, Doug lost somewhere good, really good, with his eyes closed, Dan playing until he couldn't play anymore, and me hitting the crash cymbal in one final smash, and then grabbing it, and falling headfirst, with everyone in that room, into the silence.

But mostly I dreamed of the new drummer. I became obsessed with him. In my dreams, he had a wide arch of rototoms like that guy had at the Pyramid Club that freezing night. But he played like a studio professional, like Andy White on a really good day.

I had been Pete Bested.

In my worst nightmare, I was backstage at Brownies, watching from the wings while Calamine took the stage. The new drummer not only had rototoms, but also a keyboard across his lap, which he played while simultaneously playing the drums.

A few weeks after the new horror, Julie sent me a small handwritten note on blue paper, along with a computer printout of all our shows since January, next to another list of our expenses. The expenses column—$149.75—was then subtracted from the earnings column, $415, to reveal a total of $265.25 in profits for Stephonic for 1998.

Then it was divided by four, with each member getting $66.31. There was a check enclosed for just that amount. I considered blowing my stuffy nose with it and sending it back to her.

Doug got a check for the same amount, with the same breakdown, with a Dear John letter that said,

> I'm sorry about everything. I certainly didn't want things to work out the way they did. I don't hate you, if that's what you think. We just weren't meant to be in the same band.

So this is what it came down to? A note and a check for $66.31? All that pounding, all that playing, all those ideas, all the sweat, all the heavy lifting, my bum knee. Maybe I should sue her for disability.

Then I read the blue note Julie had sent me:

> Helene,
> Here's your cut of band profits. Yippee, now you're in the money. Well, it's definite. Jimmy is moving to L.A. Aubrey and I are taking the news o.k. I'll fill you in on all the details when I talk to you.

The note was in Julie's voice. It was Julie, right there on the blue note. I really missed Julie's voice.

I really missed Julie.

It wasn't long before I heard her voice again. Yoko sent me a compilation CD of music from her travels; two dozen of her favorite songs from her favorite bands. There was Velma, with their "Astronaut" song, and Ladybug Transistor and Silver Scooter, Dressy Bessy and Kittycraft, the Sandwiches and Gerbils. Listed between "A Tribute to the Phone Calls" and "Baataa Betto" was "Document" by Stephonic.

The CD was called *Counterattack of US Indie: US Pop Life Vol. 1,* and was the first release on Yoko's label, Contact Records. Even the cover art, a blurred shot of a curved record-store security mirror, was by Yoko. I was so proud of her.

I considered throwing the CD right in the garbage, sick to my stomach from just the sight of our dead band's name. But instead, I slipped the CD out with trembling hands and placed it on the player. I forwarded to song number 11, and hunkered down on the velour couch, ready for the lyrics about Shirley Temples and Roy Rogers, penmanship and Jesus lost and found, to wash over me, ready to relive Dan's searing solo, that building crescendo and my crash and grab.

But Yoko surprised me.

The song was not "Document" but "Letters," in all its softness and tender harmony. Yoko had gotten the tracks confused. So there were Julie and Dan, spooning their guitars and vocals around each other, Doug firmly placing his bass notes between them, and me playing softly behind it all. Before we got to the second verse, I pushed STOP, shoved the CD back into its case and hid it away.

I hid it so well that I never found it again.

• THIRTY •

I came face-to-face with Julie only one time that year, by accident. Laura had a reading at the Japan Society on the Upper East Side, and, out of the dozens of friends who attended, Julie and I arrived at the door of the museum at the exact same moment. I nodded at her but looked away as she held the door open for me.

"I think Sara's saving me a seat," I said as I ran up the long staircase, away from Julie as fast as I could.

But out of the corner of my eye, I noticed that she was wearing a new shirt. A shirt I had never seen before.

That night, in bed, I made excuses for Julie for what she did. Some things in your life hurt so much that you had to make reasons for them happening, even when, usually, there was no good reason. Or maybe there were so many reasons that you couldn't count them all. Either way, there was no point in making a list.

When it came down to it, Jimmy had never really asked Julie to come with him to L.A. When she went to visit him there to see if she would like it, he told her he wanted to break up. Her first day there, Jimmy told Julie he had been cheating on her for a long time—though he assured her it was only when he was out of the country for film festivals.

I thought now that Julie must have been near a nervous breakdown in those last few weeks of the band. With what was happening with Jimmy, being too embarrassed to tell us what was going on, too embarrassed to let Martin know, after hating Martin with me for so long. Her own boyfriend was doing the very same thing. It was no wonder she snapped and kicked Doug and me out of the band. Or me at least.

A year after the band breakup, Martin and I moved into a new apartment, a place with an elevator, a place that didn't have a repaired door that had once been ripped off its hinges, a place with clean, smooth walls that didn't have dents plastered over by the super. A place with a new office, with a new phone.

So Martin and I started over, leaped from the plane one more time and hoped for a safer landing this time around. The thing about skydiving was that the more you practiced, the better you got at tucking and rolling. It took a lot of courage to make the leap with those mending broken bones, but because of them, you were all the more careful the next time around.

Laura called one afternoon, called on my brand-new phone, and told me Calamine was going on vacation for the summer. Their last show—for a while, anyway—was the next night.

"Do you think you might want to go?"

It was ridiculous really, not being able to read the music listings, carrying around this torch, this hatred for someone I had been so close to.

"Yeah. Let's go."

Before the show, I had one more nightmare. In the dream, I went to see Calamine. Martin and I were overdressed. I had on a coat with fur on the edges. We had to park our car in a lot and then we couldn't find Brownies. We had a baby with us. So we had to put big headphones on him so his ears wouldn't get damaged from the loud music.

In my dream, the show was like a play, with Dan and Julie talking and acting out little skits. It was like a cabaret. Julie had on a feather boa and a dress and lots of makeup and hardly did any singing. She jumped around onstage a lot. The drummer and bass player were both girls, which was a surprise. At the end, Julie told us she was pregnant with a baby girl. I wondered if it was Jimmy's. But then she sang a song about Jimmy moving to L.A. and becoming a jerk.

The reality was a little different. Jimmy had, of course, moved to L.A. He was doing all right for himself. He had just finished writing the screenplay for *Scooby-Doo,* and had made a fortune breathing new life into the old gang, Shaggy, Daphne, Fred, and, of course, Velma.

But I had no fur-trimmed coat to wear to Brownies. Martin didn't come along. He had to stay home and baby-sit for our six-month-old son. I had to go it alone, until I met up with Laura at the club.

Like in my dream, I drove to Brownies, but had no trouble finding it. I parked right out front around 9:15. I looked down at my outfit, nervous, like that first day with Julie, about what I looked like. I had on blue jeans, a black, short-sleeved sweater and a black leather jacket, with blue sneakers. Simple enough. And appropriate. Black and blue all over.

The guy at the door took my $6 and handed me a bracelet so I could drink. I hadn't been to a show in so long, I had forgotten about these bracelets. These hospital bracelets. Like the one I had worn not long ago in the maternity ward. "We are nurses in the maternity ward," I sang under my breath, to calm myself.

The club smelled the same, beery and smoky, but looked slightly different. The shelf off of which my snare drum had fallen onto Lauren's head was no longer there. Definitely an improvement. The area now had stools and tables. There was a little lounge at the front of the bar as well, up near the stage. It was like coming home and finding the furniture had been rearranged.

I scanned the rest of the room and didn't recognize a soul. Where was Laura? She was supposed to meet me here, for moral support. I couldn't do this alone. I looked around in a growing panic. I backed into the bar and ordered a scotch, just like the old days, except I wouldn't be playing tonight. I needed it to calm my nerves, but for a different reason. I started to get angry all over again and considered just leaving, but the guys sitting next to me at the bar were talking so loudly that I found myself completely immersed in their conversation, sucked in against my will.

"So Newark is the new Williamsburg," one guy was shouting. "It was in the *Times* the other day. Didn't you see it?

"Everybody knows Williamsburg is over. And Hoboken is overgentrified. This is the new place. I'm tellin' ya. It's the new waterfront."

"Newark is on the water?"

"Yeah. The bay, like in *Bay*onne?"

Suddenly, quietly, Dan walked in from the street and was standing right in front of me. Julie walked out from behind the stage. They came at me from both ends.

They both hugged me. First Dan and then Julie. As if they had been taken over by pods from Minneapolis. I couldn't remember Dan ever hugging anyone, not even his girlfriend.

"Your hair is so long," I said to Julie, stroking it for a second. It was long and straight and made her look so different, older somehow. Or I guess maybe she was older. Dan's hair was much longer, too, the bleached blond long ago grown out and cut off.

"I guess long hair is in," he said, nervously flicking a lock of it.

"So, let me see the pictures," Julie said, clapping her small hands excitedly.

"What pictures?"

"The pictures of the baby!" She flung her still-skinny arms up in the air.

"Oh right," I said, pulling them out of my bag. "The baby." While she looked at the baby, I looked at Julie's outfit, an orange shirt and jeans, black sneakers with white stripes. All the clothes I knew were long gone by now, old and worn, sent off to the dump or to the thrift store. We had new clothes. New lives. New people starring in them. Some people just gone from them. Gone for good.

Jimmy was among the missing, as was Doug. Dan's astronaut step-father, Charles "Pete" Conrad, had been killed just months earlier in a motorcycle accident in California. There was a big obituary about him in *The New York Times,* and as soon as I saw it, I knew exactly who it was. I turned to Dan.

"Hey, I'm sorry about your stepdad."

"Thanks," he said.

"I want you to meet Andrew," Julie said, introducing me to Jimmy's replacement, a short, cute guy with a video camera. "He's a documentary filmmaker. He's gonna tape the show."

Laura walked in then and I could feel the tension in my body start to seep out. I had an ally.

When I turned around, I saw Dave and Mary, Julie's old friends from Philadelphia. I had forgotten they had even existed.

"Hey!" Julie said to them. They came over and hugged everyone.

"How are you?" Mary asked. "It's so good to see you."

"You, too," I said.

"Dave and Mary have a baby, too," Julie said.

"Congratulations," I said.

"Hey," I said, "have you guys heard the Gordon Lightfoot song? The one we used to do? 'If You Could Read My Mind?' Some band rerecorded it. I think it was on the *Last Days of Disco* soundtrack or something."

"See?" Dan said to Julie. "We should have released that song. You blew it." He poked her in the arm.

"She always hated that song," Dan said to Dave and Mary.

That was when I spotted him, out of the corner of my eye, up onstage, setting up his kit. Julie's new drummer. He had bangs and scientist-like glasses and a red-and-white check too-cool shirt. His drums were white, just like mine. He was setting them up the same way I used to, too, with the ride cymbal down low. I was happy to see he had only one tom-tom. No rototoms. No keyboard across his lap.

"Should I introduce you?" Laura whispered.

"No, thanks. I'd rather stick a drumstick in my eye."

The bass player, I was happy to see, was big and balding, much more so than Doug. With a goatee, to balance the missing hair on his head.

Julie and Dan ran away. From me, I thought, at first, and from the low growl building in my throat. But then I realized that they had to get onstage. The show was starting. I took a deep breath and an even deeper sip from my rock glass.

The first song was a song I had never heard, about waiting for your lover to show up or something. Julie's guitar seemed slightly out of tune. And as usual, there was a big guy standing right in front of me, blocking part of the stage. But I was happy he was there. I didn't want to see everything. I felt like a kid in a horror movie, hiding behind my popcorn to avoid the gruesome scenes.

After a second unfamiliar song, the band launched into "Astronaut." I knew it right away, from Doug's stolen bass line. The new drummer played the rhythm the same as I had, with little skippy beats, the ride and the hi-hat coming in in the exact same places.

"Your version was better," Laura leaned over and whispered in my ear.

I looked at her and pretended to plunge a knife into my heart. She nodded and gave me a sympathetic look.

I noticed that the drummer wasn't singing any backup. Probably not coordinated enough, I thought, huffing. He was very ordinary, I realized, no better than me, really. And without boobs and a tight T-shirt. At the end of the song, Julie played one bar too long, screwing up the ending, just as she had so long ago with "The Next Big Thing."

I was feeling good all of a sudden. Okay. I would live through this.

"Can I grub a cigarette?" I said to Mary, leaning over to her.

"Great," her husband said. "I'm between two smoking moms."

Thank God I had the cigarette, because the next song was "Document." I began to sweat. Over the intro chords, Dan and Julie both approached their microphones and said, one over the other, "This is for Helene." I held up my lit cigarette in appreciation.

The dedication didn't make hearing it any easier. Watching this show, this spectacle, this song in particular, was like hearing a love letter, written just for you, read by your ex, in public, to another woman.

No. It was like watching your ex have sex onstage with his new girlfriend. All the moves were there, all the moves you recognized, except she was up there, too. Instead of you.

The only thing that made it bearable was that the new drummer didn't play "Document" quite as well. His buildup, his climax, was nowhere near as good as mine and Dan's.

Dave leaned into me. "Yours was better."

It was time for me to check out emotionally. This was way too much. So I turned to Laura and started a conversation, something I had hated from the audience when I was onstage.

"So how are you?" I said, loudly.

"You know they're breaking up, right?" she said, tilting her head toward the stage.

"You said it was their last show for the summer. But no. I had no idea they were breaking up for good." She nodded. A feeling of well-being washed over me, though I felt petty and small.

"How come?" I asked.

"Well, Dan wants to write more of his own songs and Julie doesn't want him to. It seems one of the reasons he brought the new drummer in was to have more control over the whole thing. He's a good friend of his. But now it turns out that the drummer has stolen Dan's girlfriend, Pauline."

"Get out!" I said, laughing.

"He's a financial investor, you know," Laura said, nodding at the drummer. "He's rich. Lives in this big loft in SoHo."

"He should be wearing a suit."

By the end of the set, Julie seemed more at ease. More confident. Before their last song, their best song, a new melodic power pop tune called "Trampoline," Julie announced to the crowd that they were going on hiatus for the summer. But now I could tell that she was lying. And I could tell, now that I knew the back story, that she was mad at Dan.

They used to play with each other up there, flirt sort of, but the chemistry was missing, I realized. Dan was about to join the pile of Julie's castoffs. "Leaving a trail of destruction that's second to none," is how Judas Priest once put it. Ah, the poetry.

When they were done, Julie rushed over with a Calamine sticker and a CD. Out of some well of politeness I didn't know existed, I offered to buy one of the CDs.

"Oh, no," she said, thrusting both into my hands. "You can have it for free."

When Julie walked off, I noticed the new drummer standing alone just a few feet away. I decided to torture him and go up and introduce myself. Why should I feel uncomfortable, when I could make him feel even more uncomfortable? And besides, now that I knew he wasn't better than me, I had a little courage. Or maybe it was just the scotch.

"Hi," I said. "I'm Helene. You're my replacement."

Before I even finished the nasty sentence, he was nodding and backing up a little, as if he was afraid I might pull a knife or something. He was so nervous and nerdy that I felt sorry for him now. Why did I have to say that?

"You probably noticed I messed up on 'Document,' then," he said, looking down at his hands.

"You probably just did that for me." I hadn't noticed actually. I was too busy gossiping with Laura.

"I was a little self-conscious," he said.

Julie bounced back over, probably worried I was about to eat his liver.

"Well, I should probably get home," I said. "The baby and all." I raised my eyebrows and shrugged. So Julie hugged me. And then Dan. There was no way in hell I was going to hug the drummer.

"Nice meeting you," I lied, sticking out my hi-hat hand for him to shake.

CODA

One day, soon after, while searching for a mix tape Tony had made me, I came across our practice tapes. Dozens and dozens of practice tapes and shows. Close to fifty of them, which I had stuffed, in my madness, into a bottom drawer near the stereo right after the breakup.

I had forgotten they were there. Or maybe I hadn't. Maybe I was waiting until I had enough courage to open that drawer. Maybe I was waiting until I had a reason to open it. And my reason was to drown out the Calamine music playing inside my head.

After the show, I had gone home and played that Calamine CD. There, among their new songs, were "Document" and "Astronaut," and the songs we had practiced but had never played out. That song that was about Martin sitting in his chair, all alone, with the Christmas lights blinking on and off. "Gone Away," we had called it. But now it was called "Flicker." Renamed, disguised, but just the same as we had left it.

Like your love letter, left behind and read aloud to another lover.

Like love letters, those tapes had sat hidden away for two years. Two years. Until that day when I was brave enough to find them. To look for them.

Letters, in a box, tied with packing string,
back in my closet among the other things I saved.
The feelings come in waves.
I should have thrown them away.

I closed the drawer, chickening out, afraid of what I might hear.

Maybe I should have thrown those tapes away. But the thought never even occurred to me.

Time passed. Martin asked Tony to be the godfather of our baby, and he gracefully accepted. Julie got married to Andrew. Elvis Costello and Cait O'Riordan got divorced. Spiral closed. Brownies stopped booking bands and renamed itself HiFi. The view from the Manhattan Bridge changed. And all the while, the drawer mocked me, called out to me, sometimes sang to me, out loud, right there in my living room. It called me a coward and dared me to open it again, until all the wounds scabbed into memories, until the whole thing seemed so silly, until I was brave enough one day to open the bottom drawer again and listen.

And suddenly, there we were.

Chords and beats, vocal harmonies and long-forgotten conversations, spilled out like the remembrance of a kiss or an embrace or a glance across a room. I fell right in, right back in love with them all over again, with the songs, with my bandmates.

On the I Hate Jane tapes, there were actual kisses and embraces and glances across the room from Martin. There were clues to what was to come: talk of the trip to Alaska, the trip to Mexico, Martin coming to practice after a long, bad night at work. His beeper going off and him running to the pay phone to call "his editor." Me sounding so stupid and happy while he was gone. I strained to hear every detail, every nuance, but sometimes the music played too loudly over the words we spoke to one another.

Later, on the Stephonic tapes, there was talk of the psychic and of the Minneapolis trip and of Yoko, and a moody Julie in early spring and Dan playing "Should I Stay or Should I Go."

But there, for a while, on tape, we sounded happy. We had all been happy. I could hear it with my own ears.

As I listened, our history began to take shape. More than two years of our life, recorded on tape. Mine and Julie's. Mine and Martin's. Doug's, Steve's, Elizabeth's, Dan's. Not the history I had created in my head, that personal history filled with imagined plots, petty excuses, and hidden motives, but the real history, recorded in real time, with real voices engaged in real conversation, documented there for my listening pleasure.

And then there was the music—overpowering and nearly impossible to describe.

Music, like love, was like that.

KNOWLEDGMENTS

alsh, Bruce Tracy, and Ann Godoff for
ce; to Julie Stepanek, Doug Mikko, Dan Crane,
ey Stapinski, Paula Spagnoletti, and Anthony Pet-
ir memories; to Irene Stapinski, Brenda Tyson, Aaron
nd the staff at Shakespeare's Sister for the peace and quiet;
nost of all to my husband, for his open mind and heart.

ACKNOWLEDGMENTS

…to Jennifer Rudolph W…

…and guidance…

…Stanley…

…for their…

PHOTO: STUART CONWAY

HELENE STAPINSKI is the author of *Five-Finger Discount: A Crooked Family History*. She has also written for *The New York Times, New York,* and *Billboard*. She received her B.A. in journalism from New York University and her M.F.A. from Columbia University. She lives in Brooklyn with her husband and two children.